Congressional Ethics

**Timely Reports to Keep
Journalists, Scholars and the Public
Abreast of Developing Issues, Events and Trends**

April 1977

CONGRESSIONAL QUARTERLY INC.
1414 22ND STREET, N.W., WASHINGTON, D.C. 20037

Congressional Quarterly Inc.

Congressional Quarterly Inc., an editorial research service and publishing company, serves clients in the fields of news, education, business and government. It combines specific coverage of Congress, government and politics by Congressional Quarterly with the more general subject range of an affiliated service, Editorial Research Reports.

Congressional Quarterly was founded in 1945 by Henrietta and Nelson Poynter. Its basic periodical publication was and still is the CQ *Weekly Report,* mailed to clients every Saturday. A cumulative index is published quarterly.

The CQ *Almanac,* a compendium of legislation for one session of Congress, is published every spring. *Congress and the Nation* is published every four years as a record of government for one presidential term.

Congressional Quarterly also publishes books on public affairs. These include the twice-yearly *Guide to Current American Government* and such recent titles as *Origins and Development of Congress* and *Powers of Congress.*

CQ Direct Research is a consulting service which performs contract research and maintains a reference library and query desk for the convenience of clients.

Editorial Research Reports covers subjects beyond the specialized scope of Congressional Quarterly. It publishes reference material on foreign affairs, business, education, cultural affairs, national security, science and other topics of news interest. Service to clients includes a 6,000-word report four times a month bound and indexed semi-annually. Editorial Research Reports publishes paperback books in its fields of coverage. Founded in 1923, the service merged with Congressional Quarterly in 1956.

Editor: Robert A. Diamond.
Major Contributor: Margaret C. Thompson
Contributors: Martha V. Gottron, Ed Johnson, Thomas P. Southwick, James R. Wagner, Laura B. Weiss.
Indexer: Diane Huffman.
Cover Design: Howard Chapman.
Production Manager: I. D. Fuller. **Assistant Production Manager:** Kathleen E. Walsh.

Library of Congress Cataloging in Publication Data

Congressional Quarterly, Inc.
    Congressional ethics.

    Bibliography: p.
    Includes index.

    1. Corruption (in politics)—United States.   2. United States. Congress—Salaries, pensions, etc.   3. United States. Congress—Rules and practice.   4. Elections—United States—Campaign funds.   5. Political ethics.   I. Title.

JK2249.C66   1977   328.73'07'6   77-4186
ISBN 0-87187-110-6

Table of Contents

Part I: Current Developments in Congressional Ethics

Part II: Historical Background

Introduction

Twenty years ago, Rep. Thomas J. Lane (D Mass. 1941-63) was warmly welcomed back to the House by his colleagues under rather unusual circumstances. Lane had just been re-elected after serving a four-month prison term for income tax evasion.

In 1976, however, House Democrats did not show the same sympathetic understanding to Rep. Wayne L. Hays (D Ohio). Instead, they forced him to resign as chairman of the House Administration Committee because of allegations by 33-year-old Elizabeth Ray that he had given her a job on the committee in exchange for her sexual favors. (Hays later resigned from Congress.)

These two incidents illustrate the changing attitude among members of Congress toward the behavior of their peers and their refusal to excuse the abuses they casually tolerated in the past.

The question that congressional observers have been asking, however, is whether that change reflected a higher ethical tone among today's members of Congress or just a greater sensitivity because of increased press and public scrutiny of the personal pecadillos of representatives.

Garrison Nelson, a University of Vermont political scientist who specializes in Congress, attributes the House Democrats' sharp response to the Hays scandal to "the higher ethical level of Congress today. The level of outrage has never been really high in the past. Tom Lane was welcomed back with open arms as his House friends forgave and forgot what he had done. But today, the winking and chuckling about 'good old Wayne' lasted for about four days and then those guys swung into action to purge him."

But others are not so sanguine about the depth of the change in congressional attitudes. "Congress is more sensitive now than it's been in a long time," acknowledged Rep. Richard Bolling (D Mo.). "But what you can't forget is that the morality of Congress has some relationship to the morality of the country. Congress is no different from the society around it."

"I'd suspect that Congress is not much different than in the past," said Rep. Barber B. Conable Jr. (R N.Y.). What is different, he added, is that "we now have a much more sensitive press."

Several observers laid the increased sensitivity to the Capitol Hill scandals to the aggressive coverage of the allegations in the national press and the fact that the scandals broke out in an election year. "You can't avoid being sensitive any more," said William M. Maury, historian of the U.S. Capitol Historical Society. "You can't hide from the scandals when TV news and newspapers are broadcasting them throughout the country. What has given them an added edge is that you have so many newsmen poking around."

Whatever the reasons for the heightened sensitivity to ethical standards, it appeared in early 1977 that members of Congress could not sweep the transgressions of some of their colleagues under the rug. No longer able to ignore the charges of unethical and illegal conduct that were widely circulated in 1976, both chambers were prompted to take steps to put their own houses in order. Shortly after the 95th Congress convened, special committees in both the House and the Senate began drawing up comprehensive new codes of ethics which were adopted by both chambers in March.

"Let he who is without sin cast the first stone. There is no one here who does not have a skeleton in his closet. I know, and I know them by name."

—Adam Clayton Powell (D N.Y.), Jan. 19, 1967

The flurry of reform-minded activity on Capitol Hill was motivated in part by public opinion polls that revealed the low esteem in which many Americans held their elected representatives as well as post-Watergate public concern about the general state of morality in government.

Pay Raise and New Ethics Code

It was also spurred by recommendations of a federal salary commission which urged that a Feb. 20 pay raise for top officials in the legislative, judicial and executive branches be tied to adoption of a strict code of conduct. Under a 1967 law, top-level pay increases, recommended every four years by a citizens' commission, took effect automatically 30 days after a President sent them to Capitol Hill unless either chamber voted to reject them. Within a few weeks after Ford sent his pay-raise proposal to Congress, it became obvious that the leaders of both houses, sensitive

1

to the repercussions of Congress going on record as approving its own pay raise, were not anxious to have the matter come to a vote. The Senate Feb. 4 turned back an attempt to block the pay raise, while the measure remained bottled up in an ad hoc subcommittee of the House Post Office and Civil Service Committee, making it impossible to bring the pay-raise to a vote on the House floor before the Feb. 20 deadline.

That maneuver, as well as the provision for automatic pay hikes, was sharply criticized by some members of the House, who in turn were accused by some of playing to their constituents. "How can we expect the American public to have confidence in this institution if we are reluctant to conduct our own affairs openly and with full debate?" said Rep. Teno Roncalio (D Wyo.) on the House floor Feb. 7.

Despite opposition, members of Congress received their $12,900 pay raise, boosting their annual salary to $57,500. Acceptance of the pay hike, however, may have been a sharp prod to adoption of new ethics codes limiting outside income and requiring full financial disclosure passed by both chambers in March. *(See p. 13)*

Scandals of the 1960s

The focus on congressional ethics of the mid-1970s was reminiscent of a decade earlier when, in the mid-1960s, scandals involving Robert G. (Bobby) Baker, secretary to the Democratic majority in the Senate, Rep. Adam Clayton Powell (D N.Y.) and Sen. Thomas J. Dodd (D Conn.) received widespread news coverage, forcing reluctant members of Congress to investigate the improprieties and subsequently take disciplinary action. "Public approval of congressional performance and public respect for individual members of Congress fell dramatically," noted Edmund Beard and Stephen Horn in their 1975 study of congressional ethics in the House.[1] "Worse, senators and representatives found that wrongdoing by one of their colleagues reflected badly on all of them. In the public mind, the sins of one were not isolated aberrations but the likely tendencies of all." The result of public pressure was the formation of ethics committees (the Select Committee on Standards and Conduct in the Senate—renamed the Ethics Committee in 1977—and the Committee on Standards of Official Conduct in the House), charged with a watchdog function over newly devised ethics codes. But by 1976, the two panels had become largely dormant due to the reluctance of many members to investigate and sit in judgment on their colleagues.

Footnote

1. *Congressional Ethics: The View From the House,* Brookings Institution, Washington, D.C.

1976 Developments: Spotlight on Scandals, Mounting Concern

In their study, *Congressional Ethics: The View from the House,* authors Edmund Beard and Stephen Horn noted a "strong tendency" on the part of congressmen "to live and let live, especially in matters of personal and political finance" and to "tolerate or even protect a member who may step out of line." This was forceably demonstrated in 1976. Unlike the Watergate scandal, which prompted both houses to launch highly publicized, lengthy investigations, most members tried to ignore the allegations of impropriety on Capitol Hill.

Only twice in 1976 did the House move to discipline a member. The first case was Hays; the second came on July 29, when the House voted to reprimand Robert L. F. Sikes (D Fla.) for financial misconduct. The Hays case prompted the House to set up a special committee to study reforms in the congressional payroll system, while the Sikes case created pressures for stricter financial disclosure laws.

But beyond those incidents, Congress declined to investigate or take any other action concerning the possible misdeeds of numerous members in 1976.

While the Hays scandal drew the most publicity, the most pervasive scandal of the year involved campaign contributions. It began in December 1975, when a special committee of the Gulf Oil Corporation reported to the Securities and Exchange Commission (SEC) that Gulf over the previous decade had contributed more than $5-million in illegal corporate funds to the campaign efforts of dozens of members.

Those named in the SEC report included some of the most influential members of the legislative branch, among them Senate Minority Leader Hugh Scott (R Pa.).

James R. Jones (D Okla.) pleaded guilty to a misdemeanor in connection with failure to report a Gulf contribution, and H. John Heinz III (R Pa.) publicly admitted having received illegal contributions from the oil company.

One Senate aide, Henry Giugni, administrative assistant to Daniel K. Inouye (D Hawaii), admitted that he lied to a federal grand jury when he denied having passed on $5,-000 in Gulf money to his boss.

Yet Congress took no action against these three or any other members implicated in the case.

Inouye declined to dismiss Giugni and the Senate Select Committee on Standards and Conduct voted overwhelmingly not to investigate Scott, even though the minority leader reportedly admitted to the panel that he had received $45,000 in Gulf money.

John J. McCloy, who headed the committee which investigated the Gulf affair for the SEC, concluded that "nobody seems able to make the Senate ethics committee do its job."

In February 1976, 18 members of Congress, including both chairmen of the House and Senate ethics committees, Rep. John J. Flynt Jr. (D Ga.) and Sen. Howard W. Cannon (D Nev.), admitted having received unreported free hunting trips from various defense contractors, an apparent violation of House and Senate rules. No formal congressional action was taken.

The Wayne Hays scandal focused the spotlight on a number of other sex-related accusations. House aide Colleen Gardner charged that her boss, John Young (D Texas), had kept her on the House payroll primarily to have sex with him, and the *New York Post* reported that Joe D. Waggonner Jr. (D La.) had been arrested in Washington on a charge of soliciting a police decoy for purposes of prostitution.

Waggonner was released without formal charges because of a District of Columbia police practice, later revised, which prohibited arresting members of Congress for misdemeanor charges while Congress was in session.

No official House action was taken against Waggonner or Young or against Allan T. Howe (D Utah), who was convicted July 23 of soliciting sex for hire from two undercover Salt Lake City policewomen.

An ethics committee investigation of charges reported in *The Wall Street Journal* on March 23 that 10 House members had filed false claims for travel expense reimbursement never got beyond the preliminary stages.

An attempt to strip Andrew J. Hinshaw (R Calif.) of his office because of his conviction on bribery charges was shouted down overwhelmingly in the House on Oct. 1.

Also in the fall, it was reported that the Justice Department and the SEC were gathering evidence concerning what one government source called "the most sweeping allegations of congressional corruption ever investigated by the federal government." The probes reportedly involved more than 20 former and present members of Congress and their ties with South Korean businessman Tongsun Park. Park was said to be the Washington operative of a ring of South Korean agents which dispensed between $500,000 and $1-million a year in cash and gifts to members of Congress and other U.S. officials in order to promote a "favorable legislative climate" for South Korea in

Washington. The allegations prompted the House early in 1977 to vote overwhelmingly in favor of authorizing an extensive investigation into the matter by the ethics committee.

Obstacles to Action

These charges of congressional misconduct, combined with the tendency to avoid taking disciplinary action, produced fairly widespread dissatisfaction with the operations of the ethics committees in both chambers.

During the Sikes debate in the House, freshman Andrew J. Maguire (D N.J.) complained that the House had "too often sidestepped or ignored" action on standards of conduct because of "the operation of the buddy system or because of the reluctance of individual members to criticize colleagues."

And R. Michael Cole, legislative director of Common Cause, the self-styled citizens' lobby which initiated the Sikes inquiry, said that "nobody takes the ethics committees very seriously...."

Several factors combined to make it difficult for the House or the Senate to act on allegations of misconduct on the part of members. The first and perhaps most important was the reluctance most members had to sit in judgment on their colleagues. Rep. Flynt, chairman of the House ethics committee, said during the debate on the Sikes reprimand, "It is never pleasant or enjoyable to sit in judgment on one's peers."

Depriving a member of his seat, the ultimate punishment, is difficult because expulsion requires a two-thirds majority vote. Moreover, the House cannot refuse to seat a person, as was attempted with Adam Clayton Powell (D N.Y. 1945-1971) in 1967, if he or she meets simple constitutional tests of minimum age (25), U.S. citizenship (seven years) and state residency at the time of election.

But beyond this, Congress had itself placed institutional hurdles in the way of any action on charges of congressional impropriety. The House ethics committee, for example, in most cases required a formal, sworn complaint from a member of Congress before investigating.

This happened occasionally, but in most instances House members were extremely reluctant to swear to charges against a colleague.

Congress also made it difficult for outside prosecutors to delve into charges of congressional misuse of campaign funds. The Campaign Reform Act (PL 93-443) passed in 1974 contained a provision reducing to three years from five years the statute of limitations on campaign law violations, a stricture which imposed severe limitations on Justice Department investigations, especially in the Gulf Oil case, which stretched back 15 years or more.

Watergate special prosecutor Henry S. Ruth in 1975 asked Congress to repeal this provision, charging that it provided special privileges for members of Congress not enjoyed by the average citizen. But Congress took no action to change this part of the law.

The most fundamental bar to congressional action on charges of misconduct, however, may have been voter apathy. Many of those charged with illegal actions, and even some of those convicted of crimes, found that their constituents really didn't mind very much.

Hays, who was the focus of one of the most widely publicized scandals in recent history, won renomination to his seat in Congress and probably would have won reelection as well had he chosen to run.

Six weeks after the House voted to reprimand Sikes for financial misconduct, the Florida Democrat was renominated by a margin of 54,000 votes and faced no opposition for re-election in November.

Jones' guilty plea on a misdemeanor charge in connection with failure to report a campaign contribution apparently had little impact on his re-election campaign.

Heinz easily won the Republican nomination to the Senate in Pennsylvania following disclosure of his Gulf contribution and also won in the November election to succeed Scott to the Senate. Hinshaw's bribery conviction clearly cost him the nomination to another term in California. Howe was defeated for re-election and various charges of misconduct against Rep. Otto E. Passman (D La.) may have played a part in his defeat in the Democratic primary election in Louisiana. But for the most part, the public seemed to react mildly to charges of impropriety on the part of their elected representatives even if the charges were proven.

Following are details of some of the major cases involving questions of congressional ethics that occurred in 1976:

Wayne L. Hays

The most widely publicized scandal of the year revolved around Rep. Wayne L. Hays (D Ohio), the powerful chairman of the House Administration Committee and Democratic Congressional Campaign Committee who had control over members' staff allowances and fringe benefits. The scandal began with a story in *The Washington Post* and ended three months later with Hays' resignation from Congress. It was the spur for major reforms adopted by the House and the House Administration Committee in the system of perquisites which Hays had managed.

The story broke on a Sunday when *The Washington Post* May 23 published a front page article which quoted a House Administration Committee secretary named Elizabeth Ray as stating that she had been kept on the House payroll primarily to serve as Hays' mistress.

"I can't type, I can't file. I can't even answer the phone," Ray said of her $14,000-a-year job.

Ray, 33, said she was not required to do any House-related work and showed up at her fifth-floor private office in the Longworth House Office Building for work once or twice a week for a few hours.

Hays' initial response was to deny the charges. But the story persisted and on May 25 he asked the House Committee on Standards of Official Conduct to in-

Wayne L. Hays

vestigate the matter and admitted that he had had a "personal relationship" with Ray. In a House floor speech, Hays said his relationship with Ray "was voluntary on her part and mine" and had taken place while "I was legally separated and single." He had obtained a divorce Jan. 15 from his first wife, the former Martha Judkins.

Hays explained his original denial of an affair with Ray by saying that "my first and overwhelming reaction was to protect my marriage and my new bride. In attempting to do so, I now realize that I committed a grievous error in not presenting the facts." On April 13 he had married Patricia Peak, who worked in his Ohio district office.

"I stand by my previous denial of Miss Ray's allegation that she was hired to be my mistress," Hays continued.

That same day 25 members of the House sent a letter to the ethics committee asking that it take up the matter. Hays, a powerful and abrasive man, had been controversial with his fellow congressmen. The Democratic Steering Committee at the start of the 94th Congress had recommended dumping him as chairman of the House Administration Committee. The Democratic Caucus had reversed the move, 111-161.

The Justice Department and the FBI entered the case soon after the Post story appeared. By May 26 a federal grand jury in Washington, D.C., began hearing testimony related to Ray's allegations.

In the meantime, the House Democratic leadership began to maneuver behind the scenes in an attempt to force Hays to resign his post as chairman of the Democratic Congressional Campaign Committee. Some members feared that the longer Hays held on to power the greater the chances that the Republicans would make him a campaign issue in the congressional elections.

By June 3 the pressure on Hays was intense. In a stormy meeting on June 1, House Majority Leader Thomas P. O'Neill Jr. (D Mass.) bluntly told Hays that he had to step down from the campaign committee and the House Administration Committee chairmanships immediately.

Hays reportedly attempted to strike a bargain with O'Neill about the campaign committee, offering to surrender the post if he could name his successor until the investigation had been completed. According to a House source, O'Neill vetoed Hays' move, telling him, "You're not nominating anybody."

That same day the House ethics committee voted 11-0 to begin an immediate investigation in the charges against Hays.

Also on June 3 the House Republicans made their first move to capitalize on the Hays scandal by asking the House to take back the responsibility for voting on increases in the allowances and perquisites for House members. In 1971 the House gave the House Administration Committee the authority to increase the perquisites without any floor vote or debate.

In the face of this mounting pressure, Hays agreed June 3 to resign as chairman of the campaign committee.

Hays received another setback on June 8 in the Ohio primary when he won renomination to a 15th term in the House, but not by the comfortable margins he had enjoyed in the past. Slates of delegates pledged to him as a favorite son presidential candidate were defeated.

The affair took an abrupt turn on June 10 when Hays was admitted to a Barnesville, Ohio, hospital after taking an apparent overdose of sleeping pills at his nearby farm. His press secretary, Carol D. Clawson, said that she did not know whether the overdose was "inadvertent or deliberate."

The hospitalization delayed, but did not change, the eventual outcome of the struggle over the Administration Committee. On June 18, Hays, still recovering in the hospital, resigned his chairmanship. He later resigned from Congress. *(See p. 7)*

On June 22 the House Democratic Steering and Policy Committee nominated Rep. Frank Thompson Jr. (D N.J.) to replace Hays as chairman of the Administration Committee.

At the same time it endorsed a 13-point reform plan put together by a three-member task force chaired by David R. Obey (D Wis.) and including Lloyd Meeds (D Wash.) and Norman E. D'Amours (D N.H.). The reform plan tightened bookkeeping and housekeeping procedures, overhauling the system of allowances and requiring full public disclosure of House spending.

Democrats Action on Ethics Reform

The House Democratic Caucus June 23 adopted 12 of the reform proposals following stormy morning and evening meetings. The package ran into unexpectedly strong opposition from members from safe districts and from others who opposed provisions that would bar them from withdrawing as much as $11,000 a year in cash.

Supporters of the reform package rejected during the caucus session four amendments that would have made it more difficult for Democrats to implement the changes and eliminated or narrowed the plan to consolidate seven separate expense accounts into a single account.

The caucus voted down a series of proposed amendments:

● By a 112-227 vote, the caucus defeated an amendment proposed by Mendel J. Davis (S.C.) that would have required the committee to report the reform proposals to the House, thus allowing Republicans to vote on the changes.

● By a 56-107 vote, the caucus rejected an amendment offered by Jonathan B. Bingham (N.Y.) that would have eliminated the consolidated account and a prohibition on members spending unused clerk-hire funds on computer and equipment rental.

● By a 71-112 vote, the caucus defeated an amendment proposed by Bob Eckhardt (Texas) that would have separated the telecommunications and travel allowances from the consolidated account.

● An amendment sponsored by Robert N. Giaimo (Conn.) to eliminate the consolidation, staff reporting and all account changes from the resolution was beaten back on a 75-148 vote.

Earlier, Majority Leader O'Neill withdrew the one controversial provision that allowed the Speaker to name the Democratic members of the House Administration Committee.

The caucus also approved Thompson as chairman of the Administration Committee and the House ratified the choice later in the day by a 295-4 vote with 106 Republicans voting present.

After the caucus approved the reform proposals they were sent back to the Administration Committee, some to be ratified and some to be cleared for further action on the House floor.

Perquisite Changes

The House Administration Committee June 28 wrapped up action on its segments of the housekeeping reform package approved by the House Democratic Caucus June 23. The committee adopted a series of orders that implemented those proposals not requiring House action.

The orders approved at the panel's June 28 meeting:

● Reduced the 20-cents-a mile allowance for automobile travel for House members to 15 cents, the amount set by the General Services Administration for federal employees, effective July 1.

● Required House members and chairmen of committees and subcommittees to certify monthly the salaries and duties of their staffs and to disclose any kinships between staff employees and any House member. This change would become effective 30 days after the Administration Committee approved the certification forms.

● Required quarterly reports of how House funds are spent. The reports would be indexed according to employees and employing offices, showing the titles and salaries. The first report under the new format was expected to cover the third quarter of 1976 ending Sept. 30.

● Required that disbursements be made only on the presentation of vouchers.

● Eliminated the separate postage stamp allowance, $1,140 in 1976, and ended the so-called "cash-out" practice that permitted members to convert unused stationery and travel allowances into cash for their personal use. These changes were not to take effect until the beginning of the 95th Congress.

● Gave the committee the power to adjust the clerk-hire allowance, $238,584 at the time, to reflect federal government cost-of-living raises.

● Revised the telephone and telegraph allowance to permit each member to have two WATS (wide area telephone service) lines to reduce costs for long-distance phone calls. If a member opted for the WATS lines, he would give up half of his annual telecommunications allowance.

● Revised the system of allowances used by members to run their offices by permitting members for the first time to transfer money from one fund to another. The new system would take effect in the 95th Congress. The Democratic leadership task force had proposed that seven separate accounts be consolidated into a single allowance.

According to Lloyd Meeds (D Wash.), one of the three-man task force that drafted the changes, the consolidated account would lead to a savings of about $1,400 to $9,000 a year.

Following is Meeds' comparison of the amounts of money involved in the two plans:

Existing System

Travel	$ 7,168
Taxi	1,280
Postage	1,140
District office	2,000
Telephone	14,062
Stationery	6,500
Equipment rental	9,000
Newsletter	5,000
District office rental	9,555
Total	**$55,705**

Consolidated System

Travel	$ 6,515
District office expenses:	
Stationery, equipment rental, and newsletter	22,500
District office rental	9,555
Telephone (without WATS service)	15,750
Total	**$54,320**

Amount to be reduced by one-half if WATS service is used.

Final Package Approved

House Democrats completed action on their package of reforms to overhaul the House's system of allowances and housekeeping procedures over the strenuous objections of conservatives in their own party and most Republicans.

The House July 1 adopted two resolutions recommended by the House Democratic Caucus that 1) es-

---

Travel and Salaries

The Wayne Hays scandal had an impact beyond the resignation of the powerful Ohio Democrat from Congress and the move by the House to reduce the power of the Administration Committee.

On June 18 the House quietly moved to undo one of the small favors Hays had performed during his years as a Capitol Hill power broker.

The vehicle was the 1977 State Department authorization bill (HR 13179). An amendment to that measure, requiring that annual foreign travel expense reports compiled by committee chairman and delegation chiefs be printed in the *Congressional Record*, was adopted by voice vote.

The reports had been published in varying form in the Record every year between 1958 and 1974. In 1973 the House approved a change in the law, sponsored by Hays, that terminated the publication of the reports.

The change was a virtually unnoticed provision in the annual State Department authorization (PL 93-126). When it came to light in 1974, Hays told *Congressional Quarterly*: "We decided we weren't going to spend eight or nine thousand dollars to let you guys [reporters] do your stories on congressional travel."

Nevertheless, public criticism of the change in 1974 resulted in the addition of a provision to the legislative branch appropriations bill (PL 93-371) which reinstated the requirement for the reports but required that they be filed with the secretary of the Senate and the clerk of the House rather than be published in the *Congressional Record*. The 1976 action fully reinstated the original requirement. *(Details, chapter on Pay and Perquisites, p. 27)*

---

tablished a 15-member commission to study the chamber's accounting and personnel procedures and 2) stripped the House Administration Committee of its unilateral power to alter representatives' benefits and allowances.

Rep. Frank Thompson Jr. (D N.J.), the committee's new chairman, also announced June 25 that he had ordered the congressional General Accounting Office (GAO) to audit his committee's books "and all accounts controlled by the committee...."

The House Rules Committee June 30 had set the stage for the sharply partisan debate on the reform package by clearing it for floor action under guidelines pushed by the House Democratic leadership. By straight 11-5 party line votes, the committee gave closed rules to the resolutions creating the study commission (H Res 1368) and abrogating the House Administration's power to change members' perquisites (H Res 1372).

The action was a victory for the Democratic leaders, who feared that the reform moves would be stalled or possibly defeated if Republicans and dissident Democrats were given the opportunity to offer amendments.

Republicans excoriated the Democrats on the House floor for trying to ram through the proposals, calling them a "cosmetic sham" designed to relieve the Democrats of responsibility for the scandals.

Attacking H Res 1368, which set up the study commission, John B. Anderson (R Ill.), chairman of the House

Republican Conference, accused the Democrats of acting in an "undemocratic and anti-reform fashion.... Where is all that sunshine you crave? Have you been frightened off by one little Ray?" he asked, referring to Elizabeth Ray.

Minority Leader John J. Rhodes (R Ariz.) called the commission a "whitewash."

The Republican motion to recommit H Res 1368 was rejected by a 143-269 vote that followed party lines. The resolution then was adopted 380-30.

The Democrats had a more difficult time passing H Res 1372, the key item in their reforms. The Republican strategy was to recommit the resolution and then try to amend it to reverse the House Administration Committee's action earlier in the week changing the members' allowances. That would have forced a House vote on the changes instituted by the panel June 28.

Rhodes called H Res 1372 a "sham and a hoax" since the Administration Committee still retained the authority to raise House perquisites to reflect changes in the cost of materials, services or office space and cost-of-living pay increases given to federal government employees.

Robert E. Bauman (R Md.) said the Democrats were using the resolution to gain political credit for ending the abuses that brought on the sex-payroll scandals. "The scandals which have been exposed are part and parcel of a system in which concentration of power allowed to accumulate in the hands of a few members led to inevitable abuse," he said. "If that is what the present system produced, need we ask whether the system must be fundamentally changed, not next year, but right now?"

The resolution ran into resistance from some Democrats, who warned their colleagues against changing the system of House perquisites too quickly. "I plead with my colleagues, let us go slowly," said Robert N. Giaimo (D Conn.), who opposed the change to a consolidated account. "We are voting ourselves an expense account, and it is going to come back and haunt us."

Defending the Administration Committee's orders, Thompson said they were "a genuine improvement in the existing accounts system, both in terms of flexibility to the member and accountability to the House and our constituents."

Richard Bolling (D Mo.), a member of the Rules Committee, said the resolution was brought to the House floor under a closed rule to make sure the Democrats' reforms were adopted. "[I]f we get into the amendment stage and into an open rule situation, because of the enormous differences that exist on both sides of the aisle and with the attitudes that are so different, we would end up with an unraveling of what I believe to be a useful package," he said.

Despite the Republican attack, H Res 1372 survived two test votes before it was adopted. A Democratic move to shut off debate on the resolution—and thus prevent the Republicans from offering amendments—was adopted 220-190. A motion by Rhodes to recommit it was defeated 165-236. The resolution eventually was adopted 311-92.

Hays' Retirement

But the House action on reform did not solve Wayne Hays' problems. Investigations of the Ohio Democrat continued in the House ethics committee and in the Justice Department. Newspaper stories raised questions about whether Hays might have been guilty of financial improprieties in his role as chairman of the House International Relations International Operations Subcommittee.

Faced with possible public hearings, Hays on Aug. 13 announced that he would retire from Congress at the end of his term.

Hays said that he had planned to retire anyway at the end of 1978, his 30th year in Congress. But he said that his current state of health "coupled with the harassment my family and I have taken from *The Washington Post,*" led to his decision to withdraw.

But still the investigations continued, and on Sept. 1, Hays took the final step, resigning from Congress.

Both the House ethics committee and the Justice Department subsequently called off their inquiries into Hays' affairs.

Robert L. F. Sikes

Only twenty-eight days after the sharp partisan debate over perquisites changes, the House July 29, without fanfare or much visible drama, voted 381-3 to reprimand Rep. Robert L. F. Sikes (D Fla.) for financial misconduct. The vote marked the first time the House had punished one of its members since 1969, when it fined Adam Clayton Powell (D N.Y.) and stripped him of his seniority.

Sikes had been charged with sponsoring legislation in Congress to remove restrictions from Florida land he owned an interest in, failing to disclose certain financial holdings and other alleged conflicts of interest.

Robert L. F. Sikes

The Sikes action began early in 1976 with an investigation into his financial holdings by Common Cause. On April 7, Common Cause filed an official complaint with the House ethics committee endorsed by 45 members of the House. In taking the action against Sikes, Common Cause Chairman John Gardner charged that "the ethics committee has exemplified the buddy system at its worst. The committee has a perfect record of never having carried out a formal investigation of any member of the House since the committee was created eight years ago."

The ethics committee responded to Gardner's criticism by voting 10-2 on July 21 to approve a 498-page report on Sikes' dealings and recommending House adoption of a resolution reprimanding the Florida Democrat.

Charges

The report cited three instances where it said Sikes' actions "have violated standards of conduct applicable to all members of Congress." They were:

● Failure to report ownership of stock in Fairchild Industries, Inc., from 1968 through 1973, and in the First Navy Bank at the Pensacola Naval Air Station, Pensacola, Fla., in 1974, as required by House rules. Although Sikes' failure to report these holdings did not appear to be "an effort to conceal" them from Congress or the public, the report declared: "The committee believes that the failure to report...is deserving of a reprimand."

● Sikes' investment in stock of the First Navy Bank at the same time that he was using his influence to obtain a charter and federal deposit insurance for the bank. "If an opinion had been requested of this committee in advance about the propriety of the investment, it would have been disapproved," the report said.

• The sponsorship of legislation in 1961 that removed restrictions on Florida land parcels without disclosing that Sikes had an interest in the same land. The committee did not recommend any punishment for this action because, it said, it took place so long ago and "at least to some extent" the circumstances "appear to have been known to Representative Sikes' constituency, which has continually re-elected him to Congress." The committee also noted that Sikes had sold some of the land after the bill he had sponsored passed the House, but before it passed the Senate. Although recommending no punishment, the committee said Sikes' involvement with the legislation "created an obvious and significant conflict of interest."

In the first two instances, the committee specified that adoption of the report would constitute a reprimand.

On another charge, the committee concluded that Sikes did not violate House rules when he voted for a fiscal year 1975 defense appropriations bill (HR 16243—PL 93-437) that contained a $73-million appropriation for an aircraft contract with Fairchild Industries. The committee determined that Sikes' ownership of 1,000 shares out of the more than 4.5 million shares outstanding in Fairchild was not "sufficient to disqualify him from voting on the bill."

Sikes denied any wrongdoing, and charged that the ethics committee conducted a "one-sided" investigation.

House Action

The floor debate on the one-sentence resolution calling for adoption of the ethics committee report recommending reprimand lasted only 20 minutes. Sikes, who did not speak in his own behalf, sat quietly and without expression behind a microphone three rows from the well of the House.

Reprimand vs. Censure. John J. Flynt Jr. (D Ga.), chairman of the ethics committee, said he saw no real difference between a reprimand and a censure, but that the committee members decided to use the word reprimand. Asked if Sikes had been dealt with "easy," Flynt replied: "As I told another House member who asked that, if it happened to you, you wouldn't think it was easy."

House Speaker Carl Albert (D Okla.), asked by reporters after the vote whether he thought a reprimand was sufficient punishment, said, "That's a pretty severe thing to have in your record as a member of Congress."

In the case of a vote to reprimand, no further action is taken against a member. Under censure, the member has to stand in the well of the House and be publicly admonished by the Speaker.

Sikes later told reporters he did not think the vote would hurt his chances of re-election to a 19th term in Congress; and indeed, he ran unopposed in the November elections.

Loses Chairmanship. Nonetheless, Sikes fared less well with his colleagues in Congress than he had with his constituents. When the 95th Congress convened, the House Democratic Caucus, anxious to demonstrate a commitment to ethical conduct, voted Jan. 26 to oust Sikes from the chairmanship of the House Military Construction Appropriations Subcommittee.

The vote of 189-93 surprised even the backers of the oust-Sikes movement who had expected to win but by a much narrower margin. The caucus the next day elected Gunn McKay (D Utah) to the chairmanship.

Supporters of Sikes argued during debate in the caucus that the House reprimand was enough punishment and that additional action would constitute double jeopardy. "How many times does a man have to stand in judgment and answer the same charges brought against him?" said John J. Flynt Jr. (D Ga.), chairman of the House ethics committee in defending Sikes before the caucus.

Sikes' opponents argued during the caucus meeting that the integrity of the House was at stake and that a failure to remove him from his post would undermine moves to tighten up the House code of ethics.

"If we are not prepared to enforce the code of ethics, then it is a futile exercise to write one," said Richardson Preyer (D N.C.), who was named to head a special committee to draft a new code for the House.

After the vote, Sikes blamed a "coalition of liberal lobbies and liberal news media" for his defeat and said that the real issue was his support for a strong national defense.

The vote against Sikes was something of a blow to the newly elected House Democratic leadership. Both Speaker Thomas P. O'Neill Jr. (D Mass.) and Majority Leader Jim Wright (D Texas) had announced that they would vote to keep Sikes in his post. O'Neill later said that his statement represented his personal view, not a leadership position.

Despite the loss of his chairmanship, Sikes remained a power in the House Appropriations Committee where he continued to sit on both the Defense Subcommittee and the Military Construction Subcommittee, one of only two Democrats to serve on the two panels most directly concerned with issues of national defense spending.

Gulf Oil Contributions

The Gulf Oil political contributions scandal which broke in December 1975 implicated dozens of members. But the bulk of public attention focused on charges that Senate Minority Leader Hugh Scott had received up to $100,000 in illegal campaign contributions from Gulf Oil lobbyist Claude Wild between 1960 and 1973.

According to Senate sources, Scott told the Select Committee on Standards and Conduct in August that he had received $45,000 from Wild, but had given the money to other senators for their political campaigns rather than keeping it himself.

The Senate committee spent 10 months trying to figure out what to do about the Scott case before calling the Pennsylvania Republican in for questioning.

Scott refused to answer reporters' questions regarding the Gulf Oil allegations. "I have denied any impropriety whatsoever. That denial stands," he told Congressional Quarterly Sept. 14 through an aide.

On Sept. 15, the ethics committee voted 5-1 in closed session not to investigate the matter. Scott retired from Congress at the end of 1976.

Meanwhile, several other senators involved in the Gulf matter were questioned by the special prosecutor's office or by a federal grand jury. Among those questioned were Strom Thurmond (R S.C.), Robert P. Griffin (R Mich.), Charles H. Percy (R Ill.) and Clifford P. Hansen (R Wyo.).

Republican vice presidential candidate Sen. Robert Dole (R Kan.) also appeared before the grand jury to answer questions about his involvement with Gulf, but denied ever having received any money from the oil company or from Scott.

Defense 'Hospitality' Probe

Seventeen members of the Senate and House acknowledged during 1976 that they visited hunting lodges as guests of major defense contractors on one or more occasions. The dates of the visit were not all known, but most appeared to have been between 1970 and 1975. These members insisted there was nothing improper in their acceptance of such invitations, and some pointed out that many of the companies involved had offices or plants in their own states or districts.

Acceptance of any gift of "substantial value" from a company with an interest in legislation was expressly forbidden by House rules. The Senate had no such regulation at the time. (In 1977, both chambers passed measures restricting acceptance of gifts from lobbyists.)

The Defense Department on Oct. 22, 1975, sent letters to 36 military officers and four civilian officials in the Pentagon admonishing them for "lack of judgment" in accepting similar hunting invitations from defense contractors.

Background

Beginning in 1961, the Northrop Corporation engaged in an extensive program of activities, some of them illegal, designed to promote goodwill for the company's products at home and abroad. An illegal $150,000 contribution to the 1972 Nixon campaign was investigated by the Watergate Special Prosecutor, the Senate Select Committee on Presidential Campaign Activities and the Securities and Exchange Commission. In addition, a class-action lawsuit was filed on behalf of Northrop stockholders and a special audit was undertaken by the corporation's accounting firm, Ernst & Ernst.

The audit revealed that the corporation had rented a goose-hunting facility on Maryland's eastern shore and that between 1971 and 1973 the lodge had been visited 120 times by the Northrop staff, 123 times by military personnel, 21 times by civilian Pentagon officials, 11 times by members of Congress, 85 times by congressional staffers and 49 times by other persons.

The audit also revealed the company's practice of allowing federal, state and local officials to ride on the corporation's private aircraft if such flights were already scheduled for company business.

Investigations of Northrop's activities by the Joint Committee on Defense Production and the Senate Foreign Relations Subcommittee on Multinational Corporations during the summer and fall of 1975 revealed that hunting facilities were used for similar purposes by other defense contractors, including Rockwell International Corp. and Remington Arms Co. Inc., a subsidiary of E. I. Dupont de Nemours & Co.

In hearings Feb. 2-3, 1976, the Joint Committee on Defense Production investigated the scope and significance of such corporate favors to Pentagon officials. Committee Vice Chairman Sen. William Proxmire (D Wis.) accused the Defense Department of lax enforcement of its own conflict-of-interest regulations and said that it had been "less than zealous" in its probe of the widely reported hunting trips by Pentagon personnel. But the committee avoided any reference to members' participation in the same activity.

Six senators and 12 members of the House had acknowledged acceptance of hospitality from at least one major defense contractor.

Legal Restrictions on Foreign Gifts

Article I, Section 9, Clause 8 of the U.S. Constitution states: "No title of nobility shall be granted by the United States and no person holding any office of profit or trust under them shall, without the consent of Congress, accept of any present, emolument, office or title of any kind whatever from any king, prince or foreign state."

At various times, Congress has granted special permission for federal employees to accept gifts from foreign governments. Most recently, the Foreign Gifts and Decorations Act of 1966 (PL 89-673) allowed officials to accept gifts worth less than $50 or more expensive gifts if refusal to accept would damage U.S. foreign relations. In the latter case, however, the gifts were required to be turned over to the U.S. government.

All other gifts from foreign governments or their agents were banned under the law. This broad prohibition against gifts from foreign governments, however, left one possible loophole. It did not explicitly include travel expenses in the definition of gifts.

In order to close that loophole, a number of federal agencies, including the State Department, have issued guidelines prohibiting their employees from accepting travel from foreign governments.

On June 25, 1974, the House Committee on Standards of Official Conduct issued an advisory opinion stating that "acceptance of travel or living expenses in *specie* or in kind by any member of employee of the House of Representatives from any foreign government, official agent or representative therefore is prohibited."

When the Senate ethics committee proposed that that body adopt a similar rule, however, the resolution (S Res 325) was quietly tabled by the full Senate on July 2, 1976.

The resolution was tabled on a motion by Senate Majority Leader Mike Mansfield (D Mont.). Mansfield, in a joint statement with Minority Leader Hugh Scott (R Pa.), had argued two years earlier that trips abroad for U.S. officials at the expense of foreign governments should be allowed because the United States operates programs to bring foreign officials to this country.

"If these U.S. programs are to continue to be effective," Mansfield and Scott argued, "they must derive from the principle of reciprocity and mutuality. They can hardly be deemed highly desirable when foreign personnel come to this nation and then frowned upon when American personnel go abroad under similar arrangements."

As a result, since June 1974 House members and employees had been expressly forbidden from accepting any gifts, including travel, from foreign governments, while senators and their employees in effect were free to decide for themselves whether the constitutional ban on gifts from foreign governments

There was, however, no ban in either house in 1976 on acceptance of gifts from foreign private, non-profit foundations. In 1977, both chambers passed rules restricting acceptance of gifts from lobbyists or from foreign nationals.

South Korean Connection

The story of South Korean efforts to influence members of the House of Representatives loomed as a major obstacle to the peace of mind of the 95th Congress. Allegations of the activities of the "South Korea lobby" emerged piecemeal for more than a year; by early 1977, many of them had not yet been proven. Nonetheless, the picture that emerged was one that could damage both the Congress and U.S.-South Korean relations.

At the end of 1976, five investigations were proceeding into the matter, including inquiries by the Justice Department, the Securities and Exchange Commission (SEC), the House ethics committee, the House International Relations Subcommittee on International Organizations and the House Judiciary Subcommittee on Civil and Constitutional Rights. As a Justice Department spokesman phrased it, the investigation was "not one for a short-distance sprinter."

The reason for the likely longevity of these inquiries was the vastness and the complexity of the alleged activities by South Koreans. The scandal emerged through the press, with newspapers including *The Washington Post, The Washington Star* and *The New York Times* providing new pieces of the puzzle throughout the last several months of 1976.

The early focus of the investigative reporting was on the activities of Washington-based businessman Tongsun Park (the westernized arrangement of his name, Park Tong Sun). Acting on behalf of the South Korean government, he was reported to have passed out large sums of money, running well into the hundreds of thousands of dollars each year since 1970, to various members of Congress. As many as 90 persons associated with Congress ultimately could be implicated in Park's largesse, although this was considered unlikely. That widely reported figure derived from a list of 90 targeted Capitol Hill figures that was found in Park's possession during a routine border search in December 1973.

In addition to Park, news reports drew attention to at least one possible Korean operative who was on the House payroll in 1976: Suzi Park Thomson, who was employed by the office of Speaker Carl Albert (D Okla.). Thomson, who was accused of being a Korean Central Intelligence Agency (KCIA) agent, was, like Park, known for extravagant parties despite her reported salary of $15,000.

Fraser Hearings

The threads of a reported KCIA presence in the United States prompted Rep. Donald M. Fraser (D Minn.), chairman of the International Organizations Subcommittee, to hold three sets of hearings on the matter in 1976. The hearings focused largely on the apparent activities of the KCIA in the fast-growing Korean community within the United States. The testimony also underscored the parallel activities of KCIA agents in other nations.

Ethics Committee Probe

With the Justice Department and SEC continuing their investigations, the House Ethics committee moved in late 1976 and early 1977 to open its own probe to determine the extent of congressional wrongdoing involving the Korean lobby. In a press conference Dec. 15, Chairman John J. Flynt Jr. (D Ga.) announced that the committee would begin a full investigation of the matter.

The committee proceeded to hire Philip A. Lacovara, a former top aide to the Watergate special prosecutor, as counsel to the investigation. And on Jan. 31, 1977, the committee voted to request the House for a $530,000 investigative budget—double the previous year's appropriation.

On Feb. 9, the House put itself overwhelmingly on record as favoring an intensive inquiry into the Korean matter, voting 388-0 to adopt a resolution authorizing the ethics committee to "conduct a full and complete inquiry to determine whether members of the House of Representatives, their immediate families, or their associates accepted anything of value, directly or indirectly, from the Government of Korea or representatives thereof." The House vote in effect pre-empted arguments of ethics committee critics that the panel could not conduct a credible probe into Korean bribery allegations and that the investigation should instead be entrusted to a new select committee.

Paid Taiwan Visits

All-expense-paid visits to Nationalist China by members of Congress and their aides became an issue in late 1976 and early 1977 as questions were raised concerning the legality of the trips.

The visits were financed by an organization called the Pacific Cultural Foundation (PCF). Between 1974, when the PCF was founded, and late 1976, 18 members of Congress and more than 100 congressional aides had taken PCF-financed trips to Asia. Numerous others had declined PCF invitations, due to uncertainty concerning the nature of the foundation and its ties to the government of Taiwan.

The State Department told those who inquired that it was under the impression the PCF was a front organization set up by the Taiwanese government to circumvent statutory restrictions prohibiting U.S. officials from accepting gifts from foreign governments. *(Box p. 9)*

Nevertheless, a number of members of Congress and their aides chose to accept the PCF claim to be a private organization and were therefore able to justify accepting the trips.

As of early 1977, neither the House nor the Senate ethics panels had made a definitive ruling on the matter. When one aide invited on a PCF trip in 1976 asked the House ethics committee for a written ruling on whether or not the trip would be proper, committee staff director John M. Swanner wrote: "This [ethics] committee has been advised that the Department of State is under the impression that the Pacific Cultural Foundation, 'although ostensibly a private organization, is closely controlled by the government of the Republic of China.'"

The letter went on to outline the rules against accepting gifts from foreign governments or their agents. But in conclusion, Swanner wrote, "In the final analysis, a determination of the propriety of acceptance of such trips depends on whether the Pacific Cultural Foundation is in fact an official agent or representative" of the Chinese government.

"The committee," Swanner said, "has no definite or conclusive evidence upon which it can make such a determination."

Criminal Actions

The following criminal actions were taken against current or former members of Congress in 1976:

Hinshaw

Incumbent Rep. Andrew J. Hinshaw (R Calif.) was sentenced to concurrent one-to-14-year jail terms Feb. 24 for two bribery convictions stemming from his first race for the House in 1972. A California jury had convicted Hinshaw Jan. 26.

Originally indicted in May 1975, Hinshaw had been charged with soliciting a $1,000 campaign contribution and accepting bribes in the form of stereo equipment from Tandy Corp., parent firm of Radio Shack stores. He was convicted on both of those charges. The jury acquitted Hinshaw on a separate charge of soliciting a bribe. Eight other charges, including grand theft and misappropriation of public funds, had been dismissed in October 1975 for lack of sufficient evidence.

Hinshaw was assessor of Orange County at the time the offenses occurred. The prosecution contended that Tandy was given an assessment reduction in return for favors to Hinshaw.

On June 30, Rep. Charles E. Wiggins, another California Republican, introduced a resolution calling for Hinshaw's expulsion from the House. Wiggins cited Hinshaw's conviction on the bribery charges and his refusal to resign. Hinshaw had been defeated for renomination to his seat in the June 8 California primary and had refrained from voting throughout 1976, as required by House rules whenever a member is convicted for any crime which could bring a jail sentence of two years or more.

On Sept. 2, the House ethics committee voted 2-10 against the Wiggins resolution. Wiggins called the privileged resolution to the floor Oct. 1, but it was tabled by voice vote without debate. The only previous cases of expulsion had involved support of the Confederacy in 1861. A common sentiment in the House was that Hinshaw should not be expelled for offenses which occurred prior to his tenure in office.

Late in the summer of 1976, Hinshaw's trial on other charges contained in the same 1975 indictment began. In this case, Hinshaw was charged with fraud and theft in connection with his use of assessor's office personnel in his 1972 campaign. On Sept. 3, Supreme Court Justice William H. Rehnquist rejected Hinshaw's plea to block this second jury trial.

Jones

Rep. James R. Jones (D Okla.) pleaded guilty to a misdemeanor Jan. 29 on a charge that he failed to report a 1972 cash contribution from Gulf Oil Corporation. There was no evidence that Jones knew he was receiving the money illegally from corporate funds.

On March 16, Jones was fined $200 in the case. He had faced a fine of up to $1,000 or a jail sentence up to one year.

Helstoski

Rep. Henry Helstoski (D N.J.) was indicted by a federal grand jury in New Jersey June 2 on charges that he solicited and accepted bribes from Chilean and Argentinian aliens in return for introducing bills to block their deportation from the United States. Helstoski and three aides were charged with bribery, conspiracy, obstruction of justice and lying to a federal grand jury.

Helstoski and his aides were accused of operating an extortion scheme between 1967 and June 1975. The indictment said Helstoski had received $5,500 on behalf of five Chilean aliens, $1,500 on behalf of two Argentinians and at least $1,735 from two New Jersey lawyers specializing in immigration cases. Helstoski denounced the charges as politically motivated, saying they were part of a "five-year vendetta" against him.

On June 25, Helstoski pleaded not guilty to the charges and was released on a $10,000 personal recognizance bond pending trial. He was defeated for re-election Nov. 2. A trial date was set for Feb. 15, 1977.

Clay

On Oct. 27, the Justice Department announced that it had decided to drop a civil suit pending against Rep. William (Bill) Clay (D Mo.) after Clay agreed to repay the government $1,754 in overpayments for travel expenses. Department officials said there was no attempt to collect any penalties from Clay in the settlement, only the actual amount the department estimated that Clay owed the government.

The Justice Department on June 4 had taken over the suit brought against Clay under the False Claims Act for recovery of double the money paid out to the Missouri Democrat in reimbursements for allegedly fraudulent travel vouchers. The suit originally had been filed by a first-year law student from Buffalo, N.Y. The student, Alan R.

Atmosphere and 'Perks'

Perhaps more significant than actual instances of criminal misconduct leading to indictment was what Anthony Marro, writing in the Jan. 30, 1977, *New York Times*, termed "the atmosphere of congressional existence" that "affects negatively, not only the way congressmen behave but the laws they pass." Members' extensive perquisites often lead them to consider themselves in a special, select class not bound by codes of conduct that govern the general public. The legislative process itself, laced with pressures from outside special interests, vote trade-offs and special favors also produces a tendency to compromise ethical standards.

Noted Marro: "what some critics see in the pattern of congressional behavior is deception—voting down pay raises while quietly increasing other benefits that the public knows little about—that is of a piece with the way Congress conducts much of its work. 'There are a lot of things they do that are devious,' says one congressional aide. 'And this sets the standards and the ethical climate.

" 'They vote down amendments and then vote up the bills,' he said, referring to a common practice in which congressmen will try to weaken, for example, a clean air act to satisfy industry, then vote for the final version so they can tell the public they favor clean air.... They're building a record to campaign on, and a lot of it is appearance instead of reality.' "

"The most pervasive form of access-buying is in campaign contributions," Marro continued. "The whole process of raising campaign money automatically confronts all congressmen with ethical decisions, since it puts them in debt to persons or groups who identify their private interests with the public good. It is not difficult for many congressmen who have received large campaign contributions to perceive the same illusory common good."

Hollander, filed the suit after reading a story in the March 23 *Wall Street Journal* which accused Clay of filing vouchers for trips to his home district in St. Louis on dates when records showed him traveling elsewhere or present and voting in the House. The Journal also implicated Clay for a relatively common practice of billing the House for auto travel expenses, when he actually had flown to St. Louis at lower cost. Under rules revised in 1975, members could receive reimbursement for up to 26 trips a year to their districts.

Clay consistently denied any fraud or improper claims, saying that any discrepancies were the result of clerical errors made on vouchers, filled out by his staff long after the trips in question were made. On June 23, Clay introduced a bill (HR 14526) to repeal the False Claims Act for future cases. The bill died at the end of the 94th Congress.

The Justice Department also announced Oct. 27 that it had decided not to file civil suits against nine other House members it had investigated for alleged travel overcharges. Department officials reportedly had determined that it would be impossible to prove that any of the nine members had intentionally committed fraud.

All nine members had been under investigation for receiving reimbursement for automobile trips to and from their home districts when they actually traveled by plane. Normally, reimbursements for auto travel are greater than those for air travel.

Most of the members under investigation claimed the overpayments resulted from clerical errors made by their staff aides. A Justice Department spokesman said at least some repayments by the House members had been made, but he declined to say how much or whether all nine had been required to make repayments.

The nine members included: Rep. Ray J. Madden (D Ind.), Margaret M. Heckler (R Mass.), Tim Lee Carter (R Ky.), Walter Flowers (D Ala.), Otto E. Passman (D La.), Bill D. Burlison (D Mo.), George E. Shipley (D Ill.), Robert E. Jones (D Ala.) and Gene Taylor (R Mo.).

Howe

Rep. Allan T. Howe (D Utah) was found guilty July 23 of soliciting sex for hire from two undercover Salt Lake City policewomen posing as prostitutes. Howe had been arrested June 12. He was sentenced to 30 days in jail and a $150 fine.

Howe appealed the municipal court decision, but on Aug. 24 a state district jury found him guilty a second time. The next day the trial judge gave Howe a 30-day suspended sentence and ordered him to pay court costs estimated at about $500. Despite pleas from Democratic leaders in Utah and the resignation of all but one of his paid campaign staffers, Howe refused to drop out of the race for re-election to the House seat he had first won in 1974. Howe's voting privilege was not affected. He was one of two freshmen elected in 1974 to be defeated in the 1976 congressional election.

Horton

Rep. Frank Horton (R N.Y.) in August was given an 11-day jail sentence for speeding. Horton had been arrested in the early morning hours of July 18 after a high-speed chase on the New York Thruway near Batavia. Police charged him with speeding and drunken driving.

After pleading guilty to the charges, Horton was sentenced Aug. 31 to the jail sentence and a $200 fine—$100 each on the two charges. He was released Sept. 7 after serving less than a week of his sentence. Officials said he had received time off for good behavior.

Hastings

Former Rep. James F. Hastings (R N.Y. 1969-75) was indicted Sept. 21 by a federal grand jury in Washington for operating an alleged kickback scheme with members of his congressional staff.

Prosecutors contended that Hastings' executive secretary and two part-time staff members in his New York district office had been involved in the scheme which allowed Hastings to use parts of their salaries for his children's college education, for purchase of an automobile and a snowmobile, for contributions to his New York State retirement plan and for other purposes. The indictment listed 26 counts of mail fraud and nine counts of false statements to House officials in connection with the fraud scheme. None of the employees was indicted.

On Oct. 1, Hastings pleaded innocent to the charges. On Dec. 17, he was convicted on 28 felony counts and was sentenced to serve 20 months to five years in federal prison.

1977 Developments:
New Ethics Codes Approved

"Congressmen see the responsibility for disciplining colleagues guilty of improper behavior as having three dimensions—each congressman personally, the House [or Senate] as an institution, and constituents are all capable of curbing a legislator's actions, although not with equal effectiveness," wrote authors Beard and Horn in their 1975 study of congressional ethics.[1] "Often the least effective and most difficult way to discipline congressional behavior is to have individual members attempt it.... A more viable approach is for the House [or Senate] to assume responsibility for defending itself against behavior that weakens it as an institution.... [T]he third approach—having the district take responsibility for the behavior of its chosen representative...could be the most effective, even if it has not always been in the past. As one member said, 'It's up to the district; if they want to send a bum here, what can we do?'

"...[T]he lack of ethical standards in Congress...[is] rooted in the nation's political institutions," the authors continued. "How, then, can the reforms be achieved that low public confidence in government seems to call for? Ironically, the very climate that has accelerated the erosion of public trust may bring forth the answer. The atmosphere surrounding a heavily publicized scandal is conducive to the reordering of old standards; indeed, it appears to be vital for such change to take place."

These observations appeared to be borne out in early 1977. Prompted by the scandals of 1976 and critical public reaction to the tendency of Congress to do nothing about them, both chambers began work on drawing up new ethics codes. With House Speaker Thomas P. O'Neill Jr. (D Mass.) riding close herd on his Democratic colleagues, the House March 2 overwhelmingly adopted a resolution (H Res 287) imposing strict new regulations on the financial activities of its members. The Senate followed suit one month later, adopting a similar ethics code. *(pp. 18, 22)*

Obey Commission

In the House, the job of drafting the new code had been given to a bipartisan, 15-member study commission (the Commission on Administrative Review), chaired by David R. Obey (D Wis.). Similarly, the Senate Jan. 18 passed a resolution creating a special 15-member committee, chaired by Gaylord Nelson (D Wis.) to formulate a comprehensive code of ethics for that chamber by early March.

The House panel was created July 1, 1976, in the wake of the chamber's sex-payroll scandals involving Wayne Hays. The commission had been recommended by the House Democratic Caucus to follow up on the housekeeping and administrative reforms adopted by the House Administration Committee in late June. The panel included five Democratic and three Republican House members and seven from the public. *(Box, p. 14)*

The commission had a tough job ahead: improving ethical standards on Capitol Hill is a complex matter, involving changes in the nature and use of perquisites, new rules on financial disclosure and acceptance of gifts and favors, limits on campaign contributions, tighter lobby disclosure regulations and a general willingness on the part of Congress to undertake a thorough self-appraisal of its conduct and character as an institution. Although the Obey commission addressed itself to only some of these issues, it soon became apparent that members of the House differed on the nature of the proposed reforms.

At hearings held on Jan. 14 and 15, 1977, the commission heard conflicting recommendations about financial regulations and enforcement of standards of conduct for members. House Speaker O'Neill said he felt the new membership of the House Committee on Standards of Official Conduct (ethics committee) would give that panel the prestige it needed to handle all questions of ethics. *(Box p. 15)*

"These appointments will mean that the ethics committee will have the [public] confidence [it] will need to handle all of these things," O'Neill said.

But Rep. Bill Frenzel (Minn.), the ranking Republican member of the commission, appeared to disagree. Supported by Peter G. Peterson, chairman of the federal salary commission, Frenzel argued in favor of some kind of outside body to audit House members' accounts and review the handling of public money by both the members and committees.

The Obey commission also heard conflicting opinions about what kinds of standards should be set for members of Congress. Peterson argued in favor of abolishing honoraria, private office accounts and other mechanisms by which

---

1. Edmund Beard and Stephen Horn, *Congressional Ethics: the View from the House*, Brookings Institution, Washington, D.C.

special interest groups could exert financial influence on members. "I have heard special interest groups speak very arrogantly about the effect of a few thousand dollars on legislation," he said.

Chesterfield Smith, the former president of the American Bar Association, urged the panel to ban all outside earned income by members, saying that serving in Congress should be a full-time job.

But a panel of members of Congress disagreed. John B. Anderson (R Ill.), the chairman of the House Republican Conference and a leading advocate of House reform, took sharp issue with the suggestion to limit outside earned income. "If you are serious about limiting outside income to between 10 and 15 per cent of a member's salary, I'll soon leave this place," he said. "I don't want to try to educate five college age children with that."

Morris K. Udall (D ariz.) objected to the proposal to limit honoraria. "You're saying that if I have all kinds of inherited wealth in stocks and bonds it's okay. But if I get out on weekends and hustle and get some money from speaking engagements it's not okay," Udall said. The Arizona Democrat said that he favored full disclosure as the best way of preventing abuses.

Commission Recommendations

On Feb. 7, the full commission endorsed a series of proposals on financial accountability recommended by a seven-member task force for the panel. The task force recommendations had been made on Jan. 31—three days before the commission released a poll of the public and a survey of House members to determine their attitudes towards various proposals to revise the rules governing financial accountability and other standards of conduct. *(Box, p. 17)*

Several of the proposals endorsed by the commission were likely to arouse considerable controversy when brought before the full House. Among them was the proposal to ban private office accounts. Private office accounts were maintained by an estimated 140 House members, purportedly to help defray expenses not fully covered by official allowances. However, the accounts were not subject to any regulations. Members were not required to reveal the sources or amounts of contributions to the accounts or even to admit maintaining them. In addition, the funds in the accounts could be used for virtually any purpose.

Obey said that the commission staff estimated that the average office account in the House was maintained at a level of $5,000 and that the largest accounts ran up to $25,000. Office accounts became an issue in late 1976 when then-House Majority Whip John J. McFall (D Calif.) admitted having received a $4,000 secret contribution to his office account from South Korean businessman Tongsun Park, the target of a Justice Department probe into allegations of influence peddling on Capitol Hill.

The task force proposal to ban the office accounts was coupled with a recommendation that the official expense allowances for members be increased by $5,000.

Another proposal likely to arouse opposition in the House limited each member's outside earned income to 15 per cent of his salary. With the Feb. 20 pay raise that increased members' salaries to $57,500, the limit on outside earned income would be $8,625 per member per year for a total of $66,125.

Earned income would include fees for speeches or articles and other so-called honoraria, as well as income from

Members of Obey Commission

The House Commission on Administrative Review is made up of eight House members and seven persons representing the general public. They are:

House Members

David R. Obey (D Wis.), chairman; Melvin Price (D Ill.), Lloyd Meeds (D Wash.), Lee H. Hamilton (D Ind.), Norman E. D'Amours (D N.H.), Bill Frenzel (R Minn.), William L. Armstrong (R Colo.), Robert E. Bauman (R Md.).

Public Members

Ralph K. Huitt, executive director of the National Association of State Universities and Land Grant Colleges; Charles U. Daly, former vice president for government and community affairs at Harvard University; Lucy Benson Wilson, former president of the League of Women Voters; William Duchessi, executive vice president of the Amalgamated Clothing and Textile Workers Union; William R. Hamilton, president of William R. Hamilton and Staff Inc., a market research company; Robert W. Galvin, chairman of the board and chief executive officer of Motorola Inc.; and Roscoe L. Egger Jr., partner in the accounting firm of Price Waterhouse.

law practices or other business activities. It would not, however, cover unearned income such as interest and dividends from stocks or bonds.

The existing ceilings on honoraria were $2,000 for a single speech, article or appearance and an aggregate of $25,000 in any single year. There was no limit on other forms of outside earned income.

The commission staff estimated that during 1975, 62 per cent of all members had income from honoraria or investments. It noted that 56 members had reported aggregate amounts of honoraria for that year ranging from $100 to the then legal limit of $15,000 (which was later raised to $25,000) and that the average income from honoraria exceeded $5,000. The staff report also estimated that 50-75 members received over $5,000 annually for personal services rendered in private business.

Another proposal adopted by the commission that stirred debate would reduce to $750 from $2,000 the limit on individual honoraria payments to members. (The task force had recommended a $500 limit.)

In other major recommendations, the commission proposed that the House:

Gifts to Members. Prohibit gifts of more than $100 in value per year to members of Congress from persons or groups with an interest in legislation, but exclude gifts of personal hospitality.

Mass Mailings. Require that mass mailings sent by representatives go third class, a change that the commission staff estimated would save $9.5-million a year in postage costs.

Use of the Frank. Require that postal patron district-wide mailings by members be submitted to the Franking Commission for an advisory opinion before mailing to avoid abuses of the frank.

Lame Duck Travel. Prohibit travel by lame duck members (i.e. those who have not been re-elected to the succeeding Congress in November or when Congress adjourns *sine die,* whichever comes first) and prohibit members from claiming per diem reimbursement for travel expenses covered by other sources, such as private organizations or other governmental agencies.

Financial Disclosure. Substantially widen financial disclosure regulations for members to cover all income, including honoraria, of over $100 from any one source; gifts of $250 or more from one source and all other gifts aggregating $100 or more from one source except gifts from a relative, gifts of less than $25 in value and gifts of "personal hospitality"; reimbursements of $250 or more from any individual source; holdings of property valued at $1,000 or more; debts of more than $2,500; securities transactions of more than $1,000.

Campaign Contributions. Ban the use of campaign funds to pay off personal debts. (House Democratic Majority Leader Jim Wright of Texas had disclosed on Jan. 26 that he had converted $98,501 of his 1976 campaign contributions to personal funds to pay off debts, a transaction which, although highly unusual, was legal under existing rules.

House Committee Approval

The House commission recommendations were split into three sections and sent to three different committees. The House Administration Committee was given jurisdiction over the section dealing with unofficial office accounts, the Committee on Standards of Official Conduct was given the section covering gifts to members, and the rest of the measure was sent to the Rules Committee.

The code cleared its first hurdle with ease as the Standards Committee voted 8-0 on Feb. 16 to report its section of the resolution (H Rept 95-21, Part 1). The only change it made was to delete a section that exempted gifts of personal hospitality and gifts of under $35 in value from the ban on gifts to members from lobbyists.

More Money for Expenses

The fireworks began in the House Administration Committee. A central target of Republican opposition to the commission recommendations was the provision to increase official expense allowances by $5,000. Bill Frenzel (R Minn.), a member of both the commission and the Administration Committee, charged that the increase was an attempt to "buy" votes for the commission package by increasing the level of spending for all members to the level of the "hogs."

In the first go around the Republicans Feb. 17 prevailed as the committee, on a vote of 12-11 struck from the resolution the $5,000 increase. When word of the committee action reached the House leadership, however, O'Neill swung into action. A second committee meeting was hastily called that afternoon and the Democrats were able to round up enough proxies from absent members to reverse the committee's previous decision. The panel voted 13-12 to reconsider the resolution, then voted to restore the $5,000 provision, and then to reapprove the resolution.

Republicans were incensed, charging in minority views attached to the committee report (H Rept 95-21, Part 2) that the procedure was a "railroad" and accusing the House Democratic leadership of "arm twisting."

New Ethics Committee Members

The House Committee on Standards of Official Conduct (ethics committee) underwent an important change of membership in 1977. Four of the 12 members designated to serve on the panel in the 95th Congress were new members. The change was not only in numbers. Generally the new members were younger and more aggressive than those they replaced.

The new Democratic members of the ethics committee, nominated by the Democratic Steering and Policy Committee on Jan. 13, were Richardson Preyer (N.C.), Walter Flowers (Ala.) and Lee H. Hamilton (Ind.). They replaced F. Edward Hebert (La.), Melvin Price (Ill.) and Thomas S. Foley (Wash.).

The House Republican Conference earlier named Millicent Fenwick (N.J.) to replace Edward Hutchinson (Mich.). Bruce F. Caputo (R N.Y.) replaced Donald J. Mitchell (R N.Y.).

House Speaker Thomas P. O'Neill Jr. (Mass.), who in effect picked the Democrats on the panel, said that his choices would give the ethics committee "a free hand to handle" all complaints about unethical conduct on the part of House members.

The choices brought praise from critics of the ethics committee. Fred Wertheimer of Common Cause, the self-styled citizens lobby that had been highly critical of the ethics committee's performance in the past, said of the new members, "They are a very impressive lot."

One of the first tasks the committee faced will be an investigation of allegations that some House members received gifts from agents of the government of South Korea in return for favorable action on legislation important to that country.

Outside Income Limit

But the biggest hurdle was yet to come. The most widely opposed provision of H Res 287 was that which restricted outside earned income to 15 per cent of a member's official salary. A crucial core of opposition came from the Democratic membership of the Rules Committee.

At committee hearings on Feb. 22, Morgan F. Murphy (D Ill.) charged that by excluding unearned income from the limit the resolution would discriminate in favor of the wealthy. "The American people are not going to be fooled by this," Murphy said. "They will perceive it as protection for the millionaires and very wealthy people around here."

Claude Pepper (D Fla.) called the limit "a gross violation of the Constitution"; Shirley Chisholm (D N.Y.) charged: "People who sit on boards of directors have their interest protected." The Rules Committee had two chores before it: to make substantive changes in the resolution and to decide the rules under which the full House would consider the measure.

After a bit of last-minute maneuvering, including a reportedly heated breakfast meeting between O'Neill and Rules Committee members the morning of the Feb. 24 committee vote, a deal was struck. Murphy and other opponents of the income limit agreed not to press their case in the committee in return for a promise that the full House would be allowed to vote up or down on the issue.

The only matter left unresolved was the leadership's desire to have a fall-back position in the form of a floor amendment that would increase the income limit to $15,000 from 15 per cent of salary ($8,625 at the current salary level of $57,500).

Opponents of any limit charged that the $15,000 amendment was merely designed to give backers of the measure room to maneuver on the floor in case the House rejected the 15 per cent limit. But a motion in the Rules Committee that would have denied the House a chance to vote on the $15,000 amendment, and forced a vote up or down only on the 15 per cent limit, failed on a tie vote of 8-8.

Thereafter all the Democrats fell into line. The committee rejected a motion by John B. Anderson (R Ill.) to allow the full House to vote to amend the $5,000 increase in office accounts. The vote was 2-14 with only Anderson and Delbert H. Latta (R Ohio) voting "aye."

On a straight party line vote of 11-5 the panel then voted down a motion by James H. (Jimmy) Quillen (R Tenn.) that would have provided for a fully open rule on the resolution.

The only major substantive change the Rules Committee made in H Res 287 was to strike a section that would have established a new committee to write the statutory ethics code. Committee member Richard Bolling (D Mo.) explained that this issue would be better dealt with by a separate resolution after the code itself had been adopted.

Money for Speeches, Articles

The panel also voted to increase to $1,000 from $750 the amount of money a member could accept for making a speech or appearance or for writing an article. The move came in response to a similar change in the ethics code that the Senate committee had made the day before at the request of Jacob K. Javits (R N.Y.). Javits, in arguing for the increase, said that there was no reason the Senate should have the same limit on speaking fees as the House, and said that the increase was justified in order to "try to preserve a measure of personal dignity for ourselves."

When Bolling presented the amendment in the Rules Committee the next day to make the same change in the House code, he said that the report on the measure would justify the amendment with a single word, printed in bold-faced type: "Dignity."

House Floor Action

Having been cleared by the three standing committees, the Obey commission proposals went before the whole

Thomas P. O'Neill Jr.

David R. Obey

Principal forces behind House ethics code

House on March 2, where they were adopted very nearly intact by a vote of 402-22.

On a key procedural vote leading to the adoption of a modified closed rule providing for floor consideration of H Res 287, only 15 of the 279 Democrats voting deserted the leadership. The vote, on moving the previous question and thereby ending debate on the rule, was 267-153: R 3-138; D 264-15.

Had the leadership lost on this vote, the rule would have been rewritten to open the ethics package to many individual floor amendments that probably would have changed the code's character dramatically. But once the issue was settled on the procedural vote, the rule as backed by the leadership was adopted by voice vote.

Democrats also held together in defeating a Republican-backed amendment to strike from the bill a section banning unofficial office accounts and increasing members' official allowances by $5,000. The vote was 187-235.

After O'Neill told the House that a section of the resolution imposing a limit on outside earned income was needed to restore the "collective integrity of the House," the House crushed an amendment to strike that section. The vote was 79-344. On final passage only a handful of disgruntled Republicans and Southern Democrats were willing to risk being labeled anti-ethics and to vote against the resolution.

Outside Income Limit

By far the most controversial section of H Res 287 was that which limited the amount of outside income a member could earn to 15 per cent of his official salary ($8,625 at the current salary of $57,500).

Backers of the provision argued that it was needed to ensure that members devoted full time to their House duties and to avoid the appearance of conflict of interest with other jobs. Opponents charged that the limit—which did not apply to unearned income such as dividends from stocks or bonds—discriminated in favor of wealthy members, that it would force many members to leave Congress in order to support their families, and that it would create a class of professional politicians.

Otis G. Pike (D N.Y.) made an impassioned speech to a crowded House chamber in which he said that the restrictions on outside income would "create a Congress of two kinds of people. Some will have large unearned income and the rest will need their political jobs in order to feed and clothe and educate their families. Whether this will be a more ethical Congress only time will tell, but I think not."

But O'Neill, in an equally strong statement, told the House that "to allow us the privilege of continuing to earn outside income, no matter how stringent a provision of financial disclosure, creates in the public mind a suspicion of conflict, a suspicion of impropriety."

Calling the limit on the outside earned income, "the heart and soul of the entire package," O'Neill told his colleagues that "the issue before us is not unofficial office accounts, honorariums, outside income, earned or unearned. The issue is credibility, restoring public confidence in this Congress." "I appreciate deeply that there are those members who will be greatly affected by this provision," O'Neill said. "It is a sacrifice we all must make."

Office Accounts

The closest vote of the evening, 187-235, came on an amendment sponsored by Frenzel to strike from the bill a

(Continued on p. 18)

Obey Commission Survey House and Public Opinion

A survey released Feb. 3, 1977, by the House Commission on Administrative Review, chaired by Rep. David R. Obey (D Wis.), indicated that both the House and the general public would endorse many of the changes in standards of conduct recommended by the commission.

The results of the survey of both public opinion and House members provided what Obey termed a "unique" insight into the opinions of average Americans and their elected representatives about the duties of a congressman and the ethical standards to which he should adhere. On many specific issues related to ethical conduct the two polls found that the majority of Americans and the majority in the House held remarkably similar opinions.

However, on several points relating to the job of a congressman—both what it should be and what it really is—there were some glaring differences. The public opinion poll also revealed that there remains a deep dissatisfaction with Congress as an institution and a widespread skepticism about the ability of Congress to reform itself.

The public opinion poll, conducted by Louis Harris and Associates Inc., was based on a survey of 1,510 Americans representing a cross section of the population 18 years and older. It cost the commission $53,000.

The members' survey was based on confidential in-person interviews of 153 of the 372 members who sat in the 94th Congress and were re-elected to the 95th Congress. The sampling was conducted by Victor J. Fisher, director of survey research for the commission, who said that it reflected a statistically representative cross section of the House.

More Information on Congress

The public survey also revealed a strong desire by many Americans for more detailed information about Congress and its activities. By a margin of 88-7 per cent the survey respondents said that they would like Congress to make more information about itself available, and large majorities favored televising House and committee meetings as a way of doing this.

District or National Interests

When asked whether they felt that a congressman should be primarily concerned with looking out for his district or looking after the interests of the nation as a whole, the public by a margin of 57-38 said that the top priority should be the interests of the district.

House members, on the other hand, by a 45-24 per cent margin said they viewed their primary responsibility to be looking after the interests of the nation.

Paying Official Expenses, Office Accounts

Both the public and the members indicated a desire to have all official expenses paid for out of public funds. The Harris poll, for example, revealed that by a 76-19 margin the public believed that congressmen should have all of their travel within their districts paid for and by a 78-15 margin that all official travel between Washington and the home district should be paid for out of public funds.

Existing rules provide for 26 free round trips a year for a member between Washington and his home district and a $2,000 allowance for district expenses, including travel in the district.

The members' survey revealed that 53 per cent of those surveyed felt a need to increase official allowances, with the travel allowance most often cited as being inadequate.

The members were not, however, unanimous in their opinion of what to do about private office accounts. Although only 10 per cent said that there was no need to change the existing arrangement, the rest split on what to do; 46 per cent said that the accounts should be permitted with some restrictions, and 30 per cent said they should be abolished.

Outside Earnings, Disclosure

Both the House members and the public reflected a strong viewpoint that service in Congress should be a full-time job. Some 54 per cent of the public and 64 per cent of the members said that members of Congress should give up their private careers entirely when elected to office.

A heavy majority of both the House (69 per cent) and the Public (63 per cent) indicated that they would like to see full financial disclosure by both House members and candidates for the House.

Conflicts of Interest

On the issue of potential conflicts of interest, the House members appeared to be more skeptical and to favor more stringent restrictions than the public.

For example, 94 per cent of the members said that they would be "bothered" by a situation in which a member received a share of the profits from a law firm that did business with the government, even if the member did not actively work for the firm. Only 59 per cent of the public said that such a situation would disturb them.

Similarly, 67 per cent of the public and 85 per cent of the members said they would be bothered by a situation in which a member received a large fee for speaking to a group that had an interest in legislation.

Negative View of Congress

Despite the similarity of opinions by members and the public on ethical issues and an overwhelming approval by the public of initiatives to tighten the congressional code of conduct, most Americans remained skeptical of Congress and its ability to reform itself.

Those surveyed continued to give Congress a negative rating by a margin of 64-22, a slight improvement over 1974 but still a long way from the 64-25 per cent favorable rating of 1965.

This negative view of the Congress as an institution, Harris found, had still not affected the public view of their individual representatives. By a margin of 40-22 per cent the public rated its representatives as positive.

(Continued from p. 16)

section banning unofficial office accounts and increasing the official expense allowances for each member to $7,000 from $2,000.

Frenzel argued that because of the closed rule, the only way he could move to kill the $5,000 increase in the official allowances was to kill the entire section on unofficial office accounts. He said that if his amendment carried he would later offer a separate resolution to kill the unofficial office accounts without the increase in official allowances.

Frenzel said that the $5,000 boost was included in the resolution "as some kind of payoff" to those members who had maintained private office accounts.

"When we get down to it, the whole point of the $5,000 was to buy out those people with slush funds. We seem to be told that the people who have engaged in what we now term to be unethical or no longer tolerable behavior have to have this $5,000 or they will not vote for the whole ethics package," Frenzel said.

But Obey, who had engaged in similar debates with Frenzel during the commission deliberations on the ethics package, said that "what we are trying to do is to meet official expenses in an official, honest, aboveboard, open fashion," and that the only way to do that was to increase the official allowances to pay for expenses that members had been meeting out of their private office accounts.

The debate heated up, with Obey referring to Frenzel's arguments as "baloney" and then retracting his statement from the record, and William M. Ketchem (R Calif.) calling the Obey proposal "the most ridiculous thing I have ever heard of."

Other Amendments

In other action on amendments proposed by committees that had reported the resolution, the House:

● Rejected by a standing vote of 14-43 an amendment to strike the exemptions from reporting requirements granted in the resolution for gifts of less than $35 in value and gifts of personal hospitality;

● Rejected by voice vote an amendment to increase to $1,000 from $750 the limit on individual fees a member could receive for a speech, appearance or article;

● Adopted by voice vote an amendment to include grandsons and granddaughters in the meaning of the term "relative" as used in the resolution's sections dealing with disclosure of gifts and financial activities;

● Adopted by voice vote an amendment to strike from the resolution a title establishing a Select Committee on Ethics.

The rule also allowed an amendment to increase the ceiling on outside earned income to $15,000 from the 15 per cent of official salary, or $8,625. However, after the landslide vote against the amendment to strike the limit altogether, no member brought up the $15,000 amendment.

House Code Provisions

As passed by the House March 2, H Res 287:

Title I—Financial Disclosure

Required House members, officers, principal assistants and professional committee staff employees to file a financial disclosure statement with the Clerk of the House by April 30 of each year beginning in 1978 to cover the preceding year's financial activities. (The 1978 statement would cover only Oct. 1-Dec. 31, 1977 activities.)

Information Covered. Specified that the disclosure statements had to include the following information:

Income. The source and amount of all income received during the year from a single source aggregating $100 or more.

Gifts. The source and value of all gifts from a single source aggregating $100 or more per year. Exempted from the disclosure requirements were gifts from relatives, gifts of personal hospitality, gifts with a fair market value of $35 or less, and gifts of lodging, food or transportation aggregating less than $250 for the year.

(The Obey Commission, which drafted the basic ethics proposals, said in an explanation of H Res 287 that it understood "personal hospitality" to mean hospitality extended for a non-business purpose by an individual, not a corporation or organization, on property or facilities owned by that individual or his or her family.)

Reimbursements. The source and identity of any reimbursements received from a single source for expenditures aggregating $250 or more.

Financial Holdings. The identity and category of value of any property held at the close of the calendar year in a

Major House Code Provisions

Ban office accounts

Limit outside income from speaking engagements, articles, other sources

Restrict gifts to members from lobbyists

Prohibit travel by lame duck members

Widen financial disclosure

Chapman

trade or business or for investment with a market value of at least $1,000. Specified that the categories within which the holdings had to be designated were less than $5,000; $5,000 to $15,000, $15,000 to $50,000, $50,000 to $100,000 and above $100,000.

Liabilities. The identity and category of value of each liability owed that exceeded $2,500 at the end of the calendar year. Specified that the categories of value were the same as applied to financial holdings *(see above).*

Exempted from the disclosure requirements mortgages for members' personal residential homes in the Washington, D.C., area or home district, or for the principal residence of any other person covered by the rule.

Securities, Commodity Transactions. The identity, date and category of value of any transaction in securities or commodities futures that exceeded $1,000 in value. Specified that the categories of value were the same as applied to financial holdings *(see above).*

Real Estate. The identity, date and category of value of any purchase or sale of real property exceeding $1,000 in value in the previous calendar year except for personal residences. Specified that the categories of value were the same as applied to financial holdings *(see above).*

Spouses. Directed that with respect to the spouse of the person reporting, the report include information about all the financial dealings which were under the constructive control of the person reporting.

Exemption. Exempted from the reporting requirements members who announced before April 30, 1978, that they would not seek re-election to the 96th Congress.

Public Inspection of Reports. Directed that all financial disclosure reports be printed and made public by the Clerk of the House and that copies of each report be kept on file by the Committee on Standards of Official Conduct for public inspection and that a copy of each report filed by a member be sent to the secretary of state in the member's home state.

Title II—Gifts, Testimonial Funds

Prohibited any member, officer or employee of the House from accepting any gifts aggregating $100 or more in value in any one calendar year from any lobbyist or lobbying organization, or from foreign nationals or their agents.

Amended House rule 43 to prohibit members from converting to personal use proceeds from testimonial dinners and other fund-raising events.

Title III—Office Accounts

Prohibited any member from maintaining an unofficial office account after Jan. 3, 1978.

Prohibited new contributions to any unofficial office account, effective on adoption of the resolution.

Increased by $5,000—to $7,000 from $2,000—the amount of money each member would have available to spend on official expenses, effective Jan. 3, 1978.

Amended House rule 43 to prohibit members from converting campaign funds to personal use.

Provided a single "official expenses" allowance for members' office costs both in Washington and the home district, rather than separate allowances for each category as currently provided.

Title IV—Franked Mail

Postal Patron Mail. Imposed the following new restrictions on use of a member's frank on "postal patron" mail—mail that does not include the recipients name:

Required that any franked postal patron mail be sent by the most economical means practical, currently third class. Effective on enactment.

Provided that after Dec. 31, 1977, the amount of postal patron mail sent annually by a member under the frank could not exceed a number equal to six times the number of addresses in the member's district.

Required that a postal patron mailing to be sent under the frank be submitted to the House Commission on Congressional Mailing Standards for an advisory opinion on whether the mailing met the restrictions on franked materials. Effective on enactment.

Mass Mailings. Imposed the following new restrictions on mass mailings—defined in existing law as newsletters and similar mailings of more than 500 pieces of substantially identical content—whether sent to a postal patron address or to a specific person:

Prohibited any mass mailing under the frank unless preparation and printing costs are paid entirely from public funds. Effective on enactment. (The provision was intended to end the practice of mailing at public expense under the frank newsletters or other material printed with private funds and labeled "Not Printed at Government Expense.")

Prohibited any member who is a candidate for statewide office from sending any franked mass mailing to residents outside his district. Effective on enactment.

Prohibited any franked mass mailing from being sent less than 60 days before any primary or general election in which the member sending the mail was a candidate. Effective on enactment.

Title V—Foreign Travel

Prohibited a member or employee traveling abroad from claiming per diem reimbursement for expenses which were met by other sources. Effective on enactment.

Prohibited a member or employee from receiving reimbursement for transportation in connection with travel abroad unless the member or employee had actually paid for the transportation. Effective on enactment.

Prohibited travel abroad at government expense for any member after the date of the general election in which the member was not elected to the succeeding Congress or, in the case of a member who was not a candidate in the general election, the date of the general election or the date of adjournment *sine die* of the Congress, whichever came first. Effective on enactment.

Title VI—Outside Earned Income

Prohibited any member from earning income at a job outside Congress in excess of 15 per cent of his official salary effective Dec. 31, 1978. The limit did not apply to unearned income—such as dividends from stocks or bonds—or to income from a family controlled business or trade in which the personal services of the member did not generate a significant amount of income.

Effective Dec. 31, 1978, prohibited any member from accepting any honorarium of more than $750. Defined "honorarium" to mean a payment of money or anything of value for an appearance, speech or article by a member.

Senate Action on Ethics Code

While the Obey commission was at work on the House side, the Senate Special Committee on Official Conduct began the task of writing an ethics code for that chamber on Jan. 26. The committee had been directed to report back to the Senate with a recommended code of ethics by March 1.

Senate Majority Leader Robert C. Byrd (D W.Va.), a cosponsor of the resolution creating the panel, said that the strict timetable was needed to make it clear that the code was tied to the Feb. 20 pay raise. *(Box, p. 21)*

The resolution also provided that the recommendations of the special committee would be made the pending business of the Senate as soon as they were reported and that debate on them would be limited to 50 hours.

But as the committee held its first organizational meeting Jan. 26 it became clear that the deadline would be difficult to meet. "The questions are a lot tougher than I thought they were," said committee Chairman Gaylord Nelson (D Wis.)

To expedite the committee's work, Nelson said that he would make extensive use of the record compiled by the special House Commission on Administrative Review.

He appointed a four-member subcommittee to draft a list of issues that the committee would have to confront. The first set of hearings were held Feb. 1.

But all this activity did not allay the concerns of committee-member John Glenn (D Ohio) who called the attempt to rush through a code of ethics in order to tie it to the pay raise "ridiculous."

"It is important that we take the time to do this job right," Glenn said. "I don't see how we can develop new information and hold the hearings we need by March 1."

While the House committee action on the ethics code had been marked by a series of partisan confrontations, the Senate exercise was conducted in a less intense, often jovial atmosphere. Nelson was able through wit and compromise to defuse many of the sharp controversies.

Provisions Criticized

Nevertheless, opposition remained, particularly to provisions limiting outside earned income and speaking fees and requiring full financial disclosure.

Daniel K. Inouye (D Hawaii), summed up the opposition in a single stinging speech on Feb. 23. "Why are we singled out of all the millions of people in the United States?" he asked the committee. "Are we that bad?" He added that he found it "insulting and demeaning in many ways" to be forced to report gifts and other details of his financial operations. He echoed Javits' contention that the limit on speaking fees would be a blow to senators' "personal dignity."

But Dick Clark (D Iowa) countered that there was "a clear conflict of interest in accepting honoraria from groups with an interest in legislation...."

The issue came to a head in the form of an amendment sponsored by John H. Chafee (R R.I.) to increase the limit on an outside earned income to $15,000. The amendment lost on a vote of 6-9.

Voting for the Chafee amendment were: Inouye, Javits, Robert P. Griffin (R Mich.), Robert W. Packwood (R Ore.), Paul Laxalt (R Nev.) and Chafee.

Voting against the amendment were Abraham A. Ribicoff (D Conn.), Thomas F. Eagleton (D Mo.), Sam

---

Nunn (D Ga.), Clark, John Glenn (D Ohio), John Melcher (D Mont.), Strom Thurmond (R S.C.), Robert T. Stafford (R Vt.) and Nelson.

Restrictions Tightened

From there on it was all downhill for the reformers. The committee did accept Javits' amendment to increase the limit on honoraria, and another Javits proposal to exempt advances for books from the outside-income limits.

But the major committee actions were all in the direction of tightening the restrictions. The panel, for example, adopted on voice vote an amendment sponsored by Thurmond that would prohibit a senator from practicing any profession for compensation.

The original committee draft had contained a provision to ban law practice. But Thurmond argued that "if a man is a member of the United States Senate what business has he practicing any profession for compensation."

The committee also adopted a sweeping amendment sponsored by Clark to prohibit discrimination against employees on the basis of race, sex, religion or handicap and to prohibit senators from requiring aides to perform personal services.

Griffin warned that the enforcement of these provisions would "turn the Ethics Committee into an Equal Employment Opportunity Commission" and predicted that large numbers of employees might make use of the grievance procedure.

"The equal opportunity employment law applies to everybody else in the United States," Clark responded. "Why shouldn't it apply to us?" His amendment was adopted by voice vote.

Another change voted by the committee would require that all statewide postal patron mailings to senators' constituents go by third class mail.

This provision was adopted by voice vote over the objections of Melcher who said that "to have third class mail is demeaning. If it is worth your writing, it is worth going first class."

In the end, despite the opposition of individual senators to particular points of the resolution, the measure passed by a unanimous vote of 15-0 Feb. 24. Nelson said that it was "the most comprehensive disclosure law in the United States," and said that it would not have been possible to pass such a sweeping code "even three or four years ago."

1977 Pay Raise Tied to Ethics Code

In a supplement to his Jan. 17, 1977, budget message, outgoing President Ford requested a salary increase averaging about 28 per cent for the top echelons of the executive, legislative and judicial branches. An integral part of the proposed increases, endorsed by President Carter, was a rigid new code of ethics applying to all three branches.

The pay raises took effect Feb. 20. According to a 1967 statute *(see below),* proposed salary increases would take effect automatically 30 days after a President submitted his recommendation unless either house vetoed the measure. Neither chamber did so.

The increases were a trimmed-down version of the recommendations made Dec. 6, 1976, by the Commission on Executive, Legislative and Judicial Salaries. The nine members of the commission were appointees of the President, Congress and the Chief Justice of the United States. By statute—the Federal Salary Act of 1967 (PL 90-206)—the commission was required to review top-level federal salaries every four years. The chairman of the commission was Peter G. Peterson, board chairman of the New York City investment banking firm of Lehman Brothers Inc., and Secretary of Commerce in 1972 and 1973.

The last pay raise voted by Congress—the only one top federal officials had had since 1969—came in 1975, when Congress approved a 5 per cent cost-of-living increase for itself and the other branches.

Ford's recommendations raised the salary of the Vice President, Speaker of the House and Chief Justice to $75,000 from $65,000; for Senate president pro tem and majority and minority leaders of both houses, to $65,000 from $52,000; and for other members of Congress to $57,500 from $44,600. The increase for members of Congress amounted to 29 per cent.

In its December 1976 report proposing the salary hikes, the Peterson commission called for a new Code of Public Conduct as "the indispensable prelude to a popular acceptance of a general [pay] increase in executive, legislative and judicial salaries.

"Such a reform must be sufficiently tangible to persuade a substantial majority of Americans that the post-Watergate era has truly begun," the commission wrote. "Such a majority is by no means persuaded now."

The code had seven elements:

● Persons covered by the code would be required to file periodic financial reports showing all income, by source and amount, reimbursements for travel and other expenses, gifts, debts and personal holdings. Such information would be made public unless there were some unusual reason for maintaining confidentiality.

● Salaries would be set high enough so that individuals would be prohibited from receiving honoraria, legal fees, gifts, or the proceeds from testimonial dinners for personal use.

● Conflicts of interest would be minimized or eliminated through tight new provisions.

● "Appropriate and accountable expense allowances" would be established, with more consistency throughout government.

● Consistent and explicit rules would be made to restrict arrangements whereby executives, judges or legislators leave public service to take private jobs, especially in institutions and industries which they had been regulating.

● Regulations governing public conduct would be broadly applicable across all three branches of the federal government.

● A mechanism would be established to fully enforce, audit and report all provisions of the new code.

Common Cause, the citizens' lobby group that had worked in favor of many of the changes embodied in the Senate code, also was pleased with the outcome.

Ann McBride, the Common Cause lobbyist who followed the Senate markup, praised Nelson for an "outstanding job," and said that the code the committee produced "is tough and meaningful and really goes to the heart of the problem."

She predicted, however, that several sections of the code, especially the limit on outside earned income, would face stiff opposition on the Senate floor.

Nelson agreed with this assessment, but said that Majority Leader Byrd was fully committed to passing a tough code and predicted that "we'll prevail on all of the major points of the resolution."

Major Senate Provisions

Although the House-passed and Senate Committee versions of the code differed in detail, the broad outlines of most of the major provisions were nearly identical.

The Senate version of the code also extended many of its provisions to employees making more than $25,000 a year. In addition, it included a number of provisions not in-cluded in the House measure. Some of these the House Commission on Administrative Review plans to consider later in the year.

Among the provisions included in the Senate resolution alone were those to:

● Prohibit members who leave the Senate from engaging in lobbying activities in the Senate for a period of one year after they retire and to impose the same restrictions on employees of the Senate with respect to the member or committee for whom they worked;

● Provide that no senator could discriminate in employment or promotion practices because of race, religion, sex or physical handicap;

● Prohibit employees from being required to perform personal services for senators;

● Prohibit employees from engaging in substantial amounts of campaign activities during office hours;

● Provide for enforcement of the code by the Senate Ethics Committee and provide that the committee must justify in public all its decisions with respect to allegations brought to it;

● Permit any two members of the committee who disagreed with a committee decision not to investigate an allegation to bring the issue directly to the floor of the Senate.

Senate Floor Action

The proposed code of ethics for the Senate reached the floor on March 17 and immediately encountered sniper fire from nearly all sides.

Even before it reached the floor, the resolution underwent a major overhaul. Objections to a number of its provisions came from members of the Senate Ethics Committee which would be charged with enforcement of the new code.

Adlai E. Stevenson III (D Ill.), the Ethics Committee chairman, said that many of the resolution's provisions would be unenforceable in the form in which they emerged from committee.

He objected, for example, to the lack of flexibility allowed the Ethics Committee in dealing with complaints about senators' conduct, and to provisions requiring the committee to deal with complaints of discrimination against employees.

To meet these objections the subcommittee that had originally drafted the resolution went back to work and came out with another version, introduced on the floor in the form of a substitute amendment by Nelson.

Nelson said that the new version of the resolution solved many of the problems raised by Ethics Committee members without altering the basic scope of the code.

But the changes did not defuse other objections to the resolution. Some senators charged that the proposed code did not go far enough, while others maintained that it went too far.

The whole issue presented a major challenge to the leadership of newly elected Majority Leader Robert C. Byrd (D W.Va.), and Minority Leader Howard H. Baker Jr. (R Tenn.). Both had supported the $12,900 pay hike senators received in February and tied their support to a pledge that the Senate would pass a tough code of ethics.

As debate opened on the resolution, it became apparent that opposition to several features of the proposed new code was stronger in the Senate than it had been in the House. Most senators, for example, were able to command larger speaking fees than House members, and consequently the code's proposed limits on outside earned income was more painful to senators than to representatives.

In addition, the Senate rules allowing unlimited numbers of amendments to be proposed presented a more difficult parliamentary challenge to the Senate leadership than it had to the House. In the House debate the leaders were able to limit the number of amendments offered to two, and to win passage of their resolution after a single day's debate.

But the back of the opposition was broken on March 22, when the Senate defeated two amendments sponsored by Edmund S. Muskie (D Maine) to modify the provisions dealing with outside earned income.

Final Passage

After two weeks of debate and action on 64 amendments the Senate April 1 adopted a new code of ethics to govern the conduct of all senators and top level Senate employees.

The 86-9 vote in favor of passage of S Res 110 by no means reflected the depth of feeling in the Senate against the new code. Nor did the action guarantee that the Senate will be any more willing in the future to investigate allegations of misconduct by its own members than it has been in the past.

Gaylord Nelson (D Wis.), the floor manager of the resolution, said after the vote that the many of those senators who voted for the measure did so out of fear of the political hazards of a negative vote.

The implementation and enforcement of the new code will be in the hands of the Senate Ethics Committee, two of whose six members—Harrison Schmitt (R N.M.) and Lowell P. Weicker Jr. (R Conn.)—voted against passage of the resolution. A third committee member, John G. Tower (R Texas) missed the final vote, but expressed strong opposition to the measure during floor debate.

Penalties for violations of the code were not changed from the traditional penalties available to the Senate in disciplining its own members—reprimand, censure, expulsion or loss of seniority.

Nevertheless, Senate adoption of the code represented a major departure from the previous, loosely worded and general code of conduct.

Chief among the provisions of the new code was a requirement that all senators and Senate employees making $25,000 or more a year disclose virtually all of their finances—income, assets, holdings, liabilities and transactions—and the sources of all income of their spouses and dependents.

Nelson said that the widespread Senate acceptance of full financial disclosure was a "milestone" because past efforts to force senators to make public their financial operations had been hotly contested.

"The Senate's vote today confirms that a quiet revolution has taken place," Nelson said. "The principle that citizens have the right to full information has been fully established."

Opposition to the code focused on several specific provisions and on a general feeling that the overall result of the code would be to create a Senate full of professional politicians.

Edmund S. Muskie (D Maine) who was recorded against passage although he did not vote, had led a fruitless fight to kill the provision limiting outside earned income, charging that it discriminated in favor of wealthy senators with large amounts of unearned income such as dividends from stocks or bonds.

Weicker argued that full disclosure alone would be sufficient to guard against conflicts of interest and that the limits on outside earned income were unconstitutional.

And Republican Senate Minority Leader Howard H. Baker Jr. (R Tenn.) expressed concern that adoption of the code would spell an end to the concept of the "citizen legislator" which, he said, had been the original intent of the framers of the Constitution.

But Majority Leader Robert C. Byrd (D W.Va.) whose lobbying tactics were crucial in persuading reluctant senators to support the code and vote against crippling amendments, argued on the floor that "the necessity of the times," and the "climate created by the errant actions of a minority of public officials," demanded that the Senate adopt the code to restore public confidence in the Congress.

Broader than House Code

The financial aspects of the code adopted by the Senate were quite similar to the financial code of conduct adopted by the House on March 2.

But the Senate code also included enforcement provisions, a section guaranteeing that senators would not discriminate against employees because of race, sex, national origin or age, and other provisions not covered by the House action.

The House Commission on Administrative Review was drafting additional recommendations to deal with these matters. The panel expected to have its suggestions before the House sometime during the summer of 1977.

Once that action is completed, Congress will then draft a comprehensive code of ethics based on the codes adopted by the House and Senate and enact the measure into statutory law so that it will cover all federal employees.

Baker Sunset Amendment

The last challenge to the code was rejected one hour before passage when the Senate voted 63-31 to table an amendment sponsored by Baker that would have terminated the code on March 1, 1981.

The tabling motion was made by Byrd, and the vote went along party lines.

Baker argued that the time limit would offer a chance to see how well the code worked and force the Senate to reexamine the measure.

But opponents of the amendment said that improvements could be made at any time through the normal legislative process and charged that the so-called sunset amendment was merely a disguised attempt to kill the code.

"If the Senate passed this amendment," said Dick Clark (D Iowa), "we will be saying to the people of this country, 'Yes, we're concerned about ethics and we're passing a tough code of conduct. But in a few years, when the heat dies down, our code will quietly self-destruct.' "

Major Provisions

As passed by the Senate April 1, S Res 110 contained the following major provisions:

Financial Disclosure

Required each member, officer or employee of the Senate making more than $25,000 a year and employed for more than 90 days in a year, each Senate employee designated to handle campaign funds, and each candidate for the Senate to file a financial disclosure statement with the Secretary of the Senate every year by May 15 covering previous year's activities.

Provided that the financial disclosure provisions would take effect Oct. 1, 1977, and that the first report, filed on May 15, 1978, would cover activities from Oct. 1, 1977, through the end of 1977.

Directed the Secretary of the Senate to compile a list of all those covered by the requirement every year.

Gifts

Prohibited any member, officer or employee from knowingly accepting or permitting his spouse or dependents to accept any gift of over $100 in aggregate value during a year from any individual or group having a direct interest in legislation before Congress or from any foreign national acting on behalf of a foreign organization, business or government.

Defined those having a direct interest in legislation as lobbyists, organizations that maintain political action funds, or officers or employees of such organizations.

Exempted from the prohibition gifts from relatives, gifts with a value of less than $35 and gifts of personal hospitality of an individual.

Directed that if a member, officer or employee unknowingly received a prohibited gift that he must, on learning of the gift, return it or reimburse the donor for its value.

Outside Earned Income

Limited to 15 per cent of his official salary the amount of outside earned income a member, officer or employee of the Senate employed for 90 days and making over $35,000 a year could receive.

Limited to $1,000 the amount of money a senator could receive as an honorarium for making a speech or appearance or writing an article.

Limited honoraria for employees making $35,000 a year to $300 per speech, appearance or article and $1,500 aggregate in any one year.

Provided that a member, officer or employee of the Senate could receive honoraria up to $25,000 a year if the proceeds are donated to charity and if no tax benefits accrue to the donor.

Defined outside earned income as income received as a result of personal services rendered if such services are material income producing factors.

Excluded from the definition of outside earned income royalties from books, income from family enterprises if the services provided by the senator or Senate employee are managerial or supervisory in nature and are necessary to protect family interests and do not require "significant amounts of time" when the Senate is in session; gains derived from dealings in property or investment, interests, rents, dividends, alimony and separate maintenance payments, annuities, income from discharge of indebtedness, distributive shares of partnership income if the services of the individual covered were not material income producing factors, income from an interest in an estate or trust, proceeds from the sale of creative or artistic works, and any "buy out" arrangement from professional partnerships or businesses related to the fair market value of his interest.

Provided that all restrictions on outside earned income would take effect Sept. 30, 1979.

Conflict of Interest

Prohibited any member, officer or employee of the Senate from receiving compensation where such compensation would occur by virtue of influence improperly exerted from his position as member, officer or employee.

Prohibited any member, officer or employee from engaging in any outside business or profession for compensation that is inconsistent with conscientious performance of official duties.

Prohibited any officer or employee from working outside the Senate for compensation without notifying his superior in writing first.

Prohibited any member, officer or employee from aiding in the progress of legislation the purpose of which was to further his own financial interests.

Provided that a member could decline to vote on a matter when he believed that voting would be a conflict of interest.

Prohibited former members from lobbying in the Senate for one year after leaving office.

Prohibited an employee on a senator's staff from lobbying that senator or staff for one year after leaving Senate employment and prohibited committee staff from lobbying any member or staff of the committee for which he worked for one year after leaving the committee service.

Provided that conflict of interest rules would take effect April 1, 1978.

Office Accounts

Provided that no member could maintain an unofficial office account into which funds are received to pay for the expenses of a member's office.

Provided that for existing unofficial office accounts no contributions could be accepted after passage of the resolution and that no expenditures could be made after Dec. 31, 1977.

Provided that expenses incurred by a member could be paid for only by personal funds of the member, official funds appropriated for that purpose, funds derived from a political committee and funds received as reasonable reimbursements for expenses incurred by a member in connection with personal services provided by the member to the organization making the reimbursement.

Prohibited members from converting political contributions to personal use.

Foreign Travel

Prohibited a senator during the last year of his term from receiving funds for foreign travel after the date of the general election in which his successor was elected or, in the case of a member who was not a candidate in the general election, either the date of the general election or of the adjournment *sine die* of the second regular session of that Congress, whichever came first.

Prohibited a senator, officer or employee from claiming funds for reimbursement for foreign travel when the reimbursement had been made by another organization and from receiving reimbursement from the government for the same expense more than once.

Permitted senators or Senate employees to take trips paid for by foreign private educational and charitable organizations if approved by the Ethics Committee.

Franked Mail

Provided that no senator or candidate for the Senate could make use of the frank for a mass mailing less than 60 days before a primary or general election in which the senator or candidate was running.

Provided that a senator could use only official funds of the Senate to pay for preparation of any mass mailing sent out under the frank. (The provision was intended to end the practice of mailing at public expense under the frank newsletters or other material printed with private funds and labeled "Not Printed at Government Expense.")

Required all mass mailings by a senator under the frank to be registered with the secretary of the Senate and the registration to include a copy of the material, the number of pieces sent and a description of the groups receiving the mailing. Required the information to be available for public inspection.

Provided that the Senate computer facilities could not be used to store any political or campaign lists and that other mail-related uses of the computer would be subject to guidelines issued by the Rules Committee.

Provided that the Senate radio and television studios could not be used by any candidate for election to the Senate less than 60 days before the primary or general election in which the candidate was running.

Provided that the rules governing franking would take effect Aug. 1, 1977.

Political Fund Activity

Effective 30 days after passage, provided that no officer or employee of the Senate may handle campaign contributions in any way except for two staff aides in Washington and one in the senator's home state who are designated by the senator to perform such functions and who are paid over $10,000 a year and who file a financial disclosure statement with the secretary of the Senate.

Provided that no member, officer or employee could utilize the services of an individual who was not an employee of the Senate or of the U.S. government for more than 90 days a year unless such individual agreed in writing to comply with the Senate Code of Official Conduct.

Prohibited senators or former senators from converting political contributions to private use.

Employment Practices

Provided that effective Jan. 3, 1979, no member, officer or employee could refuse to hire an individual, discharge an individual or discriminate with respect to promotion, pay or terms of employment on the basis of race, color, religion, sex, national origin, age, or state of physical handicap.

Ethics Committee

Charged the Select Committee on Ethics with enforcement of the Senate Code of Official Conduct.

Effective Date

Except as otherwise noted, provided that all sections of the resolution would take effect on adoption.

Historical Background

Pay, Perquisites and Patronage

For years, Congress and its members have been favorite targets of national humor. The origins of this humorous image are obscure but, fair or not, it has persisted. Perhaps the best illustration of the technique comes in Mark Twain's classic commentary: "Suppose you were an idiot. And suppose you were a member of Congress. But I repeat myself."

While the evidence is uncertain, suspicion has it that not all of the humor is lost on the members. Rep. Jim Wright (D Texas) in his book *You and Your Congressman* quoted another member as saying: "I came here to make laws, and what do I do? I send baby books to young mothers, listen to every maladjusted kid who wants out of the service, write sweet replies to pompous idiots who think a public servant is a public footstool, and give tours of the Capitol to visitors who are just as worn out as I am."[1]

In any event, it is clear that one of the fringe benefits or perquisites of serving in Congress is the opportunity to tickle the nation's funny bone. Other perquisites abound. Some are important; others are merely convenient. Some cost the taxpayers a lot of money; others simply inflate the members' self-importance. All perquisites were intended, at least when they began, to ease the burden of what can be a grinding, tedious and frustrating job.

Both the pay and perquisites of members of Congress have increased enormously since World War II. A 1975 study of the salary, staff allowances, benefits and special privileges of members of the House estimated that a representative's job was worth nearly $500,000 a year.[2]

Countering the increases in pay and perquisites, there has been a decrease in congressional patronage—the power of senators and representatives to select appointees for government jobs, and thus to bolster their political strength. Most patronage positions today are restricted to Capitol Hill itself.

A Member's Jobs

The late Rep. Clem Miller (D Calif.) once described for constituents an account of a typical day in his Washington office:

"I arise at 6:45, eat breakfast, and spend 10 minutes with the *Washington Post*.... Leave for the office at 7:55 a.m.... (Alternatively, I may breakfast at 8:00 a.m. with a veterans group, Boy Scouts, or some other group.)

...Generally at 9:00 comes the first office appointment: A trade association to discuss an industrial problem or a lobbyist to explain his position on a bill.... At 10:00 there may well be a hearing of the committee to which I am assigned, or of the subcommittee.... Frequently it seems almost impossible to arrive on time for these hearings, what with the press of office work.... The House meets at 12:00 noon.... If there is a debate on a bill, I will generally be there. Fitting lunch into this schedule often becomes difficult.... Usually I eat at my office, and relax with a newspaper from the state capital or my district. Then during afternoon hours, I am busy cramming committee meetings between duties on the floor or in the office.... About 5:00 p.m. I return to the office to work over the mail, sign letters and see people. Getting away from the office is more and more difficult. In the beginning I left at 5:45 p.m. Now I am leaving at 6:15 or 6:30 p.m."[3]

The major functions of a member of Congress are legislative and representational. Some observers also add a third: they believe that a member should "educate" the public on the major national problems and issues.

While the legislative duties of members are their most prominent ones, members are not solely lawmakers. Not only is it their function to act as the representatives of their constituents in the national government; it is unlikely that they will be re-elected if they neglect to do so. Since most members consider their own re-election as paramount, scrupulous attention usually is paid to constituent mail and the problems it brings. Some senators and representatives even make such public relations gestures as congratulating newlyweds and parents of newborn babies.

A widespread complaint is that much of this "case work," as it is known, is trivial, but few members feel that they can afford to ignore constituents, even nonvoting ones who write for help with school assignments. As a result, most of the staff and office facilities of members are given over to processing mail and running errands for the constituents. Some congressional staffs pass along constituent requests for information to the Congressional Research Service of the Library of Congress, which consequently has less time to spend on its primary duties. The member himself at times feels compelled to answer certain letters, introduce and follow private bills, talk to visitors, and even lead high school classes on tours of the Capitol.

Occasionally, a maverick member will shatter the traditional image of the infinitely patient and courteous public servant. It happens rarely, but when it does occur, the event makes news headlines. Such a maverick was Sen. Stephen M. Young (D Ohio). A liberal, Young was subjected to frequent attacks from conservatives. His acid-tongued replies were widely publicized. One Young reply began, "Dear Sir: You are a liar."[4]

The chances of getting a personal reply to a letter depend partly on the population of the state in which the writer lives. A Wyoming resident may receive a personal answer. A New Yorker is more likely to draw a standardized response drafted by a junior staff member, signed by a machine and only scanned by the member.

In recent years, a number of machines have been used to speed replies to letters. Among them are the Robotype machine and the Autopen. These machines can insert a signature and a heading on form letters while making it appear to the constituent that he has received an individual letter with a personal signature.

The Robotype machine looks like a typewriter. It is capable of reproducing identical copies of form letters without the standardized look of a mimeographed letter. Once it is set up to reproduce the body of a letter, a secretary types only the individual heading for each letter. The Autopen is a console machine with a large wheel. On the wheel is placed a metal plate with an impression of the member's signature. As the prepared letters revolve around the wheel, the metal plate stamps an imprint of the signature in the proper place on the paper.

Together, these machines make it possible for a congressional staff to answer letters after scanning them for a few seconds to see what they are about.

A Member's Workload

Political reporter David S. Broder wrote in 1962: "The main reason...that Congress does not legislate better is simply that most congressmen can no longer afford to regard legislation as the most important part of their jobs. Indeed, many of them find it very difficult to sandwich legislative work into the busy schedule of what they describe—correctly—as their more important functions. These relate to their second role, as mediators between their districts and the central government."[5]

These activities necessarily reduce the resources which members can bring to bear on legislation. Yet the technical complexities of legislation increase constantly as the code of laws, the economy and the federal government grow larger and as science, commerce, defense and foreign policy become increasingly interconnected. The problem is perhaps more acute in the Senate than the House, because senators serve on two and often three major committees, while most representatives are limited to one or two committees.

Caught by the conflicting demands of constituents and legislative duties, few members have time to perform the "educational" function except sporadically. The constant pressure of elections, however, forces many members to inform their constituents of their positions on national issues through newsletters, press releases and speeches. This activity, and efforts to promote a particular bill or approach to a national or local problem, of course add that much more to the member's workload.

The average active member of Congress—allowing for considerable variation from one office to another—frequent-

'What Ails Congress'

The growth of congressional staff and the increase in congressional expenses have been so rapid since the mid-1950s that some members of Congress have expressed their dismay.

Rep. William L. Armstrong (R Colo.), a member of the House Appropriations Committee, voted against the fiscal 1976 legislative branch appropriations bill and explained why in "Additional Views" at the end of the committee report. His statement was accompanied by tables that showed the growth of congressional employees from 5,585 in 1955 to 17,728 in 1974, and the increase in legislative branch appropriations from $70.7-million in fiscal 1955 to an estimated $802.4-million in fiscal 1976 (actual appropriation $827.5-million). Rep. Armstrong's statement follows:

"Within the last two decades congressional staffing has tripled and the overall cost of operating Congress itself has increased ten fold.

"If this increase had been accompanied by a corresponding improvement in the ability of Congress to cope with the nation's problems, I would not object. But it appears to me that the opposite is the case: Congress seems gradually less and less able to come to grips with basic issues.

"What ails Congress, it seems to me, is a lack of stomach for hard decisions, a failure of nerve and judgment rather than lack of staff and facilities, needed though these may be. Merely increasing funding for congressional operations will not overcome the basic problems which have stymied action on curbing inflation, recession, the energy crisis and other issues of utmost importance.

"I commend the committee for substantially reducing the amount of several appropriations requested by various congressional agencies. But, even so, the bill includes large increases for which no real justification has been considered or even submitted. In large part this bill simply funds the estimates of other committees without any attempt to seriously evaluate the propriety or need of such spending. While it is natural for members of the committee to defer to our colleagues in this way, by extending this courtesy we effectively eliminate any meaningful review on a large portion of the legislative appropriation which now totals approximately $700 million....

"I believe the spending of Congress on itself could and should be substantially reduced without adversely affecting the legislative process. By doing so the House would save taxpayer funds at a time when such savings are particularly necessary. More important, however, Congress would thereby set an example of prudence and restraint instead of continuing an example of self-indulgence.

"Since portions of this appropriation which are most in need of reduction merely reflect recent decisions of the full House itself, I do not intend to offer amendments which would have little or no chance of adoption. Under the circumstances, however, I am constrained to vote against the bill."

Source: U.S. Congress, House, Committee on Appropriations, *Legislative Branch Appropriation Bill, 1976,* H. Rept. 94-208 to Accompany HR 6950, 94th Cong., 1st sess., 1975.

ly puts in a 10- to 12-hour day at the office and in the Capitol before going home to dinner and two or three hours of reading related to work. During a typical day the member would probably spend time talking to lobbyists and to visiting constituents, possibly show a high school class around the Capitol, read and answer some of the large amount of daily mail, telephone the home district or state, answer questions from reporters, discuss legislation and politics with other members, attend party or regional meetings, possibly work on a speech or a newsletter to constituents, read the *Congressional Record*, newspapers, magazines and committee hearings or reports. In addition, the member would attend committee meetings in the morning and sometimes the afternoon, attend floor sessions to speak and listen to debate, vote, and wait to vote. He or she would also spend time overseeing staff work. If the member is the chairman of an active committee or subcommittee, or occupies a leadership post (for example, as a member of the whip organization), he or she would have additional time-consuming duties and additional staff aides. In the evenings, members often have combined political and social obligations. *(Washington's Party Circuit, this page)*

A Member's Perquisites

Aside from the congressional salary, a member's single greatest perquisite is a personal staff. Staff aides multiply the member's arms, legs, eyes and ears, providing the best hope of meeting the demands on the member's time. Properly used, a personal staff can function as the member's strongest ally. Misused, a personal staff becomes little more than a reservoir of wasted talents. And abused, a personal staff can turn traitor; for like the gentleman and his valet, no member is a hero to his staff.

Among the other formal, statutory perquisites are the franking privilege, immunity from certain legal actions, free office space in federal buildings, and allowances for travel, telephone and telegraph services, stationery, office expenses and equipment, plus thousands of free publications. Other benefits members receive include free storage of files and records, inexpensive use of television and radio studios, certain patronage appointments, modern recreational facilities, and discounts from Capitol Hill shops and services.

In addition, there is a vast, ill-defined collection of informal perquisites based on the deference customarily shown a VIP. Such deference appears typically in delaying the departure of a plane to accommodate the tardy arrival of a member of Congress. Other informal perquisites include free parking, assured press coverage under many circumstances, and special treatment by government agencies.

Are congressional perquisites abused? Objectively, it is difficult to tell. Probably the best answer is that members abuse their privileges about as much as such privileges would be abused by the public in general. Large-scale abuses, while rare, are uncovered periodically, touching off widely publicized scandals. Abuses that seem to recur are the employment of members' relatives as staff aides and the misuse of allowances or other funds.

Pay of Members of Congress

In Article I, Section 6, the Constitution provides: "The Senators and Representatives shall receive a Compensation for their Services, to be ascertained by Law, and paid out of the Treasury of the United States."

Washington's Party Circuit

Official entertaining is widespread in Washington. For the unwary member of Congress, what began as mere social courtesy can balloon out of control and become a social nightmare. One of the more candid descriptions of Washington's social life—as seen from Capitol Hill—was offered in a newsletter to constituents by Sen. Stephen M. Young (D Ohio). It was written in 1963.

People inquire what about social life in Washington. "Terrific" would be the answer, were a senator to attend all functions to which he is invited. Frankly, unless a senator throws in the sponge and accepts only one-fourth of the invitations, he will be out socially five or six evenings weekly. This would be a hardship in many respects. For example, inability to see "Gunsmoke," "Wells Fargo," "The Dakotas," "Wagon Train," to say nothing of wasting time needed to study pending legislation, read committee reports, etc.

More than one hundred nations have embassies in Washington. Each holds two large receptions a year plus dinners and cocktail parties to which most senators are invited. Then there are 17 State dinners. Among other dinners, make a mental note that there are 262 national associations such as the American Legion, American Farm Bureau Federation, American Trucking Associations Inc., Veterans of Foreign Wars, American Medical Association, National Association of Home Builders, U.S. Chamber of Commerce and National Association of Manufacturers. These are registered pressure groups, so-called. They filed reports admitting expenditures in excess of $5,000,000 during 1962. Many of these national associations usually invite all members of the Congress to at least one dinner a year. In addition, various state associations and citizens' organizations give dinners, cocktail parties, and receptions. They wine and dine Congressmen who attend and individual members and speakers may discuss legislative proposals they are promoting. At least 40 senators give dinners or luncheons for their colleagues and usually senators give dinners for their own state congressional delegations or a representative throws an affair to which he invites the senators from his state. In addition, a comparatively new horror has been devised—that is breakfasts to which senators are invited. The time stated is generally 8:30 a.m. The place, usually a downtown hotel, more than a mile distant from the Capitol. If a senator attends, he is fortunate to leave by 10 o'clock. Furthermore, quite frequently groups from the senator's own state visiting in Washington desire him to lunch or dine with them. These are invitations a senator appreciates receiving and likes to accept; and in turn, a senator does not keep his own pocketbook padlocked. He "wines and dines" constituents and "throws parties" to repay obligations, and also because this is an American custom we like. Regarding "pressure groups" and various professional and business associations, many Congressmen say "too busy" and are happy to pay for their own meals, and eat at home a couple evenings a week.

The constitutional language settled one sensitive contemporary issue—whether a member's salary should be drawn from state or national funds—but it left settlement of a far more delicate question up to Congress itself—deciding what the salary should be. The inevitable result was development of the salary issue into a political hot potato.

In attempts to minimize the political impact of periodic salary increases, Congress fell into the practice of wrapping up a pay increase for itself in a general pay increase for other federal workers, including at times the judiciary and the President. On a few occasions, even that tactic failed to blunt critical reaction on the part of the public.

Public reaction against congressional pay increases was strong at times, leading to wholesale election defeats for members who approved increases that their constituents considered unwarranted. Two controversial salary increases were repealed by succeeding Congresses. Frequently, a few members would refuse higher pay and return the amount of the increase to the Treasury or donate it to a public charity. Technically, every member must accept full pay. However, after receiving the salary they may return any portion to the Treasury.

Despite all the turmoil, congressional pay has risen steadily over the years. From $6 a day in 1789, it had climbed to $44,600 a year by 1975. Although the salary of members has remained unchanged for long periods of time, only rarely has it ever been reduced. Since 1946, members have been eligible to participate in a retirement system. *(Box, Retirement Benefits, p. 47)*

Early Pay Legislation

During the Constitutional Convention, a principal question surrounding compensation for members of Congress was the source of the funds. Members of the Confederation Congress had been paid by the states; those of the British Parliament were not paid at all. It was felt, however, that members of Congress should be paid, and paid by the national government.

Another question raised at the Convention was whether senators and representatives should receive equal pay. Charles Pinckney of South Carolina twice moved "that no salary should be allowed" members of the Senate. "As this branch was meant to represent the wealth of the country," Pinckney asserted, "it ought to be composed of persons of wealth; and if no allowance was to be made, the wealthy alone would undertake the service." Pinckney's motion was seconded by Benjamin Franklin but was twice rejected, six states to five states.[6]

History of Congressional Pay

Year	Salary	Year	Salary
1789-1795	$6 per diem	1907-1925	$7,500 per year
1795-1796	$6 per diem (House)	1925-1932	$10,000 per year
	$7 per diem (Senate)	1932-1933	$9,000 per year
1796-1815	$6 per diem	1933-1935	$8,500 per year
1815-1817	$1,500 per year	1935-1947	$10,000 per year
1817-1855	$8 per diem	1947-1955	$12,500 per year
1855-1865	$3,000 per year	1955-1965	$22,500 per year
1865-1871	$5,000 per year	1965-1969	$30,000 per year
1871-1873	$7,500 per year	1969-1975	$42,500 per year
1873-1907	$5,000 per year	1975-	$44,600 per year

Per Diem Compensation. One of the first—and most controversial—measures enacted by the new Congress in 1789 was a bill fixing the compensation of members. As originally considered by the House, both representatives and senators were to be paid $6 a day. The proposal for equal pay reopened the debate over whether senators, by reason of greater responsibilities and presumably higher qualifications, should receive a pay differential. At the heart of the debate was an amendment by Rep. Theodore Sedgwick (Federalist Mass.) to lower House pay to $5 per day, thus creating a $1-per-day differential in favor of the Senate. The amendment was defeated by a voice vote. On Aug. 10, 1789, the House by a 30-16 roll call passed a bill providing for payment of $6 a day to members of both chambers.

In the Senate, the bill was amended to provide that senators be paid at the $6 rate until March 4, 1795, when their pay would be increased to $8 and the pay of representatives would remain at $6. The amended bill passed the Senate on Aug. 28, 1789.

Following a House-Senate conference, the House on Sept. 11, by a 29-25 roll call, voted to fix the pay of senators at $7 a day after March 4, 1795, and by a 28-26 roll call set March 4, 1796, as the expiration date of the legislation. The Senate agreed to the House amendments on Sept. 12, and the bill was signed into law on Sept. 22, 1789, seven days before the end of the first session of Congress.

As enacted, the measure provided the first perquisite—a travel allowance for senators and representatives of $6 per 20 miles. It also provided a $6-a-day differential for the House Speaker (making his pay $12 a day), and compensation for a number of lesser House and Senate officials.

When a new pay law was enacted in 1796, only a glancing reference was made to a differential for the Senate. Both the House and the Senate passed a bill equalizing the pay at $6 a day.

Short-Lived Salary Law. In 1816, Congress voted itself a pay increase and a shift from per diem compensation to an annual salary. The Act of March 19, 1816, raised congressional pay to $1,500 a year and made the raise retroactive to Dec. 4, 1815, when the first session of the 14th Congress convened. The pay raise had passed both houses easily, but it was roundly condemned by the people. A number of members who had voted for the bill were defeated in the 1816 elections; nine members resigned over the issue. One of the election victims was Rep. Daniel Webster. He was defeated and was not elected to Congress again until 1822.

Return to Per Diem. The short session of the 14th Congress in 1817 repealed the $1,500 salary act, effective with the end of the Congress on March 3, 1817. An Act of Jan. 22, 1818, restored per diem compensation and set the rate at $8, retroactive to March 3, 1817.

Members' Salaries from 1850s to 1930s

Almost four decades later, a successful conversion to annual congressional salaries was finally achieved. An Act of Aug. 16, 1856, replaced the $8-a-day rate by a $3,000 annual salary, retroactive to the start of the 34th Congress on Dec. 3, 1855. Another retroactive pay increase—to $5,000—was approved July 28, 1866, effective Dec. 4, 1865, when the 39th Congress had convened for its first session.

"Salary Grab." In the closing days of the 42nd Congress in 1873, still another retroactive pay raise was enacted, increasing the salary to $7,500. The higher salary was made retroactive to the beginning of the 42nd Congress, in effect providing for members a $5,000 windfall ($2,500 per year for the two preceding years). Despite precedents for making the increase retroactive, the size of the increase and the windfall effect boomeranged. Congressional critics, already primed by the Credit Mobilier scandal, attacked the pay increase as a "salary grab" and a "backpay steal." Some members returned their back pay to the Treasury; others donated it to colleges or charities.

When the 43rd Congress opened in December 1873, scores of bills were introduced to repeal the increase. By an Act of Jan. 20, 1874, congressional pay reverted to the previous $5,000, and it stayed at that level until a $7,500 salary was at length sanctioned by an Act of Feb. 26, 1907. A raise to $10,000 was provided by an Act of March 4, 1925.

Government austerity was the byword as the Great Depression of the 1930s deepened. Salaries of federal employees were reduced, and members of Congress likewise had to take a pay cut. The Economy Act of June 30, 1932, provided for a 10 per cent cutback in members' salaries, dropping them from $10,000 to $9,000. The cutback was increased to 15 per cent, meaning a further drop to $8,500, by the Economy Act of March 20, 1933. Gradually the cutbacks were rescinded, and by the end of 1935, congressional salaries had been restored to the $10,000 level.

Postwar Salaries and Expense Allowances

Congress included in the Legislative Reorganization Act of 1946 a provision increasing congressional salaries from $10,000 to $12,500 and retaining an existing $2,500 non-taxable expense allowance for all members. The increases took effect at the beginning of the 80th Congress in 1947. The Joint Committee on the Organization of Congress had recommended a $15,000 annual salary and elimination of the expense allowance, but the bill was amended in the House, and the House provision was retained in the final version of the measure. The act also provided $20,000 salaries for the Vice President and Speaker of the House.

Provision for the $2,500 expense allowance had been made in 1945. The House Appropriations Committee included in the legislative branch appropriation bill for fiscal 1946 an appropriation to cover a $2,500 annual expense allowance for representatives. Although the bill did not so stipulate, the committee said the allowance probably would be tax-exempt. When the bill reached the House floor opponents called the allowance an opening wedge for inflation and a pay increase by subterfuge. But a resolution to waive all points of order, and thus thwart efforts to eliminate the expense allowance section, was adopted, 229-124. Other attempts to eliminate or change the proposal also failed, and the bill was passed by voice vote May 10, 1945.

The Senate Appropriations Committee reported the bill with a $2,500 expense allowance for senators as well. The committee amendment was defeated on the floor, 9-43, and two compromise amendments also failed. An amendment to strike out the House expense allowance was narrowly defeated, 22-28. The Senate thus passed the bill with the allowance for representatives, but not for senators.

The question came up again during Senate consideration of the first deficiency appropriation bill for fiscal 1946. The Senate Appropriations Committee offered an amendment to extend the expense allowance to senators, but the Senate rejected the plan, 24-47. Senators finally received the $2,500 expense allowance in 1946, in the fiscal 1947 Legislative Branch Appropriation Act.

Tax-Free Provision Ended. In the Revenue Act of 1951, Congress eliminated the tax-free provision on congressional expense allowances, effective Jan. 3, 1953. Also made subject to taxation were the expense allowances of the President, Vice President and Speaker of the House. The provision was offered as a Senate amendment by Sen. John J. Williams (R Del.) and agreed to on a 77-11 roll call.

Congress in 1953 created a Commission on Judicial and Congressional Salaries to study the salary question and report to Congress by Jan. 15, 1954. As passed by the Senate, the bill would have empowered the commission to raise salaries. However, the measure was amended in the House to require congressional approval for any pay increase. The commission's report recommended a $10,000 salary boost, but Congress took no action.

In 1955, Congress enacted legislation raising congressional and judicial salaries. The bill increased the salary for members of Congress to $22,500 (from $12,500 plus a $2,500 expense allowance). It also provided $35,000 for the Speaker and Vice President (up from $30,000), and retained the existing $10,000 taxable expense allowance in both cases. The increases became effective March 1, 1955.

The chief difference between the House and Senate bills was the $2,500 congressional expense allowance, which the House would have retained. Both the Senate version and the final version deleted this item. The House passed the bill Feb. 16, 283-118, and the Senate passed it Feb. 23, 62-24. The Senate rejected the first conference report Feb. 25, because it contained a compromise expense allowance provision. After that had been deleted, the second conference report was approved by the Senate Feb. 28 and by the House March 1.

Congress again raised its own salaries, and those of other federal personnel, in 1964. Members' salaries were raised by $7,500, to $30,000. Salaries of the Speaker of the House and the Vice President were raised to $43,000. The bill was enacted after the House had first killed another bill raising congressional salaries by $10,000. The first bill was rejected by the House March 12 on a 184-222 roll-call vote. Election-year worries were believed important in the defeat of the first bill. The second measure was strongly backed by President Johnson and voted upon after most of the 1964 primary elections had been held. It was passed by the House June 11 on a 243-157 roll call and by the Senate July 2 on a 58-21 roll call.

Special Salary Commission

In 1967, Congress modified a bill increasing postal rates and the salaries of federal employees by adding an amendment creating a nine-member Commission on Executive, Legislative, and Judicial Salaries to review the salaries of members of Congress, federal judges and top officers of the executive branch every four years and to recommend changes it felt desirable.

The congressionally established commission was to include three members appointed by the President, two by the President of the Senate, two by the Speaker of the House, and two by the Chief Justice of the United States. Beginning in fiscal 1969, the commission was to submit its recommendations to the President, who was to recommend in his budget the exact rates of pay "he deems advisable" for federal executives, judges and members of Congress. His recommendations could be either higher or lower than those of the commission, or he could propose that salaries not be altered. The recommendations would take effect within 30

Docking of Pay

It is often suggested that the way to curb absenteeism in Congress is to dock a member's pay for each day he fails to appear on the floor. The Constitution makes no provision for this, saying only that "each House shall be the Judge of the Elections, returns and Qualifications of its own Members, and a Majority of each shall constitute a Quorum to do Business; but a smaller Number may adjourn from day to day, and may be authorized to compel the Attendance of absent Members, in such Manner, and under such Penalties as each House may provide." (Article 1, Section 5)

The first session of the First Congress in 1789 provided for an automatic docking of pay. Salaries were $6 a day for each day of attendance.

A law enacted in 1856 provided that "The Secretary of the Senate and the Sergeant at Arms of the House, respectively, shall deduct from the monthly payments of each member or delegate the amount of his salary for each day that he has been absent from the Senate or House,...unless such member or delegate assigns as the reason for such absence the sickness of himself or of some member of his family."

Since then a few rare attempts to compel attendance have cited this law. During the 53rd Congress (1894), after a ruling by the chairman of the Committee of the Whole that the 1856 law was still in force, portions of House members' salaries were withheld.

The 1894 incident was recalled in 1914 when the House adopted a resolution revoking all leaves of absence granted to members and directing the sergeant at arms to deduct members' pay for each day they were absent. The 1914 resolution was enforced stringently for a brief time.

No docking of pay of absentees occurred for many years. The House Parliamentarian's office said there was no way of knowing when a member was away.

In 1975, the Senate included a provision repealing the 1856 law in its version of the fiscal 1976 legislative appropriations bill. The Senate Appropriations Committee maintained that the law "has no contemporary meaning," and urged its repeal. In testimony before the committee, the secretary of the Senate, Francis R. Valeo, said: "The fact is that a senator has to be, and is, on duty at all times, 24 hours a day, whether in his home state, in committee, or in the chamber.... A senator's absence from Washington and the Senate floor at no time separates him from the continuing responsibilities of his office any more than when the President is away from Washington, or the Supreme Court justices are away from the court on recess. The obligations of their office remain with them at all times." The provision was dropped in conference.

on June 3, 1968. Named to head the commission was Frederick R. Kappel, former chairman of the American Telephone & Telegraph Co. The commission, reporting in December 1968, recommended salary levels of $67,500 for the Chief Justice, $65,000 for associate justices, $60,000 for Cabinet members, $50,000 to $40,000 for Level II-V in the executive branch, and of $50,000 for members of Congress. With the exception of Cabinet members, all salary recommendations were scaled down by Johnson in his budget request. The congressional salary level was set at $42,500, an increase of $12,500 over members' previous salary, the same rate as for Level II of the executive schedule.

The new salary scales became effective March 1, 1969. Although numerous bills were introduced in 1969 to rescind the congressional pay increase and to abolish the salary commission, none was enacted.

Congressional salaries were not increased again for six and a half years, although there were some controversial attempts at raises. Because President Nixon did not appoint the second commission until December 1972, the quadrennial pay increase recommendations were delayed a year. The commission reported to Nixon on June 30, 1973, recommending a 25 per cent increase in 1974. Nixon modified the proposal to provide for 7.5 per cent increases in 1974, 1975 and 1976 for members of Congress and most officials, but with single 7.5 per cent increase in 1975 for Cabinet officers and Supreme Court justices. Under existing law, Nixon could not submit his pay recommendations until his budget message of January 1974.

Some members of Congress were impatient. The Senate on July 9, 1973, without debate and by voice vote, passed a bill which would have empowered the commission to recommend pay raises every two years and would have made a congressional increase possible by October 1973. But the House on July 30 rejected a rule (156-237) to bring the bill to the floor. Supporters of the measure said a biennial review would keep up with the rising cost of living and would avoid embarrassingly large increases after years of inaction. Opponents cried subterfuge, and noted that the commission's recommendations would come every year when there was no congressional election. Rep. David W. Dennis (R Ind.) said, "This bill is here on the cynical and insulting assumption that the American people are so stupid they won't realize what is going on."[7]

The increases recommended by Nixon were to have taken effect March 9, 1974. But members were uneasy about receiving a raise, from $42,500 to $45,700, in an election year. The Senate Post Office and Civil Service Committee on Feb. 28 reported a resolution to disapprove the congressional raise only. On March 6, the Senate voted 67-31 to invoke cloture and cut off debate on the measure, and then voted 71-26 to disapprove all pay increases. The action ended all pay-raise efforts for 1974. The House Post Office and Civil Service Committee on March 4 had reported a resolution disapproving all increases.[8]

Automatic Salary Increases

With surprising speed and ease, Congress in 1975 approved annual cost-of-living increases for its members and other top officials, tied to raises for all federal employees. The new plan was worked out secretly over several months by congressional leaders in consultation with the Ford administration. It was cleared by Congress only five days after most members had first heard of it.

days unless Congress either disapproved all or part of them or enacted a separate pay bill. Thus creation of the commission was an attempt to relieve members of Congress of the politically uncomfortable task of raising their own salaries.

President Johnson announced appointment of the Commission on Executive, Legislative and Judicial Salaries

The idea of Congress giving itself an automatic pay increase every year, based on the Consumer Price Index, arose from staff discussions in the Senate and House Post Office and Civil Service Committees after the Senate had killed the 1974 pay raise. The amount of the increase was to be left to the President when he made his regular cost-of-living recommendations for other federal employees. Sen. Gale W. McGee (D Wyo.), chairman of the Senate committee, began a series of discussions of the proposal in February 1975.

Congressional leaders met at the White House March 10 with President Ford and Chief Justice Warren E. Burger. The administration was alarmed because more than 20 per cent of the government's top officials were either retiring early or taking private-sector jobs because of the executive pay freeze. Burger was concerned because federal judges with lifetime tenure were returning to private life at the highest rate in more than 30 years. Between March 1969, the date of the previous pay raise, and May 1975 the Consumer Price Index had risen by 47.5 per cent. Although congressional salaries had not increased during that time, members had protected themselves from inflation by steadily increasing their allowances and other perquisites.

The automatic cost-of-living raise was added as a rider to a bill establishing a job safety program for postal workers. The Senate committee reported the bill on a Friday, July 25. The Senate began debating it July 28, defeated several amendments and then passed it July 29 by a 58-29 vote.

The bill cleared the House on July 30 by a one-vote margin, 214-213, after a short but furious debate. One representative called the debate "vicious, one of the ugliest, most disgusting things I've ever seen.... Members who rarely say a thing during floor debate were shouting and screaming at each other, saying, 'Don't be a hero, you want this raise as much as we do.' It was ugly."[9]

Under the legislation, the Executive Salary Cost-of-Living Adjustment Act (title II of PL 94-82), salaries for the executive schedule (and for related positions in the legislative and judicial branches) were to be adjusted each year, beginning in October 1975, by the average percentage adjustment of the general government pay schedule.

President Ford set the 1975 pay increase at 5 per cent, although his advisers had suggested at least 8 per cent. The House Oct. 1 voted 278-123 to uphold the 5 per cent increase, and the raise took effect that day. The salary of members of Congress thus increased from $42,500 to $44,600. Salaries for the Speaker and other congressional leaders also increased accordingly.

Opposition to the automatic cost-of-living raise was expected to continue both in and out of Congress. During the House debate Rep. E. G. Shuster (R Pa.) called the plan a "sly backdoor technique." He said, "The American people would be better off if Congress got a pay decrease when the cost-of-living went up and a pay increase when the cost-of-living went down."[10] (A year later, in September 1976, Congress—facing an election in less than two months—voted to deny members the automatic increase scheduled for 1976.)

The system of annual salary increases did not do away with the quadrennial Commission on Executive, Legislative and Judicial Salaries but was intended to help close the pay gap caused by inflation. A new commission was appointed in 1976. Meanwhile, the President's Panel on Federal Compensation on Dec. 1, 1975, gave Ford a broad list of recommendations for reorganizing the federal pay structures. Congressional salaries were not included, but some of the recommendations could affect Congress.

The panel recommended higher levels for the executive schedule, and also urged that the existing linkage between Level II of the executive schedule and congressional salaries should not be permitted to continue to distort or improperly depress executive salaries. Thus executive salaries could be set at levels independent of congressional salaries. The possible importance of this change was pointed out by the panel. It asserted that the failure of efforts to increase salaries in the Executive Schedule in 1973 at the time of the last quadrennial review was a consequence of the tacit equivalence between salary for Level II of the executive schedule and the salary for members of Congress.[11] Both salaries in 1973 were $42,500, and in 1976 were $44,600. In early 1977, salaries were raised to $57,500. *(Details, p. 30)*

Personal Staffs of Members

For a century after the organization of Congress, no provision was made in either chamber for personal staff for a member, unless he was chairman of a committee.

The Senate was first to provide for staff aides. In 1885, a senator was authorized to employ a clerk when Congress was in session. The rate was set at $6 per day. In 1893, the House first authorized a clerk for its members and provided $100 monthly for the clerk's salary.

Over the years the number of aides and the size of their salaries increased steadily. Staff responsibilities expanded as well, to include clerical and bureaucratic support skills, technical and professional legislative skills and political skills. Employees usually have to perform in all three areas.

In addition to their personal staffs, senior members are assisted on legislative matters by staffs of the committees and subcommittees they head. The chairman of a standing committee actually has two staffs. It is not unusual for an aide to do both committee work and personal casework for a member, no matter which payroll he or she is on. Personal staffs and committee staffs combined gave the Senate approximately 6,000 employees in 1975.[12] The House at that time had about 11,000 employees on 700 separate payrolls.[13]

House Staff Allowance

In 1975 the House increased the personal staff allowance of each representative to $227,270 a year to employ up to 18 aides in the Washington and home district offices. A cost-of-living increase on Oct. 1, 1975, boosted the total to $238,584, but at the time only one-third of the representatives were spending the full allowance and only one-third had hired the maximum of 18 aides. The unused monthly allowance does not accumulate; however up to $1,000 each month may be used to cover charges for computer and related services. The allowance was raised to $255,144 for 1977.

The staff increases have benefited mainly the junior representatives who do not have the additional help of committee staffs. Richard P. Conlon, staff director of the Democratic Study Group, an organization of moderate and liberal House Democrats, said in 1975, "New members have found they receive more complaints from constituents." He cited the case of freshman Rep. James L. Oberstar (D Minn.), whose constituent service workload was four times higher than that of former Rep. John A. Blatnik (D Minn.), whom Oberstar replaced.[14]

In 1976, the House Administration Committee instituted a series of reforms governing staff allowances (among other things) in the aftermath of the sex-payroll scandal that forced Rep. Wayne L. Hays (D Ohio) to resign as committee chairman. *(See Sexual Scandal, below.)*

The committee's reforms:

● Required House members and chairmen of committees and subcommittees to certify monthly the salaries and duties of their staff and to disclose any kinships between staff employees and any House member. This change was to become effective 30 days after the committee approved the certification forms.

● Required quarterly reports of how House funds are spent. The reports would be indexed according to employees and employing offices, showing titles and salaries. The first report under the new format was expected to cover the third quarter of 1976, ending Sept. 30.

● Gave the committee the power to adjust the clerk-hire allowance to reflect federal government cost-of-living raises.

Senate Staff Allowance. The personal staff allowance of senators depends upon the population of their states. For 1977, the annual allowance ranged from $449,063 for states with fewer than two million residents to $902,301 for states with more than 21 million. Senators may hire as many aides as they wish within the allowance, but only one may earn the maximum annual salary of $41,750. Senate staff allowances are cumulative within a calendar year, so that unused monthly allowances may be carried over.[15]

In June 1975, junior senators succeeded in amending the Standing Rules of the Senate to allow all senators to appoint up to three additional staff members for a total of $101,925 a year to help them with their committee assignments. In four days of debate the first-term senators and their allies also won the right to hire and control their own committee staff members, thus making an inroad on the seniority system. Employees in the new category are paid out of the contingency fund of the Senate. The resolution eventually was approved by voice vote on June 12.[16]

Problems of Nepotism

Nepotism has been a recurring issue in congressional annals. Some members have used their staff allowances to pay relatives and in effect supplement the member's personal salary.

On May 20, 1932, the House adopted a resolution by Rep. Lindsay C. Warren (D N.C.) which provided that: "The Clerk of the House of Representatives is hereby authorized and directed to keep open for public inspection the payroll records of the disbursing officer of the House." The resolution was adopted without debate. Few members on the floor understood its import. On the next day, however, stories based upon examinations of the disbursing officer's records were published in all newspapers. They disclosed that 97 members of the House devoted their clerk-hire allowance, in whole or in part, to payment of persons having the same names as their own. Presumably these persons were relatives. The names were published, and "nepotism in Congress" became a subject of wide public discussion.

Senate payroll information was not opened for public inspection until 1959. On June 26, 1959, the Senate by voice vote adopted a resolution requiring the Secretary of the Senate to make public the name, title, salary and employer of all Senate employees. The resolution was the outgrowth of critical newspaper stories on the withholding of payroll information, coupled with disclosures of congressional nepotism.

Touching off the new round of disclosures was a Jan. 5, 1959, news story by Scripps-Howard staff writer Vance Trimble, containing a lengthy list of relatives he said were employed by members in their offices in 1958. Trimble had obtained the names by checking out similar names on available House-Senate records. He filed a court suit to gain access to Senate payroll records.

On Feb. 23, 1959, the Associated Press published a list of 65 representatives who had persons with "the same or similar family name" on their January payrolls. Three members who were on the AP list denied that their payroll namesakes were in any way related to them.

Nepotism also was a problem for Rep. Adam Clayton Powell Jr. (D N.Y.). From the time of their marriage in December 1960 Powell employed his Puerto Rican wife— Yvette Marjorie Flores—as a paid member of his congressional office staff. Mrs. Powell remained in Puerto Rico after the birth of a son in 1962, but she continued to draw a $20,578 annual salary as a clerk whose job was to answer mail to Spanish-speaking constituents. The House in 1964 adopted a resolution aimed specifically at that situation; it forbade members from hiring employees who did not work either in the member's home district or in Washington, D.C. That provision was readopted as a part of the legislative branch appropriation in 1965. Mrs. Powell, however, remained in Puerto Rico. Following a select committee investigation of additional charges against Powell, he was excluded from the 90th Congress on March 1, 1967. The U.S. Supreme Court later ruled that the House action was unconstitutional, and Powell returned to Congress in 1969.

In 1967, Congress included in the postal rate-federal pay increase bill a provision to curb nepotism in federal employment. The provision prohibited public officials, including members of Congress, from appointing or influencing the appointment of relatives in the agency in which the official served. The ban covered all officials, including the President, but did not cover relatives already employed. And it did not prevent an official in one agency or chamber of Congress from seeking to obtain employment for a relative in another agency or chamber.

The "Congressional Handbook," prepared for all members and updated continually by the Joint Committee on Congressional Operations, lists 25 classifications of relatives whose employment by representatives and senators "is not permitted by law under the staff allowances."[17]

Political Misuse

In recent years the political misuse of congressional staff has become a more common charge than nepotism. The issue comes to the surface every election year, when some members are accused of using employees on the congressional payroll to help get themselves re-elected.

A series of articles in *The Washington Post* Feb. 16-24, 1975, charged that more than 100 Senate committee staff members had been transferred to non-committee duties in senators' offices and that others were being used in political campaigns.

Sexual Scandal

Traditionally, little has been said about members' sexual relations with their staffs. As a result, rumors of abuses have circulated from time to time, but rarely if ever have been substantiated.

1976 House Changes in Members' Benefits

The House of Representatives and its Committee on Administration adopted a number of reforms in 1976 in the aftermath of a sex-payroll scandal that forced Rep. Wayne L. Hays (D Ohio) to resign June 18 as chairman of the committee. Elizabeth Ray, a committee secretary, said May 23 that Hays kept her on the payroll to provide him sexual favors. Hays denied the assertion, but the widespread publicity of the assertion, and resulting adverse public and political reaction, led to Hays' resignation of the chairmanship. He resigned from Congress on Sept. 1, 1976.

Committee Actions

The House Administration Committee, meeting under its new chairman, Rep. Frank Thompson Jr. (D N.J.), adopted a series of reform proposals on June 28, 1976. No House action was required. They included:

● Reduced the current 20-cents-a-mile allowance for automobile travel for House members to 15 cents, the amount set by the General Services Administration for federal employees, effective July 1.

● Required House members and chairmen of committees and subcommittees to certify monthly the salaries and duties of their staffs and to disclose any kinships between staff employees and any House member. This change would become effective 30 days after the Administration Committee approved the certification forms, which it did on Sept. 1.

● Required quarterly reports of how House funds are spent. The reports would be indexed according to employees and employing offices, showing the titles and salaries.

● Required that disbursements be made only on the presentation of vouchers, effective Sept. 1.

The following were to go into effect in the 95th Congress:

● Eliminated the separate postage stamp allowance, currently $1,140 a year, and ended the so-called "cash-out" practice that permitted members to convert unused stationery and travel allowances into cash for their personal use.

● Gave the committee the power to adjust the clerk-hire allowance, currently $238,584 a year, to reflect federal government cost-of-living raises.

● Revised the telephone and telegraph allowance to permit each member to have two WATS (wide area telephone service) lines to reduce costs for long-distance phone calls. If a member opted for the WATS lines, he would give up half of his annual telecommunications allowance.

● Revised the system of allowances used by members to run their offices by permitting members for the first time to transfer money from one fund to another. The new system was to take effect in the 95th Congress.

House Actions

On July 1 the House adopted two resolutions which were also designed as reform measures. Both were attacked sharply by Republicans, but survived recommittal votes, and eventually were adopted by large majorities. One resolution (H Res 1368) established a 15-person study commission on House accounting and personnel procedures and members' benefits. The other resolution (H Res 1372) stripped the House Administration Committee in most instances of its unilateral authority to alter representatives' benefits.

H Res 1368. The resolution authorizing the study commission was adopted by a 380-30 roll-call vote after a Republican motion to recommit was rejected by a 143-269 vote that followed party lines.

The resolution created a Commission on Administrative Review, which was to be composed of eight representatives (five Democrats, three Republicans) appointed by the Speaker, and seven members of the public chosen for their backgrounds and experience, also appointed by the Speaker. The commission was to conduct a study and prepare recommendations covering the following areas: staff personnel, administration, accounting and purchasing procedures, office equipment and communications facilities, recordkeeping, emoluments, and allowances. The Commission was to report to the House by Dec. 31, 1977.

H Res 1372. The resolution dealing with the House Administration Committee was adopted by a 311-92 roll call after a Republican recommittal motion was rejected by a 165-236 vote.

The resolution would require House approval—instead of unilateral committee action—of most changes in representatives' benefits and allowances. Cases in which the committee could continue to act alone were ones in which there was a change in the price of materials, services or office space; a technological change or other improvement in equipment; or a cost-of-living increase.

The tradition was broken dramatically in 1976 when Elizabeth Ray, a House Administration Committee secretary, told *The Washington Post* May 23 that Chairman Wayne L. Hays (D Ohio) maintained her on the committee staff to provide him with sexual favors. Hays admitted he had had a "personal relationship" with Ray but denied he had retained her as his mistress. Ray told the Post she had been a committee staff member since April 1974 despite the fact that "I can't type, I can't file, I can't even answer the phone."

The case attracted wide attention, and pressure from the House Democratic leadership led Hays to resign as committee chairman on June 18. The House on July 1 adopted two resolutions establishing a 15-member Commission on Administrative Review to study House accounting and personnel procedures and members' perquisites, and stripping the House Administration Committee of its unilateral power to alter representatives' benefits and allowances. Earlier the committee had approved a series of orders that revamped House perquisites and instituted controls over payroll and personnel procedures. Newspapers reported a number of other cases of possible sexual misuse of female workers by male members. Hays later decided not to stand for re-election in 1976 and resigned his seat Sept. 1.

Senators' Use of Committee Staffs for Personal Work

A series of articles by Stephen Isaacs appearing in *The Washington Post* Feb. 16-24, 1975, described how numerous senators diverted committee staff personnel to non-committee work. The study was based on statistics, gathered by the paper's data processing staff, fed to an IBM computer.

The survey showed that about one-third of all senators were using committee staffers for business not connected with their committee assignments. About the same number of senators were using committees to attract favorable publicity by conducting field hearings in their home states; 85.5 per cent of all field hearings held in the 93rd Congress (1971-73) were held in the home states of members of the committees holding the hearings. In addition, the study found that more than 10 per cent of Senate committee employees "work not in committee offices, but in the suites of their Senate members" and were usually engaged in work for the senators rather than committee business.

As an example, the Post Feb. 19 cited the Judiciary Subcommittee on Refugees and Escapees, chaired by Sen. Edward M. Kennedy (D Mass.). The panel was authorized to spend $182,000 in 1974, but no bills were referred to it in the 93rd Congress and the panel held only two days of hearings in 1974. Eleven people were on the payroll, but only four worked in the subcommittee's office. On the diversion of staff, Kennedy said, "It does happen. There are people that are on payrolls that are working on other responsibilities." Appearing before the Senate Committee on Rules and Administration Feb. 28, Kennedy said he did not question whether one senator should have more staff assistants than another, but added that "I do resent quite deeply, as just an individual member of the Senate, not being afforded the kind of staff opportunity to meet responsibilities as a member of the Senate.

"We are competing with a major executive office that has extraordinary kinds of resources in every possible area, and we are constantly being challenged to represent our interests and represent them in an important way," he said.

Reasons For Diversion of Staff

Among the explanations for diverting committee staff to personal business were the enormous growth of constituent business (requiring letters, casework, etc.), the lack of office space in committee offices, and the fact that senators had obligations on other committees that required staff help.

In the Senate, any chairman has the prerogative as to what he will do with the committee staff, but there has been increasing pressure to distribute staff among committee members. According to the Post (Feb. 18), Sen. Henry M. Jackson (D Wash.) controlled a Senate staff budget totaling $1,901,970 a year. During the period Jan. 1-June 30, 1974, Jackson's Interior Committee employed 38 people, 31 of whom were under Jackson's control. Six others were controlled by the six Republican members of the committee. Jackson also was chairman of the Permanent Investigations Subcommittee of the Government Operations Committee; in that position, he controlled 32 of the subcommittee's 42 employees, with Republicans controlling the rest.

Commenting on the situation, Sen. Lee Metcalf (D Mont.), who had one staff member on the Interior Committee, said: "I think staff should be a professional staff that we use as a staff...and the lowest ranking person in seniority on the committee should have access to all of the staff for legislative work just the same as everybody else." But Jackson said, "I think the problem is that if each individual member has the staffing...you get away from the idea of a professional staff, acting for the whole committee."

Rules and Administration Committee

Funds for committee staffs are authorized by the Senate Committee on Rules and Administration, chaired by Sen. Howard W. Cannon (D Nev.). Of his role, Cannon said, "I can't be a policeman. I can't ask a United States senator to stand before me and swear an oath as to what he's going to do with that money."

In introducing his resolution providing for committee staff for individual senators (the measure was passed in modified form), Sen. Mike Gravel (D Alaska) said: "We all know that hundreds of people come to work in the Senate every day who are on committee payrolls who do no committee work. They perform services for members not related to committee activities.... The only (way to get staff) is to curry the favor of one's committee chairman in the hopes of gaining additional staff.... Machinations take place, well hidden from public view, under layers of seniority, senatorial courtesy, private back-scratching and negotiations. I submit that this is a rather silly process in which grown men are involved. But we all do it...."

Part of the committee staff problem may be attributed to the cross-jurisdictions of committees, with staffs of several panels handling the same issues. In March 1975, Sens. Adlai E. Stevenson III (D Ill.) and Bill Brock (R Tenn.), along with 50 other senators, introduced a resolution to establish a select committee to study the Senate committee system with a view to restructuring it so as to create more and better staffs and more effective and relevant committees. (A similar proposal in the 93rd Congress foundered when it ran up against opposition from senior Senate members.)

Sources: Articles by Stephen Isaacs in Feb. 16, 17, 18, 19, 20, 22, 23, 24, 1975, *The Washington Post;* Congressional Quarterly, Weekly Report, March 8, 1975, p. 496.

House Allowances, 1971-1975

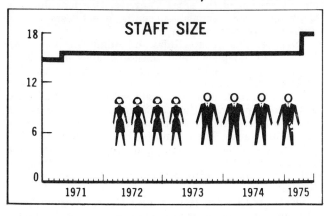

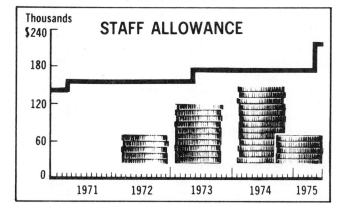

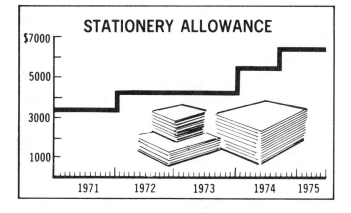

Special Allowances

The travel allowance provided in the Act of Sept. 22, 1789, fixing the compensation of members of Congress was the first of what has become a handful of special allowances that members have created for themselves through the years. Senators and representatives still receive a travel allowance. Other special allowances cover office expenses, stationery, postage, telephone and telegraph service and publications. *(Information on special allowances is taken from the House and Senate versions of the "Congressional Handbook," see p. 56)*

The various allowances have been a persistent source of trouble for members. The stationery and other allowances are susceptible to abuse. At the same time, some members

find that the amounts provided by the allowances fail to keep up with rising costs. One answer to the money problem has been for members to apply campaign contributions to certain incidental expenses.

In general, allowances are more specific and more restrictive for representatives than for senators. While representatives have often had to limit spending within each account, senators may consolidate their allowances for stationery, postage, telephone and telegraph, travel, and state office expenses "with no limitation on the amount which can be spent in any one category."[18] Many House allowances must be spent a month at a time, whereas Senate allowances usually are cumulative within a calendar year. Most allowances in the House are the same for all members, but in the Senate they vary with the population of the states.

Each legislative body largely determines its own allowances and perquisites. Occasionally members on one side of the Capitol may decide that their colleagues on the other side are trying to boost their benefits too much. On Feb. 18, 1975, the House recommitted a bill which, perhaps inadvertently, would have amended Senate rules to allow senators and their aides to collect $35 per diem in expenses while traveling to, from and within their home states. Rep. Les Aspin (D Wis.) sent letters to all representatives, saying, "The new freebie will allow senators while they are out campaigning to rake off an extra $35 daily bonus."[19] Then on June 1 the representatives increased their own per diem to $50 for official business trips.

That incident was unusual. In contrast, the House Administration Committee on May 20, 1975, added a newsletter allowance and increased the allowances for staff, travel and telephone service without even asking members whether the perquisites were needed. A resolution approved in 1971 (but reversed in 1976) gave the committee the power to set allowances without a vote of the full House.[20]

Following a sex-payroll scandal that forced Rep. Wayne L. Hays to resign as chairman of the House Administration Committee, the committee in 1976 instituted a number of reform measures dealing with (among other things) the special allowances of representatives. In addition to making a series of specific changes, the committee reforms permitted House members for the first time to transfer funds from one allowance category to another. The new transfer system was to take effect in the 95th Congress.

Travel Allowance

The travel allowance of 1789—$6 for each 20 miles—has been altered to reflect increased mobility of the nation.

House. Representatives are allowed 26 free round trips each year to and from their home district. Their staffs are allowed six free trips a year. Six extra staff trips are permitted if they are deducted from a member's quota of 26. As recently as March 1971 each House office was allowed only 12 round trips a year.

Representatives may choose to withdraw their travel allowance in cash, up to a maximum of $2,250 a year. Until 1977, any remainder not used for travel could have gone toward members' personal expenses, if they paid income taxes on it.

As part of its reform package, the House Administration Committee in 1976 reduced the 20-cents-a-mile allowance for automobile travel for House members to 15 cents, the amount set by the General Services Administration for federal employees. The new rate became effective July 1, 1976.

The committee also ended the "cash-out" practice of allowing members to withdraw the unused balance of their travel allowance. This change was to become effective with the beginning of the 95th Congress.

Senate. The travel allowance for Senate offices is based on the cost of 40 round trips a year for states with fewer than 10 million people and 44 round trips for states with more than 10 million. The states' distance from Washington is figured in the computation. The Senate travel allowance makes no distinction between trips by senators or their staffs and it sets no limit on the number of trips to be taken each year.

Per Diem Travel. Members are reimbursed for travel on official business that is in addition to visits to their home districts or states. Representatives can receive $50 per diem for such travel within the United States. Senators and their staffs normally receive $35 per diem, but may be reimbursed for a maximum of $50 a day.

Stationery Allowance

House. Each representative is allowed $6,500 a year to purchase stationery and office supplies. Until 1977, members could convert the allowance into cash to pay for other publications or gifts for constituents, or for personal expenses provided they paid income taxes on it.

In 1976, the House Administration Committee eliminated the "cash-out" option as part of its reform package. This change was to become effective at the start of the 95th Congress.

In addition to the annual $6,500 allowance, each representative is allowed 40,000 brown "Public Document" envelopes a month without charge; the envelopes may be used anytime in a calendar year.

Senate. The stationery allowance for a senator's office ranges from $3,600 to $5,000 a year, depending on the state's population. It is part of the consolidated allowance of senators which may be used for a variety of official expenses. In addition to the cash allowance, each senator receives allotments of white envelopes and letterheads, blank sheets and brown "Public Document" envelopes, all based on the state's population.

Postage Allowance

The franking privilege of members of Congress applies only to regular surface mail. Special allowances are required for airmail and special delivery stamps.

House. Until 1977, each representative's office received a postage allowance for use on official mail that was ineligible for franking. In the 94th Congress, which began in 1975, the annual allowance was $1,140. Unused allowance balances could not accumulate.

In 1976, the House Administration Committee eliminated the postage allowance, effective with the start of the 95th Congress, as part of its reform efforts.

Senate. Senators whose states are east of the Mississippi River receive an annual postage allowance of $1,390; those whose states are wholly or partially west of the Mississippi receive $1,740 a year. It is part of the senators' consolidated allowance.

Telephone and Telegraph Allowance

House. Each year a represenative is allowed 125,000 message units—for long-distance phone calls, telegrams and cablegrams—with the units freely transferable between the member's home district office and Washington office.

Unused units from one session may be carried over to a subsequent session of the same Congress. One long-distance telephone minute equals four units, one telegram word equals two units, and so on.

Senate. The Senate Rules and Administration Committee fixes telephone and telegraph allowances. Each senator may make 3,000 long-distance calls a year, totaling not more than 15,000 minutes. A senator from a state of more than 10 million persons is allowed an additional 1,500 calls a year (not more than 7,500 minutes). In addition, a senator is given a flat $2,200 a year for calls that exceed the per-call allowance. The committee uses a complicated formula to determine the telegraph allowance, based on state populations and Western Union rates from Washington. Both formulas go into a senator's total consolidated allowance.

FTS, WATS for Senate and House. Beyond these basic telephone and telegraph allowances, many members have access either to a nationwide, leased-line Federal Telecommunications System (FTS) or to wide-area telephone service (WATS) provided by telephone companies. The House Administration Committee in 1976 revised representatives' telephone and telegraph allowances to permit each member to have two WATS lines to reduce costs for long distance calls. If a representative chose to use WATS lines, half the annual telecommunications allowance would have to be given up. The change was part of the committee's reform package.

Newsletter Allowance

House. Since 1975 each representative has been allowed $5,000 a year for production and printing of newsletters, questionnaires and similar correspondence eligible to be mailed under the frank. The allowance about covers the cost of two newsletters a year. When the House Administration Committee first authorized the allowance, the chairman, Rep. Wayne L. Hays (D Ohio), said it would "assist members with district communication" and free them "from the necessity of private fund-raising." But Rep. Bill Frenzel (R Minn.), one of the committee members opposed to the new allowance, called it a "re-election campaign gimmick" that only increased the power of incumbents at the taxpayers' expense.[21]

Senate. Some services for printing and bulk mailing of newsletters, questionnaires, excerpts from the *Congressional Record* and other items are provided without charge by the Senate's Service Department. Senators receive a monthly printing allowance, based on state population, but they sometimes use part of the stationery allowance, trade-offs from other accounts, or private resources to cover newsletter expenses.

Office Allowances

House. The Washington office of a representative is provided free of charge. In 1975 a lobby group, Americans for Democratic Action, figured the average size of a member's office and the average rent for office space in Washington, D.C., and estimated that the free office saves each representative about $10,480 a year.[22] Office furnishings and decorations, housekeeping and maintenance all are free. Each member receives $5,500 a year to purchase electrical and mechanical office equipment, and $750 a month to lease equipment. The allowances are not cumulative.

In their home districts representatives are allowed up to three offices. Space in federal buildings is free. If private space must be rented, members are allowed $200 a month ($2,400 a year) for each office, or up to $500 a month in unusual circumstances. The home offices are allowed an aggregate allowance of $27,000 for furnishings and equipment. An annual expense allowance of $2,000 is shared by all home offices.

Senate. The Washington office and furnishings for senators are provided free, as are housekeeping and maintenance services. Senators do not have allowances to buy or lease office equipment because it is provided by the sergeant at arms of the Senate.

A senator's home state office space is allocated according to the state's population. Within the allowed square footage there is no limit to the number of officers. Offices are provided free in federal buildings or leased from private owners at the GSA regional rate. Senators receive an aggregate furniture and equipment allowance of $20,500 for 4,800 square feet of office space, increased by $500 for each additional 200 square feet. All furnishings are provided through the General Services Administration. The expense allowance for home offices is part of the senators' consolidated allowance. Each senator also is allowed to rent one mobile office for use throughout the state.

Publications Allowance

In addition to their special allowances for office operations, communications and travel, members of Congress receive a number of free publications. Some are used directly in the member's work—a complete set of the U.S. Code and supplements, four subscriptions to the *Federal Register,* and office copies of the *Congressional Record* and the *Congressional Directory.* Others are offered as gifts to constituents. Besides three personal copies, representatives are allotted 68 subscriptions to the *Congressional Record* and senators are allotted 100. Members and their staffs receive engraved copies of the annual *Congressional Directory.* Representatives may distribute 33 copies and senators 58 copies.

Members also receive allotments of special publications to send off to constituents. One of the most popular is the Yearbook of the Department of Agriculture. Each representative was allotted 400 copies in 1975, worth $2,280.[23] Unused Yearbooks and certain other publications may be turned in to the Government Printing Office for exchange or credit toward other books and pamphlets. Among the gifts members may choose to distribute are wall calendars and pamphlets on American history, the legislative process and historic documents.

Americans for Democratic Action calculated in 1975 that each representative was allowed $10,659 worth of free publications.[24] But is is impossible to make an accurate estimate because members also receive, and use, hundreds of bills, annual reports from federal agencies, budget documents, manuals, published hearings and committee reports. Senators are given an unabridged dictionary and stand as part of their office furnishings.

Abuses of Allowances

With so much money involved in the special allowances, some members inevitably have taken advantage of them. Some abuses have been blatant and illegal. Others resulted from genuine confusion over what was proper or improper.

One classic example of abuse of the allowance for office expenses came to light in 1959. A Scripps-Howard dispatch on March 4, 1959, disclosed that Rep. Randall S. Harmon (D Ind.) was collecting $100 a month for use of the front porch of his home in Indiana as a district office. The incident was widely publicized and led to further news stories on the use that members make of their district offices. Randall was defeated in the 1960 elections.

Before travel allowances were made so generous, it was common for members to draw from other accounts to pay for their trips back home. On the other hand, members could pocket their travel allowance and pay for transportation with other funds. The postage allowance is frequently used because members find ways to trade in their sheets of stamps for cash.

Another abuse of travel funds was reported in 1976 by *The Wall Street Journal.* On April 30 it reported that a number of members filed reimbursement vouchers for 1975 automobile travel to their districts when they actually had traveled at lower cost by airline. Others had received reimbursement for trips on dates when the *Congressional Record* showed they had been in Washington voting on legislation. On June 18 *The Washington Post* reported the Justice Department had asked the House for financial records of nine members who allegedly overcharged the government for travel expenditures. The Post listed the names of the members as Reps. Ray J. Madden (D Ind.), Margaret M. Heckler (R Mass.), Tim Lee Carter (R Ky.), Walter Flowers (D Ala.), Otto E. Passman (D La.), Bill D. Burlison (D Mo.), George E. Shipley (D Ill.), Robert E. Jones (D Ala.), and Gene Taylor (R Mo.).

The stationery allowance is easily abused because its use is not specified and because representatives until 1977 were allowed to add the entire $6,500 a year to their annual salary. If they use it as personal income they must cover stationery expenses in some other way. In practice, most members deplete their stationery allowances on routine business and never withdraw the cash for personal use.

In both the House and Senate, stationery allowances routinely are used to purchase ashtrays, cuff links, pen and pencil sets and other souvenirs for constituents—especially at the end of the year. It is no secret that the funds cover a lot of official Christmas shopping.

In the House, stationery funds not spent during a given term are carried over in a member's account. The remainder served as a retirement bonus for some members. Early in the 94th Congress, 77 retired or defeated members withdrew a total of $198,306 from their accounts. The largest withdrawal was $23,611 by H. R. Gross (R Iowa), for years the House's leading opponent of federal spending, who said it was "one of the smallest withdrawals made over a 26-year period."[25] In 1976, the House Administration Committee eliminated the "cash-out" option. This change was to become effective at the start of the 95th Congress.

Increases in Allowances

Congress increased the special allowances so much in the early 1970s that the amounts themselves were criticized as improper. Americans for Democratic Action concluded in August 1975 that the total pay and perquisites of representatives, including special allowances, had risen by over $112,000 since the end of 1973—an increase of 30 per cent in about a year and a half.[26] The cost-of-living pay increases that took effect Oct. 1, 1975, added another $13,500 to that total.

The Washington Star reported Nov. 12, 1975: "Since 1970, consumer prices have risen by 39 per cent. In Congress, meanwhile, the legislators have raised allowances for staff salaries by 71 per cent, 116 per cent for stationery supplies, 63 per cent for special postage, and 275 per cent for the rental of district office space."[27]

Not all the critics of higher allowances were outside of Congress. Rep. Marjorie S. Holt (R Md.) chose not to increase her personal staff in 1975 when the maximum was raised from 16 to 18. "Increase the staff and you've got to increase the amount of paper you buy," Rep. Holt said. "Then you've got to buy more furniture for them. That means you need more rooms. And when you build more rooms you've got to hire more policemen to protect them."[28]

'Slush Funds' of Members

Despite all the allowances, many members still find their incomes insufficient to meet certain expenses associated with their duties. Thus they have established special accounts of private funds. The polite name for them is "office accounts" or even "constituent service accounts," but they are most frequently referred to simply as "slush funds."

Slush funds may be leftover campaign contributions, any donations from individuals or organizations, or part of members' personal wealth. They are used for many purposes: newsletter expenses, family or staff travel, lunches for constituents, public meetings, parking fees, opinion polls, flowers for funerals, mailings of Christmas cards, office coffee, and just about any job-related expense not covered by the allowances.

Slush funds essentially are not regulated. Some members report all sources and uses of slush funds; others avoid any mention of them.

A representative who requested anonymity told *Parade* magazine in 1975: "Office funds—or newsletter funds, office accounts, research and information funds—whatever they're called—are the last refuge for members of Congress who want to take unlimited amounts of money from any source, spend it on whatever they please and report it nowhere."[29]

The *Parade* article said at least half of the representatives were believed to have slush funds, although "a survey shows that most of the funds are relatively small—about $5,000 a year, most of it collected in small contributions from constituents."[30]

A Senate rule requires senators to file reports on the receipt and disposition of all contributions over $50, whether campaign gifts or not. Many senators handle slush funds through their campaign committees, and some keep more than one office account so that the amount does not appear embarrassingly large. Even so, a senator's slush fund may total tens of thousands of dollars a year.

The Federal Election Commission issued a regulation July 30, 1975, to apply the contribution and spending limits of the campaign finance law (PL 93-443) to the slush funds of members throughout their terms in Congress. When that was strongly opposed by Senate leaders, the commission Sept. 30 issued a compromise regulation that treated office accounts as campaign funds only for the last two years of a senator's term and the second year of a representative's term.

A Senate amendment to accept the revised regulation defeated Oct. 8 by a 47-48 vote.

However, both chambers in March 1977 took steps to rectify abuses in the use of unofficial office accounts. Members would be prohibited from maintaining such accounts after January 1978. Moreover, effective immediately, contributions to unofficial office accounts were banned, as was the conversion of campaign funds to personal use. *(pp. 18, 22)*

Members' Honoraria

For many years members of Congress, especially senators, have supplemented their income by delivering speeches, making public appearances and broadcasts, and publishing articles for fees and royalties. Until 1975 there were no restrictions on such earnings, and it was not unusual for prominent or popular members to earn more from honoraria than from salary.

The era of no restrictions ended Jan. 1, 1975, when the campaign finance law took effect. It limited honoraria for members and other federal officials to $1,000 for any single appearance or article and a total of $15,000 a year.[31] *(See next page for 1976 change in limitations.)*

Senate. Senators, with larger constituencies and far more national publicity, always have received more than representatives in honoraria. In 1973, senators collected a record high of nearly $1.1-million. In 1974, the last year before the new law took effect, 77 senators reported honoraria totaling $939,619. Only 22 senators exceeded the $15,000 level, but they earned 69 per cent of the total. In 1975, with the new law in effect, 81 senators reported earning $637,893. The leading earner was Sen. Herman E. Talmadge (D Ga.), who reported $14,980.

The pattern of honoraria earnings followed a trend established over the years in which committee chairmen and members of committees with jurisdiction over economic issues reported the highest earnings.

In 1975 for the eighth straight year, colleges and universities spent more on Senate honoraria—$136,172 among 50 senators—than any other group. Jewish groups paid $33,500 to 19 senators; medical, dental and pharmaceutical associations paid $30,612 to 26 senators; labor groups paid $22,380 to 19 senators.

Senators were not required to report how they used their honoraria, but a few did so. Some used the funds to cover office expenses and other official activities, but most of the honoraria reported were donated by the senators to charitable institutions.

House. Reporting requirements were different in the House, where members must list activities for which honoraria were received but need not reveal the amount. In 1975, 231 representatives reported honoraria for speeches, writings and media appearances.

Of the total, 56 also reported their earnings, which came to $253,470. The leading earner was Rep. Shirley Chisholm (D N.Y.), who reported $15,000.

The leading provider of House honoraria in 1975 was the Grocery Manufacturers of America, which was listed on the reports of 20 representatives. The Brookings Institution appeared on the reports of 17 members. Other major contributors were the American Bankers Association and the American Podiatry Association.

Seven representatives reported honoraria from 20 or more sources.

(Reporting requirements of other outside earnings by members of Congress are discussed in Ethics in Congress, p. 111.)

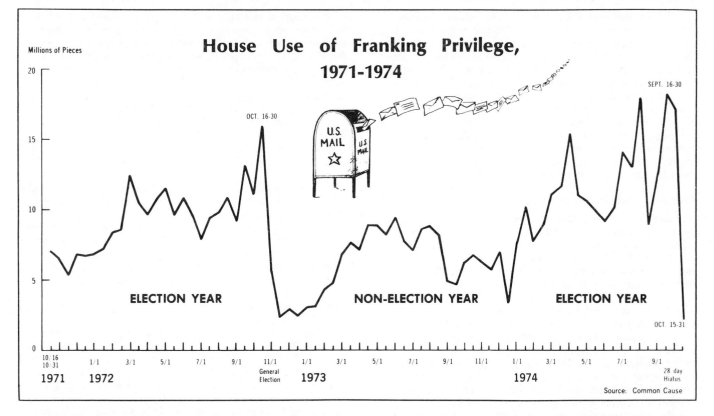

House Use of Franking Privilege, 1971-1974

Millions of Pieces

ELECTION YEAR

NON-ELECTION YEAR

ELECTION YEAR

OCT. 16-30

SEPT. 16-30

OCT. 15-31

U.S. MAIL

1971   1972   General Election   1973   1974   28 day Hiatus

Source: Common Cause

1975 Rule Modified. The 1975 restrictions on honoraria were in effect for less than a year and a half. They were loosened considerably in May 1976 when Congress approved the Federal Election Campaign Act Amendments of 1976 (PL 94-283). The issue of honoraria was the last to be settled by conferees before the legislation could be passed. The House-approved bill had not changed the existing limits; the Senate bill had eliminated all restrictions on honoraria.

In the conference committee, Sen. Mark O. Hatfield (R Ore.) led the fight for increasing honoraria limits. Hatfield had been the Senate's third-highest recipient of honoraria in 1974, taking in $45,677 for 47 speeches before the $15,000 annual ceiling had gone into effect. He was opposed by Rep. Wayne L. Hays (D Ohio), who suggested only a slight increase to permit senators and representatives to receive $2,000 per individual event and a total of $20,000 annually.[32]

The 1976 law finally raised the limit on honoraria for members of Congress and federal employees to $2,000 for each event and a total of $25,000 a year. However, the $25,000 limit was a net amount; booking agents' fees, travel expenditures, subsistence, and expenses for an aide or a spouse to accompany the speaker could be deducted from the total honoraria in reaching a net amount. The law did not change existing reporting requirements.

Franking Privilege

One of the most valuable of members' perquisites is the frank, the privilege of mailing letters and packages under their signatures without being charged for postage. For fiscal 1976, Congress appropriated a total of more than $62-million for its members and officials to send an estimated 322 million pieces of postage-free mail during the year.

The franking privilege is actually older than Congress itself. The first Continental Congress accorded its members mailing privileges, and one of the first acts of Congress under the Constitution was to continue the practice. Except for a brief time—the franking privilege was suspended for a few months in 1873—the privilege remained virtually unchanged. In 1973 Congress updated franking laws for the first time since the 19th century and established machinery for self-policing of franking practices.

Franking consists of a member's autograph or its facsimile on the envelope or package where stamps normally appear. Members submit three to five copies of their signature to the House Office Supply Service or the Senate Printing Clerk, and the most legible copy is selected for reproduction. Originally, franking was allowed on mail received by members as well as on mail sent.

Title 39 of the U.S. Code, which contains the rules of the franking privilege, limits it to correspondence "in which the Member deals with the addressee as a citizen of the United States or constituent." Members of Congress are not authorized to use the frank for letters in which they are acting as a personal friend, a candidate or a member of a political party.

The U.S. Postal Service keeps records of all franked mail as it passes through the post office in Washington. Every three months it sends Congress a bill for the cost of mail sent by members. The Postal Service computes the amount by weighing a random sample of the sacks of mail it receives each day from Congress. The rate of reimbursement is based on average weight, and was set at 14.3 cents per piece for fiscal 1976.

Neither the Postal Service nor its predecessor, the Post Office Department, has inspected franked mail to determine whether any members were abusing the privilege by sending personal or political correspondence postage-free.

41

Until 1968 the Post Office would issue rulings on specific abuses if private citizens made official complaints, and would ask the offending members to reimburse the Post Office. But the rulings were not binding, so some members refused to pay. On Dec. 27, 1968, the Post Office Department ruled that it no longer would attempt to collect from individual members who allegedly had abused the frank. The Postal Service has continued this policy.

No person allowed franking privileges may lend the privilege to any person, organization or committee, except House and Senate committees. Violators can be fined. Surviving spouses of members may use the frank for six months after a member's death.

Franked Mail Controversies

Special uses of the frank occasionally lead to controversy. In the early 1960s Congress had a fight each year over whether mail addressed to "occupant" could be sent under the frank. A compromise was finally adopted which permitted representatives to send some "occupant" mail but forbade senators from doing so.

The 1968 Post Office decision not to collect for franking abuses was followed by lawsuits taking some members to court. A 1970 decision awarded Democratic challenger John V. Tunney an injunction preventing incumbent Sen. George Murphy (R Calif.) from using the frank to send out campaign material. But a 1968 judgment had denied an injunction against similar use of the frank during a campaign by Rep. Jacob Gilbert (D N.Y.). In 1972 alone, 12 cases of alleged violations were brought before the courts.

In one franking case, a court decision was not necessary. In Georgia, the disclosure that Rep. Fletcher Thompson (R 1967-1973) was sending mail all over the state via the frank was considered a major reason he lost a race for a Senate seat. Thompson had sent a mass mailing at a cost to the taxpayers of more than $200,000, and Sam Nunn, his opponent, made it a campaign issue and was elected.

Conflicting court decisions, and a reluctance of many judges to rule on questions of congressional propriety, resulted in general confusion about proper use of the frank. The many disputes during the 1972 campaign convinced some members of Congress that new legislation was necessary. In addition, the House Post Office and Civil Service Committee in a 1973 report (H Rept 93-88) noted a marked increase in the amount of mail sent from Congress since the Post Office stopped policing use of the frank—from 178 million pieces in 1968 to an estimated 288 million pieces in 1973.[33]

1973 Franking Law

On Dec. 17, 1973, Congress approved HR 3180 (PL 93-191), which placed specific guidelines on the types of mail members could send free under the frank, set up mechanisms to rule on individual cases, and restricted the sending of mass mailings by members during the four weeks preceding congressional elections. The bill's sponsor, Rep. Morris K. Udall (D Ariz.) succeeded in establishing definitions of the franking privilege that were acceptable to most members and that represented little change from established practices. Udall said the issue was whether Congress would define the privilege or whether "the judges are going to write the law for us."[34]

The 1973 law provided the following:

● Authorized use of the frank "to expedite and assist the conduct of official business, activities and duties."

● Permitted use of the frank for mailings of any of the following: communications between members and the executive branch, newsletters and press releases dealing with legislative activity, public opinion polls, nonpartisan information on elections or voter registration, and biographies or pictures if sent in response to a specific request.

● Prohibited use of the frank for mailings that included purely personal communications, holiday greetings, information about the family of members, or political solicitations.

● Provided that material from the *Congressional Record* could be franked only if it would qualify as frankable on its own.

● Established a House Commission on Congressional Mailing Standards to make rulings on disputes arising in House election campaigns under the law.

● Assigned to the Senate Select Committee on Standards and Conduct the responsibility to make rulings on disputes arising in Senate election campaigns under the law.

● Prohibited mailings of more than 500 pieces of identical mail for the 28-day period immediately before an election by members who were candidates for re-election except for responses to inquiries, communications to government personnel, and news releases to the media.

The reforms did not anticipate every kind of abuse. Late in 1975 Congress voted to close a loophole in the 1973 law that had allowed former Rep. Frank M. Clark (D Pa.) to send out a franked newsletter mailing to his former constituents two months after his term had expired. The new legislation permitted former members to use the frank for 90 days after leaving Congress, but only for mailings to help close down their offices.

Increasing Use and Cost

Both the use and the cost of congressional franking increased enormously in the early 1970s. In 1970, members of Congress and others authorized to use the frank sent 190 million pieces of mail that cost a total of $11,224,000. For fiscal 1976 the volume and cost had jumped to 322 million pieces and $46,101,000. The 1976 appropriation was $7.3-million more than that for 1975. The Senate Appropriations Committee found in June 1975 "that the funds for fiscal year 1975 have been exhausted and that the reimbursements to the U.S. Postal Service are out of cycle by approximately $19-million."[35]

1977 Reforms in Use of the Frank

Early in 1977, both chambers took steps to place tighter restrictions on the use of the frank, passing resolutions directing that any franked mail henceforth be sent by the most economical means practical. The House measure prohibited any member who was a candidate for statewide office from sending any franked mass mailings to residents outside his district. The resolutions also banned any franked mass mailings to be sent less than 60 days before any primary or general election in which the member sending the mail was a candidate. Only material paid for from official funds could be sent under frank. *(Box, House Use of Franking Privileges, p. 43)*

Travel Abroad—Junketing

Special allowances are available to members of Congress traveling abroad on government business. As

(Continued on p. 44)

Congressional Use of the Frank

Matter that may be franked

Official business, which shall include all matters which directly or indirectly pertain to the legislative process or to any congressional representative function generally, or to the functioning, working or operating of the Congress and the performance of official duties in connection therewith.

Mail matter which is frankable specifically includes but is not limited to: (1) the usual and customary newsletter, press release or questionnaire; (2) condolences and congratulations; (3) nonpartisan voter registration or election information or assistance; (4) mail matter which constitutes or includes a biography or autobiobiography of any member or member-elect, or of their spouse or other members of their family (or a picture, sketch, or other likeness of any member or member-elect), and which is mailed as a part of a federal publication or in response to a specific request therefor, and is not included for publicity purposes; (5) mail matter between members, from a member to any congressional district office (or between district offices), or from a member to a state or local legislator; (6) mail matter to any person and to any level of government regarding programs, decisions and other related matters of public concern, including any matter relating to actions of a past or current Congress; (7) mail matter including general mass mailings, which consist of federal laws, regulations, other federal publications, publications purchased with federal funds or containing items of general information.

Public documents printed by the order of Congress.

The *Congressional Record,* a reprint, or any part of it.

Seeds and agricultural reports

Nonpolitical correspondence relating to the death of a member.

Mailgrams

Source: The Commission on Congressional Mailing Standards.

Persons authorized to use frank

The Vice President, members and members-elect, the secretary and sergeant-at-arms of the Senate, an elected officer of the House (other than a member), the legislative counsels of the House or the Senate. Members of Congress includes senators, representatives, delegates, resident commissioners.

Term of use expires 90 days after the individual leaves office.

The Vice President, members, the secretary and sergeant-at-arms of the Senate, an elected officer of the House (other than a member). (Members of Congress includes senators, representatives, delegates, resident commissioners.)

Term of use expires on the first day of April following the expiration of their term of office.

Members of Congress (senators, representatives, delegates, resident commissioners).

Members of Congress (senators, representatives, delegates, resident commissioners).

Term of use expires the 30th day of June following the expiration of their term of office.

The surviving spouse of a member.

Term of use expires 180 days after the member's death.

The Vice President, members and members-elect, the secretary and sergeant-at-arms of the Senate, an elected officer of the House (other than a member), the legislative counsels of the House or the Senate. Members of Congress includes senators, representatives, delegates, resident commissioners.

(Continued from p. 42)

defined by William L. Safire's *The New Language of Politics,* "An overseas tour by a congressman or candidate is described by him as a *fact-finding trip,* and as a *junket* by his opponents, who usually add 'at the taxpayer's expense.' "[36]

A Congressional Quarterly survey published July 17, 1976, showed that 308 members of Congress had taken at least 544 trips abroad at government expense during 1975. The trips by members and their staff and committee aides cost at least $1,349,412.50. The travelers included 55 senators and 253 representatives, or 57.1 per cent of the members in 1975.[37]

Members generally undertake foreign travel on congressional (usually committee) business or by executive request or appointment. Members traveling abroad on committee business or as delegates to meetings of certain parliamentary groups are required by law to make public annually the government funds used. No public reports are required on other foreign trips.

Defense and Criticism of Members' Trips

As long as members of Congress have been taking trips abroad at government expense, there have been arguments between those who say that such travel is valuable and those who say it is a waste of time and money.

Defenders of foreign travel point out that it enables members to develop insight and to gain first-hand information needed for intelligent legislating and appropriating of funds. They say that such trips help members to overcome prejudice and provincialism and to spread goodwill, as well as giving them the chance to center their attention on foreign affairs and U.S. programs abroad.

Those who oppose overseas travel argue that trips at government expense are mainly a waste of the taxpayer's money. They say that visiting members expect to spend only a minimal amount of time on official business abroad, that they make unreasonable demands on U.S. personnel in the countries they visit, and that they sometimes damage American prestige through tactlessness or give foreign officials the impression that their comments reflect administration policy.

Critics also assert that the true cost of travel can be easily obscured, since expenses are not completely itemized or audited. Sometimes no cost of transportation is reported when flights are furnished by the State Department or the Department of Defense. Commercial airline fares and some other expenses are not always listed if they are defrayed out of Senate and House expense allowances.

Efforts To Control Travel Costs

Congress first initiated some control over members' foreign travel with the passage of the Mutual Security Act of 1954 (PL 83-665), which allowed congressional committees to use counterpart funds in their travels overseas. Members were required to make a full report to an appropriate oversight committee (House Administration, and Senate Rules and Administration), indicating the total amount of currency used and the purposes for which it was spent.

Public reporting in the *Record* was first required by amendments passed in the Mutual Security Act of 1958 (PL 85-477). The reports for 1958 were published in 1959. Members had to make itemized statements to their committee chairmen, showing the amount and dollar equivalent of counterpart funds they spent, plus the purposes for which the money was used, including lodging, meals, transporta-

Controversial Travel

Foreign travel at public expense traditionally has been a sensitive topic for some members of Congress. In past years, the press has reported on a number of such trips, or junkets, as they sometimes are called.

Probably the most notorious junketeer in Congress in recent years was the late Rep. Adam Clayton Powell Jr. (D N.Y.).

In one of his more celebrated trips in 1962, Powell traveled through Europe for six weeks accompanied by two assistants—Corinne Huff, a receptionist in his office, and Tamara J. Wall, an associate labor counsel for the House Education and Labor Committee, of which Powell was chairman.

According to one report, Powell's itinerary included London, Rome, Paris, Vienna, Spain and Greece. He requested State Department assistance to obtain tickets to the Vienna film festival, reservations at various European night clubs and a six-day cruise on the Aegean Sea.

Powell justified the trip on grounds that he and his two companions needed to study equal employment opportunities for women in Common Market countries.

'Lame-Duck Junkets'

In an example of "lame-duck" junketing, Sen. Edward V. Long (D Mo.) and Rep. Barrett O'Hara (D Ill.) both managed lengthy trips abroad after Congress had adjourned in 1968.

Both men had been defeated in primaries earlier in the year and were not returning for the new Congress. Long and his personal secretary traveled through 19 countries in six weeks. His administrative assistant explained that the trip was made for the Senate Banking and Currency Committee "to study export insurance and the Export-Import Bank." Officials of the bank subsequently said they never had been notified or consulted about the trip. O'Hara made a month-long journey to Africa accompanied by several staff members. In 1977, both chambers passed measures banning such lame duck junkets.

Hays' Headwaiter

In 1963, press reports revealed that Wayne L. Hays (D Ohio) had invited the headwaiter in the House dining room to accompany him to Paris for a NATO parliamentarians' conference. Hays reportedly had designated the waiter, Ernest Petinaud, to serve as a liaison man. One article reported that Hays was "unapologetic, calling Petinaud a fine American and an envoy of goodwill."

Source: CQ Weekly Report, May 18, 1974, p. 1292

tion and other reasons. Each committee was required to report this information to the proper oversight committee within the first 60 days of each session. The 1958 bill changed the Senate committee to Appropriations. Within 10 days of receipt, the two committees had to publish the reports in the *Record.*

In 1961, Congress required mandatory publication in the *Record* of individual itemized expenditures (Legislative

Newspaper Says Members 'Travel in Luxury'

A front-page story in *The Washington Post* July 6 provided an unusually detailed look at congressional globetrotting.

The story was based on vouchers and other State Department documents not open to the general public. Post reporters gained access to the voluminous records by filing a request under the Freedom of Information Act (PL 89-487, PL 93-502).

The documents showed how public funds had been used in 1975 and 1976 for congressional sightseeing trips, banquets in exotic restaurants and rental of chauffeured Rolls Royces. Such information is not available from congressional travel reports filed with the House Administration Committee or the Senate secretary.

Nor does Congressional Quarterly solicit cost information when it queries members of Congress each year about their foreign travel.

The Post story turned up several instances where members who did not respond to CQ questionnaires, or whose trips did not appear on committee travel reports, were shown to have traveled abroad at government expense. *(Below)*

The State Department arranges most congressional travel overseas. When so authorized by House and Senate leaders or committee chairmen, the department's congressional travel office routinely wires U.S. embassies in the countries to be visited and instructs them to spend U.S.-owned foreign currencies to buy airplane tickets, provide hotel accommodations and pay $75 per diem allowances for traveling members.

The State Department records examined by the Post showed that in 1975 the department had handled $1.7-million worth of travel expenses for members. This is almost $400,000 more than reported by Congress. For 1974, Congress reported costs of $796,000 while State Department records showed $975,000.

Middle East Delegation

Typical of the special congressional delegations that do not report their expenses for foreign trips was a group of 23 House members who accompanied Majority Leader Thomas P. O'Neill Jr. (D Mass.) on a Middle East tour during the 1975 Easter recess. Special, one-time delegations such as O'Neill's are exempted from the reporting requirements because of an internal congressional ruling that the law applies only to routine committee travel and certain long-standing formal delegations. State Department records showed that the O'Neill trip cost more than $20,000, not counting Air Force transportation. Included were stops in London, Athens, Cairo, Tel Aviv and Barcelona.

The delegation drew per diem expenses of $7,500 in Greece, $7,000 in Egypt and $3,300 in Spain. Incidental expenses included $2,600 for local transportation in Greece and Spain (including sightseeing), $1,500 for a reception in Cairo and $4,000 for other entertainment in Egypt that included a tour of the Pyramids and a dinner aboard the luxury barge *Omar Khayyam*.

Among those who took the trip, according to a list provided Congressional Quarterly by O'Neill's office, were nine House members who did not respond to CQ's 1975 travel survey. They were Tom Bevill (D Ala.), Silvio O. Conte (R Mass.), Eligio de la Garza (D Texas), Albert W. Johnson (R Pa.), Dawson Mathis (D Ga.), Melvin Price (D Ill.), Charles B. Rangel (D N.Y.), James H. Scheuer (D N.Y.) and Bob Wilson (R Calif.).

Another member who appeared on O'Neill's list was former Rep. Richard Fulton (D Tenn. 1963-75), who resigned to become mayor of Nashville. In response to the CQ survey, Fulton reported taking no foreign trips in 1975. Other House members who did not respond to the CQ survey, but who turned up in State Department records, were:

Robert L. Leggett (D Calif.). The Merchant Marine and Fisheries Committee reported Leggett's trip to Switzerland for the Law of the Sea Conference, but only per diem and air transportation costs were shown.

State Department documents showed that while in Switzerland Leggett was provided with a car and driver for four days at a cost of $600. A day of sightseeing accounted for $300 of the total.

Wayne L. Hays (D Ohio). State Department records showed that Hays made seven trips abroad in 1975, three more than the number shown in available House reports. Further, the documents show that Hays drew $6,000 more than his allowable per diem expenses through procedures that allowed him to draw on special accounts in his capacity as chairman of some delegations. No report on these extra sums was required. Justice Department sources told the Post that Hays was under investigation for possible misappropriation of the account funds.

Charles C. Diggs Jr. (D Mich.). State Department records showed Diggs visits to Asian countries that did not appear in reports filed by the International Relations Committee. The reports included two visits to Africa.

Daniel J. Flood (D Pa.). The Appropriations Committee reported a Flood trip to Europe, but did not specify $900 spent for Flood's rented car during a four-day visit to Paris. The committee reported Flood's return cruise on the liner *Queen Elizabeth II* as simply four days "aboard ship."

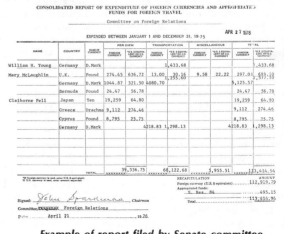

Example of report filed by Senate committee

Branch Appropriations Act (PL 86-628)). It also stipulated that appropriated dollar funds be reported along with counterpart funds (Mutual Security Act of 1960 (PL 86-472)).

In 1963, the House took further steps to curb junketing, allowing only five House committees to use committee and counterpart funds for foreign travel. Ten other committees were restricted to travel within the United States, but could ask the Rules Committee for permission to travel abroad. Such requests would receive "respectful consideration," the Rules Committee chairman said.

In 1967, the Committee on House Administration banned the use of credit cards for transportation and accommodations and required uniform accounting and reporting from all House committees on a monthly basis.

In 1967, Rep. H. R. Gross (R Iowa) revealed that on 12 occasions during a single trip in 1966, five members collected their per diem twice by traveling to two countries in the same day. The House Committee on Standards of Official Conduct issued an ethics report March 14, 1968, calling for "clearer guidelines" regulating use and reporting of expenditures. One response of the House was to amend several committee travel authorizations to specifically limit collection of per diem rates to one period of time, regardless of the number of countries visited.

Then in October 1973, Congress passed a State Department authorization bill that contained a provision eliminating the requirement for disclosure in the *Congressional Record*. The change was engineered by Rep. Wayne L. Hays (D Ohio), chairman of the Foreign Affairs subcommittee where the bill originated. Hays also was chairman of the Committee on House Administration and a champion of generous perquisites for members.

Hays claimed he changed the old law to trim down the *Record*. "We decided we weren't going to spend eight or nine thousand dollars to let you guys (reporters) do your stories on congressional travel," he said. He told Congressional Quarterly that "there was no desire on anyone's part to cover up anything."

For a long time, Hays said, he has been "trying to cut the size of the *Record* down" and that "this was just another useless bit of using up space in the *Record*."[38]

Nevertheless, the effect of the change was to substantially reverse two decades of reform efforts aimed at preventing abuses of foreign travel and providing full public disclosure. Under the revised law, the detailed breakdown by committee and members was no longer published in the *Record*, and committees were no longer required to make public a separate accounting of tax dollars spent on travel for members and staff. There was no way to check the dates of arrival and departures in various countries, making it impossible to tell how long senators and representatives stayed abroad.

In the same amendment deleting the reporting requirements, Congress voted itself a 50 per cent increase in per diem allowance for foreign travel—from $50 to $75 each day.

Newspapers throughout the country printed stories about the congressional move and editorialized heavily against it. As a result, an amendment to the fiscal 1975 legislative branch appropriations bill (HR 14012—PL 93-371) reinstated language from the old law requiring that consolidated, detailed reports on foreign travel be made each year. But instead of being published in the *Record*, the amendment specified that the reports be made available to the public by the clerk of the House and the secretary of the

Senate. The law was signed by the President Aug. 13, 1974. It made no provision for the reports of such groups as the U.S. delegations to the Interparliamentary Union and the North Atlantic Assembly.

Still more changes were made in 1975 through amendments to the fiscal 1976 legislative branch appropriations bill (PL 94-59). It required all committee reports and all parliamentary delegation reports to be filed in only two places—the secretary of the Senate and the House Administration Committee. Rep. Hays thus gained control of the House foreign travel reports through his chairmanship of the committee.

The 1975 changes did not affect the requirement that all consolidated reports be filed within 60 days of the beginning of each session of Congress, but they did specify that the reports be open to public inspection. The changes became effective when the 1975 reports were filed in March 1976.

In 1976, the House adopted an amendment to the fiscal 1977 State Department authorization bill (HR 13179) requiring that annual foreign travel expense reports once again be printed in the *Record*. The House action was one of a number of reform developments following a sex-payroll scandal in which Hays, under pressure, resigned as chairman of the House Administration Committee. On May 23, 1976, Elizabeth Ray, a committee secretary, said Hays had kept her on the committee payroll to provide him with sexual favors. Hays resigned from Congress Sept. 1.

Sources of Travel Funds

Even before the reporting law was weakened in 1973, the information contained in the *Congressional Record* usually was the minimum required by law. It told where a member went, how long he stayed and how much he collected in government per diem payments. The listings rarely told why lawmakers went outside the United States. And they did not indicate the sources of the money used by members of Congress when they left the country on official business.

Some of the funds and facilities used for activities abroad by members include:

Appropriated Funds. Money is appropriated by Congress to pay the expenses, travel included, of its committees for routine and special investigations. Some committees also have confidential funds, which chairmen may spend without specific accounting.

Counterpart Funds. Members traveling abroad are allowed to use American-owned counterpart funds (foreign currencies held by U.S. embassies and credited to the United States in return for aid, and which may be used only in the country of origin). This surplus foreign currency generally is now disbursed on a $75-per-diem basis by embassies.

Representational Funds. American embassies and consulates abroad are allocated sums for official entertaining. Some of these funds are used for hospitality purposes for visiting members of Congress.

Contingency Funds. Emergency money is provided embassies to help stranded or financially strained American travelers. These funds usually are reimbursed when the traveler returns home.

Agency Funds. Many members of Congress travel as guests of government agencies, which have money appropriated for trips to their overseas posts. The Departments of State and Defense are the agencies most called upon to arrange travel.

Military Transportation. Members often travel without charge on ships of the Military Sea Transportation Service and planes of the Military Airlift Command.

Areas Visited by Members

Because of changes in the reporting law that began in 1973, the statistics for members' travel abroad in 1975 are incomplete. U.S. territories and possessions are not recorded as foreign travel. These include the U.S. Virgin Islands, Puerto Rico and Guam.

Areas visited by members in 1975, for both government and non-government trips, are shown below:[39]

	Senate	House	Total*
Western Europe (including Turkey)	60	291	351
Asia	22	105	127
People's Republic of China	7	18	25
South America	3	24	27
Middle East	19	81	100
Australia and New Zealand	0	3	3
Caribbean	7	15	22
Cuba	2	3	5
Africa	7	41	48
Russia and Eastern Europe	17	37	54
Canada	12	18	30
Mexico	10	16	26
India, Pakistan, Bangladesh and Sri Lanka	3	14	17
Antarctica	0	1	1

* Because most members visited more than one area on each trip, the number of areas visited is greater than the number of trips reported.

Additional Benefits

In addition to their pay, staff, allowances and other perquisites, members of Congress benefit from many other services, courtesies and special favors that go along with the job. It is impossible to compile a complete list of these other benefits or to compute their precise value. Selected additional benefits are described below:

Life Insurance. Regardless of age or health, members received $45,000 in term life insurance coverage under a group plan. The government matches one-third of the premium. An additional policy for $10,000 also is available, with the extra premium determined by the age of the member.

Health Insurance. Members are eligible for a generous health insurance plan. The government pays up to 40 per cent of the premium.

Health Care. A staff of doctors and nurses stands by in the Capitol to give members free medical care while at work. Services include physical examinations, laboratory work, electrocardiograms, ambulance service and supplies of prescription medicine. First aid stations in most House and Senate office buildings offer help for members and their staffs.

Taxes. Because members live in two places—their home towns and Washington, D.C.—federal tax law allows them to deduct up to $3,000 a year for living expenses in Washington. In October 1975 the House Ways and Means Committee attempted to raise the deduction to $44 a day while Congress is in session. If the rule had been in effect in

Retirement Benefits

Congress included in the Legislative Reorganization Act of 1946 a provision, recommended by the Joint Committee on the Organization of Congress, initiating a retirement system for senators and representatives. The Act brought members of Congress under the Civil Service Retirement Act, permitting them, at their option, to contribute 6 per cent of their salaries to a retirement fund. Retirement annuities were to be calculated at 2½ per cent of average salary multiplied by years of service, but could not exceed 80 per cent of a member's final congressional salary. A member became eligible for benefits upon retirement from Congress if the member was at least 62 years old and had served a minimum of five years (except in cases of disability).

In 1954, Congress liberalized the pension law and also adjusted retirement benefits for legislative employees. The basic rate of contribution remained 6 per cent of salary, but the bill included the congressional expense allowance in the salary computation. It also provided for reduced retirement benefits at age 60 and made other minor changes in the program. In 1956 the contribution rose to 7½ per cent. Further changes were enacted in 1960, although the basic retirement benefits were left unchanged.

In 1969, Congress again liberalized the pension law for both members and legislative employees. Retirement benefits were increased by specifying that the annuity computation formula would use an employee's average annual earnings during the highest consecutive three-year period, rather than during a five-year period, as had been required. The method of computing annuities for congressional employees was liberalized by eliminating a 15-year limitation on number of years of service for which the annuity would be computed at 2½ per cent of average pay. Other benefit changes also were made. In addition, the contribution of members of Congress was increased from 7½ per cent to 8 per cent, and the contribution of congressional employees from 6½ per cent to 7½ per cent, beginning in January 1970. The government matches participants' contributions to the plan.

With enactment in 1969 of a law making modifications in the federal pension system, government retirees became eligible to receive a bonus in their pensions every time the cost of living went up by 3 per cent over the previous base period for three consecutive months. In such situations, they became eligible for an extra 1 per cent "kicker" payment.

The idea behind the kicker was to make up for the delay between the time the cost of living began to rise and the time it rose high enough to trigger a raise in pensions. However, because the kicker was then included in the base for the next raise, it had a multiplier effect, which some critics charged went far beyond its intent. Responding to this criticism, Congress in September 1976 repealed the law authorizing the 1 per cent "kicker" and replaced it with a system that would adjust the pensions automatically every six months without the 1 per cent bonus.

* U.S., Congress, House. Committee on Post Office and Civil Service, Civil Service Retirement System, Hearings before the Retirement and Employee Benefits Subcommittee, Serial No. 94-56, 94th Cong., 1st sess., Nov. 14, 1975, pp. 88-89.

Members' Recording Studios

Nearly all the perquisites of members of Congress give incumbents certain campaign advantages over their challengers. For example, a member's staff, the franking privilege, and special allowances for travel, office expenses, stationery, newsletters, telephone and telegraph services—all at public expense—may improve the member's chances of being re-elected. In addition, incumbents have inherent news-making powers which their opponents lack.

One of the greatest advantages—and perhaps a decisive one as electronic campaigning grows in importance—is the availability of radio and television recording facilities. The House Recording Studio, located in the Rayburn House Office Building, and the Senate Recording Studio, located in a tunnel between the Capitol and the Russell Office Building, are available to all members.

In theory the recording studios are designed to help members communicate with their constituents. Tapes recorded at the studios can be mailed to local stations for use in regular news or public affairs programing. In fact, much of the work performed at the studios is frankly campaign material.

Studio productions are subsidized with public funds. Tapes and films are produced at cost, and the film or tape is available at congressional stationery rooms. Members are billed individually each month. They may not pay in cash. Representatives may use their stationery allowance to purchase audio and video tapes.

Both recording studios are extensive. Color films for television are processed in-house within 24 hours. Teleprompter machines are available. Telephone "beeper" reports can be sent simultaneously to several broadcast stations. Members must design their programs and write the scripts, but the studios suggest a variety of formats and provide such services as TV sets and makeup. Members are urged to make appointments for filming and taping on a regular basis.

It is impossible to estimate the recording studios' value to members, but they are a bargain by any measure. Opponents of incumbent representatives and senators are charged full rates by commercial recording studios; they must pay for most of their broadcast time; and they are seldom seen and heard over the airwaves except during brief campaign periods.

Source: *Congressional Handbook: U.S. House of Representatives; Congressional Handbook: United States Senate.*

Library. The Library of Congress provides members with free manpower and facilities to produce research, speechwriting and responses to constituents' questions. About 800 employees in the Library's Congressional Research Service work exclusively for members.

Books. The Library of Congress gives away to members and their staffs excess books that pile up every month and are not suitable for the Library's collections. Some members send the books to libraries and schools in their district or state. Many volumes wind up in the homes of congressional staff.

Legal Counsel. The Office of Legislative Counsel, with offices on both sides of Capitol Hill, assists members in drafting bills, resolutions and amendments. Its staff provides confidential help on legislative matters only and does no personal legal work for members.

Recreation. Members of Congress have their own free health club, with a modern gymnasium in the Rayburn House Office Building and another in the Russell Office Building. Facilities include swimming pool, paddleball court and sauna.

Food. Government-subsidized food and facilities are available to members, staff and visitors. The Capitol and office buildings contain seven public restaurants and cafeterias, three members-only dining rooms, and six carry-out services. In addition, members may reserve several private dining rooms or arrange banquets and parties in caucus rooms with low-cost catering from the House and Senate restaurants.

Loans. In the House only, members may receive personal loans through the Sergeant-at-Arms Office in amounts equal to the salary due them for the remainder of the current Congress. In theory, at the beginning of a term a representative could borrow double his annual salary of $44,600 if the full amount was repaid within two years. In fact, most loans are of much smaller amount and for shorter duration. Any loan must be repaid by the end of each term. Interest rates are set by commercial banks, for whom the sergeant at arms serves as the agent. Representatives may obtain the loans for virtually any purpose. The Senate has no comparable procedure for making loans to its members.[41]

Merchandise. Stationery stores located in the Capitol office buildings sell many gift items as well as normal office supplies, all at cost or slightly above. Members and their staffs can buy such things as wallets, briefcases, pocket calculators, typewriters, and drinking glasses and ashtrays with the seal of either the House or the Senate. Christmas cards also are available at bargain prices.

Parking. Each representative gets a free Capitol Hill garage space for personal use, plus four additional spaces and one outside parking permit for staff use. Each senator gets two garage spaces and several outside permits for staff. By 1976 parking spaces in prime business areas in Washington were rented for as high as $70 a month.

Grooming. Eight government-run barber and beauty shops in the office buildings give free or inexpensive haircuts to members and staff. Congress also has two in-house beauty shops that are much less expensive than private salons in Washington.

Photographs. The Senate spends at least $149,000 in public funds for what amounts to individual photographic service for senators. Democrats and Republicans maintain separate staffs and darkrooms in the basement of the Capitol. The photographers, who may earn more than $30,-

1974, a senator could have deducted as much as $7,392, and a representative could have deducted up to $6,996. The committee later dropped the idea and voted instead to instruct the Internal Revenue Service (IRS) to determine the amount to be deducted by applying "rules of reasonableness."[40]

The IRS maintains an office on Capitol Hill to help members prepare their income tax returns. Congressional staff also receive help when droves of IRS employees visit the Capitol each year at tax time.

000 a year for taking hand-shaking shots of senators and constituents, are listed on public payrolls as "clerks" and "assistant clerks."[42]

Representatives have photography services in the Rayburn Building, but their photographers are paid from party campaign funds. In both the House and Senate, cameras, film and supplies are purchased with party campaign funds.

Office Decorations. The U.S. Botanic Garden will supply members' offices with three small potted plants every month and one large plant every three months. Members may request cut flowers as well.

Members may decorate their offices also with free wall maps, scenic photographs, reproductions of paintings and charts—all of which are framed and installed at no cost to members.

Other Benefits. Among the services and perquisites available to members are the following:

● Free storage space and storage trunks are provided for members' files and official records.

● Congressional license tags provided for each member permit unrestricted parking while on official business anywhere in Washington.

● American flags flown over the Capitol and certified by the Architect may be purchased at cost and presented as gifts.

● Members and staff may have packages wrapped free of charge for mailing, a service used heavily during the Christmas season. For years the man who does this for Senate offices has been called "Jack the Wrapper."

● Each year members give away thousands of wall calendars published by the Government Printing Office or the U.S. Capitol Historical Society. The Senate ordered 62,700 calendars for 1975, at a cost to the public of $30,465.[43]

● Members are allowed to accept free transportation on non-commercial carriers—primarily company planes—under certain circumstances. *(Details, Ethics in Congress, p. 114)*

Political Patronage in Congress

While the pay of members and their staffs has increased sharply and the perquisites of members have grown enormously, political patronage in Congress has decreased through the years. Patronage is supposed to be one of the advantages of holding political office, but many members of Congress always have regarded it as a nuisance.

As defined by William L. Safire's *The New Language of Politics,* political patronage means "governmental appointments made so as to increase political strength."[44] Senators and representatives once pulled the political strings on thousands of federal jobs. On Capitol Hill and back home, a powerful member could place scores of persons in such jobs as local postmaster, health inspector, tax collector, welfare commissioner and even custodian of public morals. The congressional patronage empire thus provided members with a healthy payoff list for political supporters.

Today on Capitol Hill, the only jobs remaining under patronage are those that generally require no special skills or technical knowledge. Elevator operators, doorkeepers, mail carriers and clerks comprise the bulk of the posts still available to patronage dispensers. All in all, a member now finds the available patronage jobs of little help in

strengthening his political position or rewarding his campaign supporters.

Andrew Jackson was the first President to give open support to political patronage. But when he spoke out in favor of patronage, the number of public jobs requiring technical skills was not large. The few misfits who slipped in through patronage appointments seemed to do little damage to the general efficiency of the government.

As the business of government grew more complex, and as it expanded, the inadequacies of the patronage system became glaringly apparent. The Pendleton Civil Service Act of 1883 made the first assault on the patronage system. Thereafter, successive statutes and executive orders virtually removed patronage rights on the state level from members of Congress. Ninety-five per cent of the persons now employed by federal agencies are hired under the merit system or Civil Service. *(Box, Origins of Civil Service, p. 50)*

Members of Congress do have a voice in presidential appointments when the President is a member of their party. The Nixon administration filled about 6,500 jobs when it took office in 1969, and many of the appointments were made after consultation with members. Jobs filled by the administration included Cabinet and subcabinet positions, White House staff posts and jobs in federal regulatory agencies, as well as some lesser positions exempt from Civil Service.

Congressional influence in these appointments is limited by the discretion of the President. Many of the appointments require Senate confirmation, but none requires prior consultation. A member's role in White House patronage affairs generally depends on his personal relationship with the President.

Patronage Machinery

There are more than a thousand acknowledged patronage jobs on Capitol Hill itself. The 435 representatives and 100 senators are responsible for filling these posts. Patronage privileges are meted out to members of Congress under a puzzling combination of written rules and contradictory traditions. The exceptions to the written procedures are so numerous and diverse that they have all but usurped the rules.

House. Of the two chambers of Congress, the House has the more clearly defined methods for distributing patronage jobs among its members. The five-member Patronage Committee of the majority party is ostensibly in control of all patronage jobs on the House side.

The committee assigns a small quota of the jobs to the minority party at the beginning of each session. These are jobs like those of clerk or page in the minority cloakroom. The remaining patronage jobs are divided among the state delegations, and the senior majority member of each delegation is responsible for distributing them among the other representatives from the state.

The Patronage Committee was first established by a caucus of Democratic representatives in 1911. Three members of the Ways and Means Committee were chosen by the caucus to distribute patronage positions to members. Committee chairmen were excluded from the general distribution of patronage because they already had the power to make appointments to committee staff positions.

When the Republicans won a majority in the House in 1918 they set up their own Patronage Committee, with rules that generally followed the Democrats' example.

Origins of Civil Service

American political patronage reached its peak in the post-Civil-War era, when senators spent much of their time keeping track of patronage in their states and were allowed to dictate major appointments.

In 1881, for example, both of New York's senators resigned after President James A. Garfield refused to nominate their choice for the lucrative position of Collector of the Port of New York.

Both senators expected the New York legislature to express its support by re-electing them. But before the legislature could meet, Garfield was assassinated by a disappointed patronage seeker.

Public revulsion over the assassination and the excesses of patronage led two years later to passage of the Pendleton Act, the first major attempt at civil service reform in America.

The Pendleton Act set up a three-man bipartisan board, the Civil Service Commission, and empowered it to certify applicants for federal employment after competitive examinations.

The original Act covered only about 10 per cent of federal employees, but its key provision gave the President power to expand the civil service classifications by executive order. A series of such orders and additional legislation in the following years removed from politics nearly all nonpolicy-level jobs in the government.

Following Garfield's assassination, Civil Service received unexpected support from the new President, Chester Alan Arthur.

In 1884, the Pendleton Act produced one more disappointed office seeker—its sponsor, Sen. George H. Pendleton (D Ohio). Pendleton was defeated for reelection by Henry Payne, an outspoken advocate of the patronage system.

In outlining the machinery for handling patronage assignments, the parties did not mention how the Speaker of the House might use his influence in the distribution of patronage. They failed also to say how behind-the-scenes bargaining for a crucial vote might involve paying off a reluctant member with a patronage job or two. Maneuvering of this kind is part of the system of exceptions by which patronage is distributed.

When Rep. Carl Albert (D Okla.) was elected Speaker in 1971 the membership of the Democrats' Patronage Committee was increased from three to five.

Patronage distribution has become highly informal, according to Rep. B. F. Sisk (D Calif.), a member of the Patronage Committee in the 1970s. He said the committee has no list of patronage jobs on Capitol Hill and does not know how many exist at any one time. For members who are not committee chairmen, seniority is a leading factor in obtaining patronage jobs. But this is not a formal rule, Sisk said, and no seniority quota exists. State delegations are still assigned quotas, however, and some of them have worked out their own systems of distribution. Majority members of the New York delegation, for example, pool their patronage jobs in order to obtain what they feel is an equitable distribution.[45]

Senate. There is a three-member committee for distributing patronage jobs among senators. The majority leader is in charge of the process. The minority party is granted about 20 per cent of the patronage posts in the minority cloakroom and a like proportion of such jobs as pages and telephone operators for the minority side of the Senate. The other jobs are distributed by seniority and as the majority leader may choose.

The minority party is not satisfied with its 20 per cent. Kenneth Davis, an aide to Senate Minority Leader Hugh Scott (R Pa.), complained about Democratic control of Capitol patronage in 1975. "We don't have 38 per cent of the patronage jobs around here," Davis said, "which we should have if they were divided equitably."[46]

What Are Patronage Jobs?

Many of the patronage jobs on Capitol Hill are filled by college students needing financial assistance. They work a shift as an elevator operator or chamber doorman and then go to classes. The turnover rate is high, but in most cases it does not greatly affect the efficiency of the operation.

An exception is the Capitol Police force, where the jobs require special skills and where patronage was sharply reduced in the early 1970s. As recently as 1971, patronage appointees constituted 25 per cent of the total force. By 1975 there were no patronage police jobs on the Senate side (486 positions) and only 109 out of 627 positions on the House side. Patronage appointees are required to meet the same standards and to undergo the same training as other members of the Capitol Police.[47]

There are almost no official figures on patronage, and members seldom admit which jobs they control. Some of the patronage positions are described below.[48]

House. The Office of the Doorkeeper oversees the largest number of patronage jobs in the House. Nearly all of the 301 positions authorized in 1975 were filled by patronage. The doorkeeper supervises officers of the press galleries, doormen for the visitors gallery and the House floor, custodians, barbers, pages, and employees of the House Document Room and the "folding room," which distributes newsletters, speeches and other materials for representatives.

The clerk of the House also had 301 employees in 1975, but relatively few were hired through patronage. The sergeant at arms of the House has partial responsibility for the Capitol Police, but the immediate office staff numbered only 16 in 1975 and none was a patronage employee. The House post office had 94 full-time employees in 1975, nearly all of them hired on a patronage basis.

Other patronage jobs in the House, less clearly defined, include several in the offices of the majority and minority leaders, the parliamentarian, the minority sergeant at arms, and the whips of both political parties.

Senate. The sergeant at arms of the Senate, who has partial responsibility for the Capitol Police, also supervises a large number of patronage employees. Among them are Senate pages, doormen, custodians, officers of the Senate press galleries and employees of the Senate post office.

The secretary of the Senate, an administrative official, had a staff of 175 in 1975, some of whom were patronage employees. There is a scattering of Senate patronage jobs in the offices of the majority and minority secretaries, the majority and minority leaders, and the party whips.

Architect's Office. Although the architect of the Capitol has an immediate staff of about 70 to assist him in his administrative tasks, he was responsible for a total of 1,781 employees in 1975. Most served in support of the House and Senate office buildings. Among the patronage employees supervised by the architect were 155 elevator operators, who each earned $7,715 a year. (The number of elevator operators was reduced in 1976.)

Other Positions. While patronage is generally restricted to non-skilled jobs, there is a group of Capitol Hill officials (technically not of patronage status) whose jobs depend on the influence of sponsors or the swing of party control. The House doorkeeper, the House and Senate sergeants at arms, the secretary of the Senate and the clerk of the House work for all members of their respective houses, but are elected by the members by strict party-line votes.

Party leadership generally plays an important part in the election of these non-patronage officials. The postmaster of the House and Senate are elected by the members of each chamber, but under the sponsorship of some senior member.

An example of the influence of House leaders in patronage appointments occurred in 1969 when the job of chief printer became vacant following the death of Truman Ward, who had held the post for 48 years. The print shop had developed into a profitable operation, printing speeches, newsletters and other material needed by House members. The chief printer receives a salary and is allowed to keep all the profits he can make.

Print shop employees and many members believed the job would go to shop foreman Robert Cutter, a veteran printer who had served as Ward's assistant since 1954 and directed the operating during Ward's illness. But the selection was up to House Majority Leader (later Speaker) Carl Albert (D Okla.), and Albert bypassed Cutter in favor of David R. Ramage, a resident of Wewoka, Okla., in Albert's home district. Ramage was not a professional printer but a loyal Democrat who had served 15 years as a clerk in the House stationery room.

Committee Staffs. The selection of committee staffs is supposed to be based on a candidate's administrative credentials and expertise on the subject matter. To a degree this is the case, but most committee staff jobs are filled by appointees of the majority party. Members hire the employees they want.

Personal Staffs. The personal staff of a senator or representative naturally includes persons chosen for partisan reasons. A member is hardly likely to hire a supporter of the opposition party. Members may hire and fire their personal staff at will—such employees are not protected by Civil Service—and in many congressional offices the staff turnover rate is quite high.

Debate Over Patronage

The use of patronage to fill positions requiring special skills or knowledge has been on the decline since 1883, when the Pendleton Civil Service Act removed 10 per cent of federal employees from the system of partisan appointments. Since that time the inequities, inefficiencies and justifications of patronage employment have been debated almost annually in Congress. The congressional patronage empire has so dwindled that some senior members count themselves fortunate if they can appoint a Capitol policeman, a few elevator operators and a mailman in the Senate or House post office.

Members of Congress lost one source of patronage in 1969 when the Nixon administration decided to remove 63,-000 postmaster and rural carrier appointments from politics

Congressional Employees

Federal civilian employment in Congress, Oct. 1955-1975.

Year	Senate	House	Total
1955	1,962	3,623	5,585
1956	2,342	3,965	6,307
1957	2,378	4,005	6,383
1958	2,516	4,082	6,598
1959	2,700	4,217	6,917
1960	2,643	4,148	6,791
1961	2,713	4,774	7,487
1962	2,889	4,968	7,857
1963	2,982	4,952	7,934
1964	3,071	5,020	8,091
1965	3,219	5,672	8,891
1966	3,294	6,190	9,484
1967	3,587	6,365	9,952
1968	3,632	6,446	10,078
1969	3,847	6,874	10,721
1970	4,140	7,134	11,274
1971	4,624	8,169	12,793
1972	4,626	8,976	13,602
1973	5,078	9,531	14,609
1974	5,284	12,444	17,728
1975	6,143	11,264	17,407

Sources: Civil Service Commission; U.S. Congress, House, Committee on Appropriations, *Legislative Branch Appropriation Bill, 1976*, H. Rept. 94-208 to Accompany HR 6950, 94th Cong., 1st sess., 1975.

and to use special boards to select candidates for the positions.

Previously, the jobs were filled by the Postmaster General upon the recommendation of the representative from the district in which the vacancy was located, provided the representative belonged to the same party as the President. If the representative belong to the opposition party, the choice went to either of the state's senators, if they belonged to the President's party. If the state had no members of the President's party, the state's national committeeman from the President's party was entitled to chose a candidate.

Nixon's Postmaster General, Winton M. Blount, approved no patronage appointments to postal jobs after he took office early in 1969. Legislation placing the appointments under a merit system was soon introduced. The Postal Reorganization Act of 1970, (PL 91-375), which established the U.S. Postal Service, put an end to post office patronage and relieved members of both power and problems.

In the fiscal 1976 legislative branch appropriations bill, approved July 22, 1975, Congress ordered a study to see if up to 50 per cent of the elevator operator jobs could be abolished. Sen. Dewey F. Bartlett (R Okla.) pointed out that many Capitol Hill elevators were automatic and did not need operators. He said that if half the jobs could be abolished patronage salaries could be cut by $540,000.[49]

For years a leading spokesman for patronage reform in the House was Rep. Joel T. Broyhill (R Va.), who was besieged by office-seekers from his suburban Washington district. In addition to the inconvenience of having his office used as an employment agency, Broyhill complained that patronage jobs on Capitol Hill were unfair to those who held them. He called the patronage market "cruel, costly and ugly" and said that all 31 of the patronage employees he had sponsored in 1954 were dismissed the next year when control of the House passed from the Republicans to the Democrats.[50]

Congressional defenders of patronage argue that most jobs remaining under the system require no special ability or training; and because the pay is rather low, they do not attract persons with families to support. They point out also that job turnover is so high that most patronage employees tend to leave within a short time regardless of what happens to their party in congressional elections.

Opponents of patronage point out that it disregards not only merit but also financial need. Critics note that many members of Congress fill patronage slots with the children of influential people from their districts. Some do seek out and sponsor disadvantaged scholarship students in the District of Columbia, but there seems to be little evidence that this is a widespread practice.

Appointments to Service Academies

One remnant of the patronage system has not only survived over the years but has continued to expand. Congressional appointees to the three major service academies account for more than three-fourths of their combined enrollment.

Until 1902, the privilege of appointing candidates for admission to the service academies was enjoyed only by representatives, the idea being to apportion academy enrollment on a national population basis. Each congressional district was to supply one appointee every four years, thus giving each class maximum geographic variance and allowing equal numbers of appointments from variously populated areas.

Eventually, senators and representatives alike were authorized to have as many as five appointees enrolled in each academy at one time. In December 1975 this added up to about 9,950 appointments in an enrollment total of 12,662, or nearly 79 per cent.[51]

In appointing young men and women for cadetships at the academies—U.S. Military Academy, West Point, N.Y.; U.S. Naval Academy, Annapolis, Md.; and U.S. Air Force Academy, Colorado Springs, Colo.—members of Congress have wide leeway in making their choices. Most senators and many representatives do not personally handle the screening of candidates. The job of selecting nominees usually falls to an administrative assistant in the senator's state office or the representative's home district.

Selection Methods. It was in 1964 that Congress set the quota of five cadet appointees in each academy at any one time. Either of two methods of selecting appointees may be used, the choice being left to the member.

● The general listing method allows for only minimal congressional influence in the selection. A list of as many as 10 candidates is submitted to each of the respective academies. Scholastic and physical tests are given the candidates and the one making the best combined performance wins the appointment.

● The principal-alternate method allows the member far greater discretion over the appointment. Again, a list of as many as 10 candidates is submitted to the academy, but

each candidate is ranked in order of the member's preference. If the first-preference candidate meets the academic and physical entrance requirements, then that candidate wins the appointment regardless of how well the other candidates perform. If the first-preference candidate does not fulfill the entrance requirements, then the first-alternate is considered and so on down the list until a qualified candidate is found.

The principal-alternate method may be used by a member when he feels that a particular young person has outstanding potentialities in some area that is not weighted heavily in the entrance requirements, such as creative talents or outstanding athletic ability. Of course, the method can be used also to ensure the appointment of a member's relative, if qualified, or the relative of a friend.

Requirements. Before candidates can be considered for appointment, they must submit to scholastic, physical and medical testing. No candidate may be older than 21. He or she must be of "good moral character" and must never have been married. Candidates must also be United States citizens, unless they are entering one of the academies on a special program for foreigners. Persons already in military service who wish to attend one of the academies may take the annual competitive examination. If they score well they will be appointed.

Other Academies. A member of Congress also may nominate as many as 10 persons for appointment to the Merchant Marine Academy, New London, Conn. The candidates must take a nationally competitive examination to win appointment. No nominee on any member's list is guaranteed appointment. The highest-scoring candidates are appointed to the freshman class, regardless of who nominated them. No congressional appointments are made to the U.S. Coast Guard Academy, New London, Conn. Interested applicants contact the academy and take national examinations.

Evolution of Academy Appointments

West Point. The system of congressional appointments to the three major service academies had an obscure beginning in 1802 when Congress established what is today the U.S. Military Academy at West Point, N.Y. Congress envisioned the academy as an institution that would serve a dual purpose—teach cadets to be both officers and engineers.

Out of the initial class of 10, three had come from civilian backgrounds, the others from the Army. The three civilians were recommended by representatives and appointed by the Secretary of War. The course of study was unstructured, lasting for as long as a cadet cared to stay. Discipline was virtually nonexistent; compensation consisted of $16 a month and two daily rations.

Congress took an active interest in the academy when the United States declared war in 1812. Bold plans were drafted that year to create a standing Army of 145,000 men. But Congress had ignored requests from West Point for additional funds, and by 1812 the academy had graduated only 71 cadets.

After 1812, enrollment was expanded to 250, and representatives were told they should appoint only men between the ages of 14 and 20 who had excelled in their preparatory schooling. Officials in Washington, however, had no intention of limiting appointments to these specifications. Thus the academy had cadets ranging in age from 12 to 25. A Pennsylvania boy who had only one arm was appointed, and a married cadet kept his wife in a boarding house just outside the post and visited her every night.

As the prestige of West Point grew, increasing numbers of young men vied for appointments. By 1820 the President made all appointments to the academy with recommendations from members of Congress and the Secretary of War. Consideration for appointment was based on a boy's poverty and the service that his family had rendered the nation.

Naval Academy. In 1839 after years of demanding an academy to match the Army's facility at West Point, the Navy started an eight-month school in Philadelphia. Under pressure from the Secretary of the Navy, Congress in 1845 established a permanent facility at an old Army post called Fort Severn in Annapolis, Md. Money was appropriated the following year and a formalized curriculum was drafted. For the next seven years, all midshipmen at Annapolis were selected by the Secretary of the Navy from the ranks of enlisted men. Not until 1852 did Congress include the Naval Academy in the patronage appointment system. Every member of the House was allowed one appointed cadet in each academy at one time.

In 1862, after the Naval Academy had been moved temporarily to Newport, R.I., when Annapolis was threatened by the Confederacy, a representative's quota was raised to two appointments to both the Military and Naval Academies. After the Civil War, however, quotas were again cut to one per representative.

World War I. The demand for qualified officers in both the Navy and Army continued to grow during the years preceding World War I. In 1900 representatives were given two appointive positions and, for the first time, senators and territorial delegates also were granted appointment privileges—a quota of two per member at each academy. Quotas were increased to three in 1917 and to five, two years later. By 1919 the enrollment at the two academies was being filled also by appointments from the District of Columbia (5), from the ranks of enlisted men (100) and by presidential selections (25).

World War II. After the First World War, appointments were cut back to three a member (1923) and the other appointive categories also were reduced. By 1928, however, congressional quotas were again hiked to four. Presidential appointments were increased to 40 and for the first time (officially), the Vice President was given two places to fill.

During the 1930s, the number of congressional appointments to the military academies rose and fell in proportion to the size of military appropriations bills. But after the United States became involved in World War II, appointments were raised to five a member. After the war, the number was again cut to four.

Air Force Academy. When the Air Force Academy was established in 1954, it received a period of grace from the traditional patronage appointment system. During the Academy's first four years in Colorado Springs, candidates were selected for appointment under a strict geographic quota system. Each state was alloted a percentage of appointments in proportion to its population. Members of Congress were to draw up lists of aspiring candidates who were then tested on a statewide basis. The most highly qualified candidates from each state were admitted. By 1958, however, the Air Force Academy was using an appointment system similar to those in use at West Point and Annapolis except that more of the air cadets were con-

gressional appointees. By 1975, 85 per cent of the cadets were appointed by members.[52]

Changes in 1964. Congress approved legislation in 1964 providing for a doubling of the enrollment at West Point and the Air Force Academy by 1971 (Annapolis already had a substantially larger enrollment than the other two schools). The bill called for an eventual increase of the maximum capacity of each of the two academies from 2,529 cadets to 4,417. To provide for the increase, members of Congress were again given a five-cadet quota. Another section of the bill provided for appointment of the best qualified 150 of the "alternates" who failed of appointment under the principal-alternate system.

Women Cadets. The military procurement authorization bill for fiscal 1976, approved by Congress in June 1975, included an amendment to allow women to enter the three service academies. The legislation did not change any procedure for appointment, nor did it set quotas for women cadets. The academies began accepting women in 1976.

Patronage Reform. In 1969 Sen. Thomas J. Dodd (D Conn.) sponsored legislation to remove all academy appointments from the patronage system. It provided that any person desiring an appointment would be allowed to take a national examination, but that only the most qualified from the entire field would be appointed. The bill died in the Senate Armed Services Committee.

Academy appointments are the last sizeable part of the congressional patronage system, and members appear reluctant to let it slip away from them.

Legislative Budget

The legislative branch, like any government department or agency, operates on a budget, and the expenditures proposed in the budget have to be authorized and appropriated by Congress. However, there are some distinctive differences.

The legislative branch appropriations bill is prepared by Congress and is not subject to revision by the Office of Management and Budget. Nor is there a central point at which the legislative budget is screened on Capitol Hill. The clerk of the House and the secretary of the Senate are responsible for preparing appropriations requests for offices within their respective jurisdictions. In practice, they do little more than pass along requests submitted to them by others.

Legislative budget requests are reviewed by the Legislative Appropriations Subcommittee of each house. Traditionally, much of the legislative budget has gone unchallenged in both the Senate and House. But this acceptance became less prevalent in the late 1960s and the 1970s as many expenditures were subjected to closer scrutiny. Even once routine expenditures, such as for mail allowances or staff assistance, generated controversy as voters grew more disenchanted with government spending. Large congressional projects, such as construction of new office buildings, always generated considerable controversy and opposition in Congress.

The power of the Appropriations Committees to control the legislative budget, although considerable, has been less than absolute because large sums, such as salaries, are almost uncontrollable and because some items, such as office allowances, are authorized by other committees and by the full Congress and must be paid when the obligations are made by individual members.

(Continued on p. 55)

Legislative Branch Appropriations, Fiscal 1955-1977

Fiscal Year[1]	Senate	House of Representatives	Joint Items	Architect of The Capitol	Botanic Garden	Library of Congress	Government Printing Office	General Accounting Office[2]	Total[3]
1955	$14,665,223	$27,424,770	$1,542,225	$6,115,800	$223,100	$9,399,636	$11,325,000	($31,981,000)	$70,695,754
1956	16,315,720	31,123,305	2,542,120	21,163,890	246,000	9,767,937	11,650,000	(31,981,000)	92,808,972
1957	21,226,615	35,499,240	2,598,395	34,998,200	253,600	10,637,608	12,190,400	(34,000,000)	117,404,058
1958	22,271,890	37,827,705	2,638,065	17,009,000	275,500	11,647,500	13,175,000	(36,050,000)	104,844,660
1959	23,473,180	39,337,765	2,468,936	30,638,225	972,500	12,411,591	13,995,190	(37,000,000)	123,297,387
1960	26,406,345	42,398,065	2,929,430	27,412,900	327,500	14,302,790	15,020,350	(41,800,000)	128,797,380
1961	26,643,940	42,492,485	3,508,785	25,493,700	352,300	15,230,000	15,749,200	(41,150,000)	129,470,410
1962	28,421,840	47,856,835	4,090,090	19,256,600	489,000	17,193,700	18,124,000	(43,000,000)	135,432,065
1963	29,601,160	48,150,725	4,255,355	18,252,500	452,000	19,431,930	26,333,600	(43,900,000)	146,477,270
1964	30,675,350	50,131,550	6,271,369	33,279,500	454,500	20,488,800	26,992,000	(45,700,000)	168,293,069
1965	31,397,625	53,777,945	6,319,415	22,010,800	500,000	23,333,100[4]	26,062,000	(46,900,000)	210,300,885
1966	36,379,790	66,414,730	8,856,977	25,640,100	467,000	25,905,700	26,329,000	(46,900,000)	189,993,297
1967	39,655,180	77,676,145	9,716,988	14,281,000	504,600	29,974,100	42,655,900	(48,500,000)	214,463,913
1968	44,125,205	80,368,670	11,311,660	15,308,600	584,500	37,141,400	34,059,000	52,800,000	275,699,035
1969	47,082,247	85,039,420	12,711,299	15,614,700	565,000	40,638,000	39,000,000	57,500,000	298,678,396
1970	54,837,660	104,813,635	13,233,322	24,036,100	599,800	43,856,300	39,950,000	63,000,000	344,733,817
1971	60,929,464	110,526,455	14,558,775	36,568,126	672,800	50,396,600	65,382,000	74,020,000	413,104,220
1972	76,034,419	136,768,970	38,428,390	96,553,200	763,350	68,462,250	56,329,900	89,208,000	562,548,479
1973	82,046,675	145,266,770	26,151,320	102,574,500	811,300	79,104,450	88,874,100	98,065,000	622,894,115
1974	97,453,593	162,511,395	36,315,230	52,374,300	884,700	86,820,450	112,871,000	109,450,000	658,680,668
1975	111,135,870	185,546,445	45,789,324	68,288,500	1,018,000	98,990,000	129,065,000	124,989,000	764,822,139
1976	118,837,000	206,407,000	54,796,000	40,755,000	1,205,000	116,231,000	145,266,000	135,930,000	827,547,000[5]
1977	137,279,875	241,773,550	55,488,860	60,479,500	1,164,900	137,895,200	140,827,400	150,580,000	943,400,485[6]

1. 1972-75 includes supplementals.

2. Until fiscal 1968, the General Accounting Office was not regularly funded in the Legislative Branch Appropriations Act. GAO figures in parentheses are for years when appropriations were provided in other bills.

3. Beginning in fiscal 1969, the total includes funds (not included in individual for Senate, House, etc.) appropriated to liquidate contract authority. Contract authority allows agencies to enter into contracts ahead of appropriations, but requires appropriations in following years to pay off (liquidate) the contracts.

4. Includes $149,000 as a supplemental appropriation for fiscal 1964.

5. Includes $6,485,000 for the Office of Technology Assessment.

6. Includes $6,624,000 for the Office of Technology Assessment; $9,319,200 for the Congressional Budget Office; $268,000 for the Copyright Royalty Commission; and $1,700,000 for the Cost-Accounting Standards Board.

Source: Senate Appropriations Committee.

(Continued from p. 53)

A second barrier to tighter budget control in the legislative branch is the traditional rule of comity, by which each chamber is considered sovereign over its own affairs. Only rarely will one chamber interfere with a spending proposal for the other chamber.

A recent case in which the rule of comity was broken occurred in 1968 when the House of Representatives rejected a Senate-passed bill authorizing acquisition of land for future expansion of the Dirksen Office Building.

The accompanying box shows funds appropriated for the legislative branch over a period of 23 years. The appropriations provide funds not only for Congress itself but also for the major congressional supporting agencies, such as the Library of Congress, the General Accounting Office and others. These are the agencies most commonly funded in the legislative branch appropriations acts. Figures in the table represent regular appropriations; sums provided in supplemental appropriations have not been included except as indicated in footnotes. *(Table, p. 54)*

Footnotes

1. James C. Wright, *You and Your Congressman* (Coward-McCann, 1965), p. 17.
2. *ADA Special Report: Advantages of an Incumbent Seeking Re-Election* (Americans for Democratic Action, Aug. 25, 1975).
3. Clem Miller, *Member of the House: Letters of a Congressman*, ed. John W. Baker (Charles Scribner's Sons, 1962), p. 66.
4. *The New York Times*, Oct. 25, 1969.
5. David S. Broder, "Portrait of a Typical Congressman," *The New York Times Magazine*, Oct. 7, 1962, p. 31.
6. James Madison, *Notes of Debates in the Federal Convention of 1787*, with an Introduction by Adrienne Koch (Ohio University Press, 1966), p. 198.
7. Congressional Quarterly, *1973 Almanac*, p. 780.
8. Congressional Quarterly, *1974 Almanac*, pp. 663-65.
9. Congressional Quarterly, *Weekly Report*, Aug. 9, 1975, p. 1803.
10. Congressional Quarterly, *Weekly Report*, Aug. 2, 1975, p. 1684.
11. *Staff Report of the President's Panel on Federal Compensation* (Government Printing Office, 1976), p. 60.
12. From interview with staff of Senate Disbursing Office, Nov. 17, 1975.
13. From interview with staff of the Committee on House Administration, Nov. 13, 1975.
14. Congressional Quarterly, *Weekly Report*, June 21, 1975, p. 1292.
15. *Congressional Record*, 94th Cong., 1st sess., Oct. 30, 1975, p. S 18983.
16. Congressional Quarterly, *Weekly Report*, June 14, 1975, pp. 1235-36; June 21, 1975, p. 1294.
17. U.S., Congress, Joint Committee on Congressional Operations, *Congressional Handbook-U.S. House of Representatives*, 93rd Cong., 2nd sess., November 1974, p. 23; *Congressional Handbook-U.S. Senate*, 94th Cong., 1st sess., July 1975, p. 22.
18. *Congressional Handbook-U.S. Senate*, p. 3.
19. Congressional Quarterly, *Weekly Report*, Feb. 22, 1975, p. 411.
20. Congressional Quarterly, *Weekly Report*, June 21, 1975, pp. 1291-93.
21. *Ibid.*, p. 1291.
22. *ADA Special Report*, p. 2.
23. *Ibid.*, p. 3.
24. *Ibid.*
25. *The Washington Star*, Sept. 22, 1975.
26. Americans for Democratic Action, press release of Aug. 25, 1975.
27. William Taaffe, "The Costs of Keeping Congress Exceed Other Inflation," *The Washington Star*, Nov. 12, 1975.

28. *Ibid.*
29. Robert Walters, "How Some Congressmen Tap Extra Funds," *Parade*, Aug. 24, 1975.
30. *Ibid.*
31. Honoraria figures used in this section were taken from Congressional Quarterly, *Weekly Report*, July 31, 1976. pp. 2050-2060.
32. Congressional Quarterly, *Weekly Report*, April 24, 1976, p. 997.
33. Congressional Quarterly, *1973 Almanac*, p. 723.
34. *Ibid.*, p. 724.
35. U.S., Congress, Senate, Committee on Appropriations, *Legislative Branch Appropriations, 1976*, S. Rept. 94-262 to Accompany H.R. 6950, 94th Cong., 1st sess., 1975, p. 25.
36. William L. Safire, *The New Language of Politics: A Dictionary of Catchwords, Slogans and Political Usage*, rev. ed. (Collier Books, 1972), p. 196.
37. Congressional Quarterly, *Weekly Report*, July 17, 1976, pp. 1883-1902.
38. Congressional Quarterly, *Weekly Report*, May 18, 1974, p. 1289.
39. Congressional Quarterly, *Weekly Report*, Aug. 23, 1975, p. 1837.
40. Edward Stephens, "Bill Holds Tax Break for Congress," *The Washington Star*, Nov. 23, 1975.
41. From interviews with staff of the Committee on House Administration, House Sergeant at Arms and Senate Disbursing Office, March 17, 1976.
42. Congressional Quarterly, *Weekly Report*, March 9, 1974, p. 638.
43. Congressional Quarterly, *Weekly Report*, July 12, 1975, p. 1475.
44. Safire, *New Language*, p. 483.
45. Congressional Quarterly, *Weekly Report*, April 10, 1970, p. 966.
46. Congressional Quarterly, *Weekly Report*, Dec. 13, 1975, p. 2719.
47. Interview with Capitol Police Chief James M. Powell, Sept. 29, 1975.
48. Employment figures for 1975 are taken from fiscal 1976 budget hearings before the House and Senate Legislative Branch Appropriations Subcommittees.
49. *The Washington Star*, July 10, 1975.
50. Congressional Quarterly, *Weekly Report*, April 10, 1970, p. 969.
51. Enrollment figures for December 1975 were provided by the Washington offices for the three academies. West Point had 4,113 cadets with about 75 per cent congressional appointees; Annapolis had 4,302 with 76 per cent; and Colorado Springs had 4,247 with 85 per cent.
52. *Ibid.*

Selected Bibliography

Books

Ambrose, Stephen. *Duty, Honor, Country: A History of West Point.* Baltimore: Johns Hopkins Press, 1966.

Beise, J. Arthur. *The Brass Factories.* Washington: Public Affairs Press, 1969.

MacCloskey, Monro. *How to Qualify for the Service Academies.* New York: Richards Rosen Press Inc., 1964.

Madison, James. *Notes of Debates in the Federal Convention of 1787.* Introduction by Adrienne Koch. Athens, Ohio: Ohio University Press, 1966.

Miller, Clem. *Member of the House: Letters of a Congressman.* Edited by John W. Baker. New York: Charles Scribner's Sons, 1962.

Ripley, Randall B. *Congress: Process and Policy.* New York: W. W. Norton & Co. Inc., 1975.

Safire, William L. *The New Language of Politics: A Dictionary of Catchwords, Slogans and Political Usage.* rev. ed. New York: Collier Books, 1972.

Tacheron, Donald G., and Udall, Morris K. *The Job of the Congressman.* Indianapolis: Bobbs-Merrill, 1966.

Wright, James C. *You and Your Congressman.* New York: Coward-McCann, 1965.

Articles

ADA Special Report: Advantages of an Incumbent Seeking Re-election. Washington: Americans for Democratic Action, Aug. 25, 1975.

Boeckel, Richard M. "Wages and Hours of Members of Congress." *Editorial Research Reports,* Oct. 13, 1937, pp. 297-320.

Broder, David S. "Portrait of a Typical Congressman." *The New York Times Magazine,* Oct. 7, 1962, pp. 31, 97-99.

"Congressional Perquisites and Fair Elections: The Case of the Franking Privilege." *Yale Law Journal,* April 1974, pp. 1055-99.

Stephens, Edward. "Bill Holds Tax Break for Congress." *The Washington Star,* Nov. 23, 1975.

Taaffe, William. "The Costs of Keeping Congress Exceed Other Inflation." *The Washington Star,* Nov. 12, 1975.

Walters, Robert. "How Some Congressmen Tap Extra Funds." *Parade,* Aug. 24, 1975.

Government Publications

U.S. Congress. House. *Report of the Clerk of the House of Representatives.* Washington: Government Printing Office, 19—.

U.S. Congress. House. Committee on Post Office and Civil Service. Special Ad Hoc Subcommittee, *Use of the Congressional Frank, Hearings on H.R. 3180.* Committee Serial 93-1, 93rd Cong., 1st sess., 1973.

U.S. Congress. Joint Committee on Congressional Operations. *Congressional Handbook-U.S. House of Representatives.* 93rd Cong., 2nd sess., November 1974. Updated November 1976.

——. *Congressional Handbook-U.S. Senate.* 94th Cong., 1st sess., July 1975. Updated November 1976.

——. *Court Proceedings and Actions of Vital Interest to the Congress: The Franking Privilege of Members of Congress. Special Report, Pursuant to Section 402(a)(2) of the Legislative Reorganization Act of 1970.* 92nd Cong., 2nd sess., 1972.

U.S. Congress. Senate. *Report of the Secretary of the Senate.* Washington: Government Printing Office, 19—.

U.S. Congress. Senate. Committee on Appropriations. *Legislative Branch Appropriations, 1976.* S. Rept. 94-262 to Accompany H.R. 6950, 94th Cong., 1st sess., 1975.

U.S. Congress. Senate. Committee on Armed Services. *Report Relating to the Nomination and Selection of Candidates for Appointment to the Military, Naval and Air Force Academies.* 88th Cong., 2nd sess., Feb. 6, 1964.

U.S. Congress. Senate. Committee on Post Office and Civil Service. *Congressional Franking Reform: A Compilation of Legislative History.* Committee Print, 93rd Cong., 2nd sess., 1974.

U.S. Congress. Senate. Committee on Rules and Administration. Ad Hoc Subcommittee to Consider the Reimbursement of Actual Travel Expense of Senators. *Travel Expenses of Members of the Senate; Hearings on S.3231.* 92nd Cong., 2nd sess., 1972.

Campaign Financing

The cost of running for the offices of senator, representative or President rose to dizzying heights in the decades after World War II and spawned a variety of ploys to fill the treasuries of candidates.

With the cost for some offices going into the millions and for most offices into at least the tens of thousands of dollars, candidates increasingly turned for help to wealthy individuals and business, labor and other organizations with well-filled coffers.

Money became the dominant influence on the election process, and the influence on public affairs of generous givers grew accordingly. But the public saw very little of this. Campaign financing was a sub rosa activity.

The result—the inevitable result, in the opinion of some critics of the campaign financing system—was the Watergate scandal of the Nixon administration. Watergate became the code word in the 1970s for governmental corruption. And although there were many aspects to the scandal, money in politics was at its roots. John Gardner, chairman of the self-styled citizens' lobby Common Cause, gave this analysis: "Watergate is not primarily a story of political espionage, or even of White House intrigue. It is a particularly malodorous chapter in the annals of campaign financing. The money paid to the Watergate conspirators before the break-in—and the money passed to them later—was money from campaign gifts."[1]

Indeed, the "smoking gun" evidence that precipitated Richard Nixon's resignation in 1974 was the disclosure that for almost two years he had concealed his knowledge that the June 1972 break-in of Democratic national headquarters had been financed by private contributions to Nixon's re-election campaign.

Included in the unprecedented catalog of misdeeds were specific violations of campaign spending laws, violations of other criminal laws facilitated by the availability of virtually unlimited campaign contributions, and still other instances where campaign funds were used in a manner that strongly suggested influence peddling or—at the very least—gave the appearance of gross improprieties in the conduct of public life.

Congress Responds

Watergate focused public attention on campaign spending at all levels of government. The public concern forced Congress to enact legislation in 1974 and in 1976 to reform the way that federal elections were financed. (Many state governments did the same for their elections.)

But Congress had begun to move even before Watergate. In the early 1970s, it had approved the concept of paying for an election with public tax money. This was done in 1971 through a check-off provision on federal income tax returns that allowed a taxpayer to put aside a dollar of his tax payment to help pay the costs of a presidential campaign.

Also in 1971, Congress in another law required disclosure of campaign contributions to candidates for federal office and placed limits on the amount of money candidates could spend. The law was greatly expanded and strengthened in 1974, and again in 1976 after the Supreme Court had struck down certain parts of the two earlier statutes.

Taken together, the 1971-76 laws provided public financing through federal tax dollars of presidential campaigns and nominating conventions (although not of congressional election campaigns), placed limits on private campaign contributions to federal candidates, required essentially complete disclosure of contribution sources and expenditure purposes and set up an independent commission to oversee and enforce the law. In a period of less than five years, Congress rewrote the manual of financing federal elections.

Issues Raised by Big Expenditures

Americans became concerned over the orgy of political spending mainly because it struck at the heart of the general assumption that every able and honest citizen of a democracy should have a chance to seek public office whether the person is rich, poor or somewhere in between. It follows that an aspirant for public service should not have to become obligated during a campaign to contributors who will expect him to vote for or against specified measures if elected. There is, however, no simple way to control campaign financing. Regulations to cope effectively with the problem of runaway costs must meet several requirements. The regulations must:

● Be enforceable; that is, they must not have the effect of unreasonably restricting use of the means of publicity

necessary for a meaningful election contest. (If the rules are unrealistic, they will encourage evasion.)
- Have as equal an effect as possible on the candidates who are already in office and well known and the candidates not previously in the public eye.
- Be tightly drafted, to guard against loopholes.
- Avoid curtailment of freedom of expression.

The laws of the 1970s attempted to meet these requirements. But by doing so they ran certain risks. Restrictions imposed on campaign financing, if too severe, may trespass on the constitutional rights of individuals, as the Supreme Court found in 1976. Tight restrictions may interfere also with the fulfillment of the democratic process. That is, it does take money to win elections, and citizens should be encouraged to contribute and participate.

High Costs of Campaigns

Until quite recently when specific accounting was required by law, there were few topics in American politics about which less was known than the cost of election campaigns. But one fact is certain: modern political campaigns for Congress and the presidency are terribly expensive. The most detailed and reliable figures supplied into the mid-1970s showed that costs were rising with every presidential campaign.

The Citizens' Research Foundation (CRF) of Princeton, N.J., founded in 1958, was regarded for years as the most comprehensive source of itemized campaign contributions and expenditures. According to CRF estimates, in 1952 the total cost of campaigns for all elective offices in the United States was $140-million. These costs rose to an estimated $155-million in 1956, $175-million in 1960, $200-million in 1964, $300-million in 1968, and $425-million in 1972. After economic and political adjustments were made, the actual increase in campaign costs over the 20-year period was estimated at 45 per cent.[2]

The amount of spending per vote cast increased enormously during that time, from an average of $2.27 in 1952 to $5.66 in 1972. Spending per eligible voter, many of whom did not vote in primaries or general elections, jumped from $1.40 to $3.04 in the 20-year period.[3]

Increased use of the broadcast media, particularly television, has accented the growing problem of campaign costs. Television and radio, a major source of news for Americans, are ideally suited to large constituencies. Television emerged after 1952 as the dominant form of communications in presidential and some congressional campaigns. The spurt in broadcast time spending testified to the increase in use of television and radio. Total charges for political broadcasts in general elections at all levels of government increased from $9.8-million in 1956 to $59.6-million in 1972.[4]

A large share of the total spending for all campaigns is devoted to the presidential nominations and elections. But the costs of congressional campaigns have increased as well. In 1970, the reported total primary and general election costs of all campaigns for the House and Senate was an estimated $71.6-million. In 1972, the outlays for House and Senate campaigns came to $77.2-million; that too was an estimate, and the totals for the year may have been several million dollars higher.[5]

The high costs of individual campaigns for Congress have been striking. Wisconsin Gov. Gaylord Nelson (D) spent less than $200,000 in 1964 to win a seat in the Senate; six years later he spent more than $450,000 to retain it, even

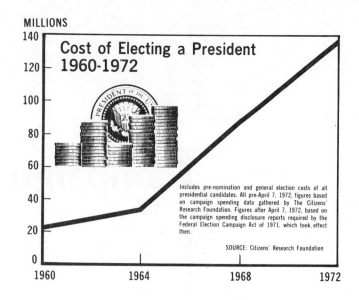

MILLIONS

Cost of Electing a President 1960-1972

Includes pre-nomination and general election costs of all presidential candidates. All pre-April 7, 1972, figures based on campaign spending data gathered by The Citizens' Research Foundation. Figures after April 7, 1972, based on the campaign spending disclosure reports required by the Federal Election Campaign Act of 1971, which took effect then.

SOURCE: Citizens' Research Foundation

though he did not face strong opposition. In the 1970 California race for the Senate, Democrat John Tunney spent $1,338,200 to defeat Republican incumbent George Murphy, who spent $1,946,400. Campaigns for seats in the House also can be expensive. In 1972, Democratic House candidates in Connecticut averaged expenditures of $74,400; Republican candidates averaged $86,800.[6]

Campaign Expenditures

To be sure, the costs of campaigns have soared since the mid-20th century. But the price tags on elections were a public concern before then. Will Rogers noted in his syndicated newspaper column of June 28, 1931: "Politics has got so expensive that it takes a lot of money to even get beat with."

There are many reasons why the costs of campaigning keep going up. One is the general economic inflation that makes everything else more expensive. Another is the increasing number of citizens who are eligible to vote and who must be reached by the candidates. The widespread use of television in political contests has added greatly to the costs. Public opinion polling, never a cheap venture, has become common even in local campaigns. Mail costs have gone up; in 1976 every first-class letter to voters cost 13 cents to mail, in addition to the costs of preparation, printing and return postage. Transportation has grown steadily more expensive. Finally, all the costs associated with political organization have increased—office space, accommodations for volunteer workers, canvassing, communications and the hiring of specialists to direct campaigns in the field.

Political Consultants

A well-heeled non-incumbent candidate in a typical campaign for an important political office may enlist the services of a professional political consultant, a computer firm, a pollster, an advertising agency, a film-maker, a speechwriter, a television and radio time-buyer, a direct mail organization and possibly an accounting firm.

The cost of such services for a tight House race easily could run to more than $100,000 per candidate in the early 1970s—exclusive of television time expenses.

The political consultant may visit his candidate's state or district only occasionally, preferring instead to closet himself with poll results, computer breakdowns of voting patterns and demographic profiles. He prefers to plan a campaign as early before the primary as possible. He generally prefers newcomers for whom he can build an image. He is expensive. Some consultants command $500 a day for their full-time personal services.

A well-versed campaign consultant must be qualified to work in public opinion surveys, electronic data processing, fund-raising, budgeting, media, research, public relations and press services, advertising and volunteer recruitment. Some participate in policy decisions as well.

No organization has the talent or resources to take on all these jobs at once, but some offer prospective clients a "package" of related services. This practice assures that one firm will be responsible for victory or defeat. Some experienced politicians, however, still prefer to draw on a variety of experienced individuals and firms for their campaigns. Other firms act only as consultants for work contracted out to other individuals or agencies.

For a large enough fee, professional experts in this field will manage every step in a campaign from the candidate's announcement of availability to the post-election victory party. They will conduct opinion polls to determine what issues most concern the voters and even what kind of clothes it would be advantageous for the candidate to wear. They will accept responsibility for fund-raising, recruitment of volunteers, research, computerization of voting and demographic patterns of the electorate, preparation of brochures and documentaries, speechwriting, advertising, holding of rallies, trips through neighborhoods, and every other activity needed for an effective campaign.

Professional campaign management has become one of the most expensive elements in American politics, and questions have been raised as to the effectiveness of political consultant firms. Since only one candidate wins, all the others can conclude that they have sent their consultation money down the drain.

Polls

William R. Hamilton and Staff is a division of a Washington public opinion and marketing research firm, Independent Research Associates Inc., one of dozens of such firms that play an increasingly important part in campaigns. "In the past," says a Hamilton booklet, "candidates have gone through entire campaigns without polls; in today's politics, however, the chances are about five to one that the opposition is making his campaign decisions based on knowledge of how the voters feel about the candidates and issues."

Hamilton, whose firm did more than 125 studies for political, governmental and commercial clients from 1963 to 1971, recommends a basic, in-depth poll prior to any major campaign activity. Trained resident interviewers in randomly selected urban blocks or rural areas of a particular constituency interview five to eight probable voters in each area. The interviewer spends about 45 minutes to an hour with each voter.

When campaign funds are "extremely scarce," Hamilton recommends a telephone poll in place of an in-the-home poll. He also offers "telephone panel-backs," or follow-up polls, and scout studies—quick spot studies—of a particular group of voters.

The cost of Hamilton's statewide personal interview poll of 300 to 800 probable voters ranged from $5,000 to

Reasons for Higher Costs

Bills for campaigning for public office were higher than ever in the late 1960s and early 1970s chiefly because of the following developments:

● Enlargement of the electorate (the number of persons to be reached in campaigning) by the coming to voting age of the postwar bumper baby crop and by expansion of opportunities for voting by blacks.

● Revitalization of the Republican Party in the South, making it necessary for southern Republicans—and Democrats—to campaign more vigorously.

● Decline in straight-ticket voting; that is, the rise of independent voting, which resulted largely from virtual disappearance of old-style party machines in the precincts. Split-ticket voting requires each candidate for each office to intensify his efforts to get elected.

● Growing use of radio and television to reach prospective voters.

● Increase in numbers of young volunteer workers, whose services, though nominally free, are costly to administer, involving maintenance of headquarters, transportation of canvassers, arrangement of "socials" to sustain enthusiasm, and other expense items.

● Use of computers to categorize voters for specialized appeals.

● Growing reliance on costly public opinion surveys geared to campaigners' needs.

● Use of other new and costly campaign techniques, including "packaged" campaigns managed by political consultants.

● Inflation.

Source: Adapted from David Adamany, "Money for Politics," *National Civic Review*, April 1970, pp. 192-93.

$10,000. Telephone polls usually accounted for about 50 to 60 per cent of the costs of a personal interview poll, or $2,500 to $5,000. Telephone follow-ups ranged from $750 to $2,500.[7]

Broadcasting

The Federal Communications Commission reported that candidates for all offices—President, Senate, House, governor and local positions—spent $59.6-million for television and radio broadcasts in 1972. In 1970, when there was no presidential election, the total was only $400,000 less.

The 1970 total was almost double that for 1966, the previous non-presidential year. The totals include commissions paid to salesmen and others responsible for the broadcast advertisements.

Clearly, candidates increasingly are relying on radio and television to gain recognition for themselves and to explain their programs to the voters. But there are campaigns where television is not much of a factor, either because of the location of media markets or the area's political makeup. For example, only a rare congressional candidate from Manhattan could afford substantial television time at New York City rates. Candidates from New Jersey have the same problem, because that state has no television stations of its own and depends on New York facilities.

In rural areas candidates still find it more effective to get out and meet the voters in person. Citizens of sparsely settled states who know their senator by his first name are less likely to pay attention to half-hour television specials in which the candidate describes his record. Spot announcements and reminders are supplemented by billboards, posters, cards and—most of all—handshakes and personal greetings.

Print Advertising

Broadcasts cannot handle all political advertising. Some information from candidates has to be read because it is too complicated to be flashed over the airwaves. Politicians long ago learned the importance of getting their printed name before the voters exactly as it will appear on the ballot. Despite radio and TV, political consultants still emphasize print advertising.

Agencies determine the execution of posters, billboards, brochures, newspaper and magazine ads and handouts. Although some politicians discredit the effectiveness of newspaper ads, the medium consumed 10 to 15 per cent of the total budget of a modern statewide campaign in 1970.

Billboards are bought by market, rather than by state, and by what are called "showings," according to Jack Bowen of a Washington advertising agency, Bailey, Deardourff and Bowen. A showing is a projection of the percentage of people in an area who will see a billboard message at least once a week. Billboards are bought in advance, by the month. In the New York metropolitan area in 1971, Bowen said, a billboard for one month at a 100 showing would total 232 different boards costing $34,160. At a 75 showing, or 174 boards, the cost would be $25,620.

In the Billings, Mont., area, a 100 showing, or 14 boards, would cost $1,050; a 75 showing, or 11 boards, $825. In Atlanta, Ga., a 100 showing, or 80 boards, would cost $8,630; a 75 showing, or 60 boards, would cost $6,480.

Persons buying billboards for a presidential campaign, Bowen said, usually buy within a selected list of 50 to 100 top markets.[8]

Besides the agency fee, campaigns must pay for the advertising itself. Ad agencies also handle such campaign paraphernalia as buttons, bumper stickers, balloons, posters and placards, hats, brochures, printed speeches and position papers, costume jewelry and even paper dresses. For national or statewide elections, campaign committees often produce favorable books about their candidates.

Staff and Office Expenses

Although headquarters and staff generally account for less than 20 to 30 per cent of most campaign budgets, a long-time aide to a western senator refused to estimate a probable cost for his boss' next campaign. "It depends on who you find," he said, "a retiree who will work for just about expenses or someone you hire away from a full-time job. Staff costs are among the imponderables."[9]

As long as the campaign continues, dollars flow from campaign headquarters not only for broadcasts and professional expertise, but also for a myriad of campaign services of other kinds. Some expenditures are made directly for equipment, supplies and services. Others take the form of contributions by a national committee to a local committee, or vice versa, to help the recipient committee pay its bills. Some costs are peculiar to the process of running for office; others, such as the Social Security tax on payrolls, are common to any business enterprise.

At campaign headquarters, costs continue through election day for items such as rent, supplies, utilities and salaries of some employees. There are expenses for transporting voters to the polls if not enough persons volunteer for such duty. And poll-watchers may have to be paid.

The administration of a campaign's volunteer work force is costly. Indirect expenses include recruitment drives, maintenance of headquarters, transportation of canvassers, social events to sustain enthusiasm and other items.

Speechwriting and Reseach

Speechwriters and researchers are usually included on the campaign staff, but occasionally freelance writers are hired. Commercial research firms and clipping services are often contracted to provide extensive background information and continuous updating on candidate publicity.

Professional gag men have been retained by parties or candidates at least as far back as the Herbert Hoover-Al Smith campaign, but these have been partisan volunteers whose activities were kept as secret as possible. Today the candidate's joke writers have been openly credited with making or breaking several campaigns.

Transportation

Reported campaign travel costs may be considerably inflated since as much as half the total is reimbursed by the organizations of reporters traveling with candidates. The reimbursement is for flying on a plane provided by the campaign or in the candidate's plane, and occasionally for ground transportation such as press buses. Substantial portions of travel costs can be recouped when the candidate and his staff fly with enough reporters.

Transportation accommodations vary widely among candidates—from flying private jets to riding tourist-class on commercial airlines. All travel costs have increased, however, and in large states or national campaigns they can use up a lot of the candidates' budgets.

Free Goods and Services

Some candidates receive goods and services without charge from their supporters. For instance, a friend may lend his private plane to a candidate or may lend a building rent-free for an office. Incumbents have certain financial advantages, too, such as computerized mail files of correspondence during their tenures.

Furthermore, when campaign totals are given, they represent committed costs, not actual expenditures. Some of the debts from the Kennedy, McCarthy and Humphrey campaigns of 1968 were settled for less than their full amount, for example.

Pre-Nomination Expenses

The most comprehensive estimates of campaign spending generally date only from the primaries, but it has been argued that campaigns and their attendant expenses begin several years before the nomination contests. For example, Richard M. Nixon's extensive travel in 1966 on behalf of Republican congressional candidates made him a major presidential contender after the Republicans' impressive election results that year. The 30,000-mile tour, including the salary and expenses of one assistant, cost $90,000. The money was raised independently of the campaigns.[10]

Mr. Nixon's first campaign planning session for his 1968 presidential race was held in early January 1967. He spent about $10-million during the next 19 months before he became the Republican Party's nominee.

Pre-nomination and post-nomination campaign organizations are often almost identical. The number of workers increases as election day nears. So do expenses. But the campaign managers, press secretaries, policy advisers, pollsters, advance men, schedulers and speechwriters, researchers and political intelligence staff have been hired months earlier.

Primary elections, especially presidential preference primaries, can be enormously expensive. Since the stakes are so high, campaign offices in primary states often open months before an election. And nominating conventions present candidates with still more campaign costs.

Effectiveness of Spending

The extent to which an election can be won by out-spending the opposition is debated during and after almost every political contest. But big campaign spenders say they can point to better-than-random correlation between financial outlay and victory. Other political consultants analyze the situation this way:

● The majority of voters have made up their minds about the candidate they will vote for by the start of the campaign. Unswayed by bids for their favor during the campaign, they will vote for their pre-chosen candidate.

● About 10 to 15 per cent of the electorate, the voters who are "independent and susceptible" when the campaign begins, often hold the balance of power.

● The candidate with the most money cannot be sure of winning to his side enough of the undecided voters to give him a victory, but the candidate with less money may be unable to present his case adequately to the crucial group of undecided voters.

Campaign Fund-Raising

Obviously, before candidates can spend money on their campaigns they have to raise the funds. Where the money comes from is no less important than where it goes after it is turned over to the politicians. Campaign fund-raising traditionally was among the better kept secrets of American electoral politics. But again, the excesses of the Watergate scandals in the early 1970s brought about considerable reform. The most significant change was the beginning of public funding of part of the campaign process.

The changes in federal campaign finance laws are discussed in detail later in the chapter. This section describes the general methods and sources of campaign fund-raising.

The reform measures of the 1970-75 period, which originally imposed strict limits on campaign contributions and expenditures and provided for the public financing of presidential campaigns, were supposed to curtail drastically the role of money in campaigns. Candidates were expected to devote less effort to wooing contributors. Overall campaign spending was expected to be reduced. Challengers and incumbents were supposed to be placed on a more equal footing than in previous campaigns, because big money at last had been de-emphasized and the spending and fund-raising advantages of incumbents had been curbed.

But campaign financing law was altered in the winter and spring of 1976, first by a Supreme Court decision and then by new legislation. The over-all effect was to void recent restrictions on campaign contributions. However, the post-Watergate political climate and the economic down-

turn of the previous three years made 1975 and early 1976 a difficult period in which to raise money. Even before the temporary $1,000 limit on donations was lifted, many previously generous donors made only small contributions.

The cumulative effect of these difficulties was to push candidates to seek new givers to make up for the loss of large contributors and the slowness of fund-raising. Several campaigns in the past were able to expand greatly their contributor base and to tap large numbers of people who had never given before. Barry Goldwater did that on the Republican right in his 1964 presidential campaign. So did George McGovern on the Democratic left in his 1972 campaign. And Alabama Gov. George C. Wallace found many new small contributors to finance his 1968, 1972 and 1976 presidential campaigns.

Direct Mail

Direct mail is the only way that large numbers of small contributors can be reached. But increases in postage rates and paper prices pushed the cost of a direct-mail fund-raising letter to more than 20 cents, far too high a price if a mailing has a low response. Many candidates and political fund-raising organizations found in 1975 and 1976 that direct mail was not bringing in as much money as in previous years. The exceptions, according to reports for 1975, were Wallace and Republican presidential contender Ronald Reagan, whose conservative constituencies yielded them good direct-mail returns. Historically, the political extremes have found direct mail a much better source of money than have moderates.[11]

Millions of letters soliciting funds are sent out by computers in an election year. With the increasing need for large sums of money and the use of computer techniques by direct mail professionals, mass mail solicitation has become the most important means of fund-raising in a number of major political campaigns.

According to direct mail specialist Richard Viguerie, "direct mail comes close to being a science. We know the importance of the color of envelopes, length of letters, personalized variables in letters, because we've tested all of these variables. The results are analyzed...and the success of each variation is measured.

"It's exciting what can be done," Viguerie said, "but you seldom find a client who is interested in using all of this information in a sophisticated manner." Most users of direct mail are interested in geographic and financial breakdowns—for example, all of the contributors in a given state who have contributed $10 or more to a conservative cause.[12]

Direct mail works against the traditional premise that in order to finance large campaigns a candidate has to rely on big business, labor and large contributors. A small contribution goes to a candidate or committee with a personal commitment by the donor. It comes from people who expect nothing in return.

Direct mail experts estimate conservatively that there are more than 500 million names on computers. An official of the Direct Mail Advertising Association has said that "people's names get on lists because people exist.... Only hermits could avoid getting on lists but then they'll probably get on somebody's list of hermits."[13]

The collection of personal data by direct mail list brokers has raised questions similar to those concerning credit data banks. Lists include information on what publications an individual reads, what charities he contributes to, what candidates he is supporting financially and his stands on political issues. And the lists are available for sale by the list brokers.

Buying and selling political mailing lists has become a successful business. Periodicals and book clubs sell lists to all comers. Viguerie sells lists of anything from "active Americans" to "retired military" to conservative Republicans. The United Nations International Childrens Emergency Fund (UNICEF) has sold its lists to the Democratic National Committee and the 1970 Campaign Fund. The Internal Revenue Service sells aggregate income statistics about taxpayers broken down by zip code. This is valuable to identify high-income communities for fund-raising.

Interest Groups

Special-interest groups spent an estimated $13-million on campaign contributions and related political activities in the first eight months of 1974, according to a study of reports filed with federal officials.[14]

A total of 526 groups representing business, labor, agriculture, doctors, educators and other interests reported expenditures of $15.3-million by Aug. 31. About $2-million of this was simply transfers of cash between national groups and their state committees, however. In addition, the same political committees reported another $12.9-million in cash on hand ready for use before the November elections.

The reports, required by the Federal Election Campaign Act of 1971, provided the first timely, comprehensive picture available during an election year of total campaign spending. With seven weeks to go in the 1974 campaigns, spending by special-interest committees already was running about $2-million ahead of the previous record for an entire non-presidential year. Similar groups reporting spending $11-million on the 1970 election campaigns, according to records then available.

Part of the increase could be attributed to the tougher reporting requirements of the 1971 law, which replaced the Federal Corrupt Practices Act of 1925, often described as more loophole than law. But a larger flow of campaign dollars from some older groups and a proliferation of new committees also added to the record outpouring of funds.

The biggest spenders by category as of Aug. 31 were labor, $6.3-million; medical and health professionals, $3.9-million, and business, $2.2-million. These were gross figures, not adjusted for transfers. Actual labor spending, for instance, was closer to $5-million.

Teachers, contributing through new political action committees, joined the top spenders for the first time, disbursing $682,833 and reporting another $740,999 in cash available for the final weeks of the congressional campaigns.

The largest amounts are usually spent on campaigns in the final weeks before an election. By combining expenditures through Aug. 31 with cash on hand, it was possible to calculate the total funds available as of that date to various groups for political spending in 1974.

Business Executives

Executives of the largest defense-related contractors gave eight times more money in 1972 to the campaigns of President Nixon and other Republican candidates than to their Democratic counterparts.

Officers and directors of these companies gave $2,555,740 to Republicans and $319,983 to Democrats, according to data compiled by the Citizens' Research Foundation of Princeton, N.J.[15]

The amounts, as well as the margin by which Republicans were favored, were up sharply from 1968. A similar Citizens' Research survey for that presidential election year showed Republicans favored 6 to 1 in donations. They received $1,235,402, compared with $180,550 for Democrats.

Both surveys covered campaign gifts reported by officials of the companies ranking among the top 25 contractors to the Defense Department (DOD), Atomic Energy Commission (AEC) and National Aeronautics and Space Administration (NASA).

The three agencies were the federal government's largest buyers of military and other hardware. DOD spent more than $20-billion a year on weapons systems and equipment. The AEC (later broken into two agencies) supplied nuclear warheads for bombs and missiles. And NASA rocketry helped the development of intercontinental ballistic missiles.

The old Federal Corrupt Practices Act of 1925 required no reporting of campaign gifts made before the nominating primary or convention. This loophole ceased as of April 7, 1972. The change did not affect the long-standing prohibition on campaign contributions by corporations. Executives of corporations may make campaign contributions as individuals.

Because of overlapping on the DOD, AEC and NASA lists, the survey covered 52 separate companies rather than a total of 75. Forty-six of the 52 companies had officials who gave to political campaigns. Not all the officers and directors of these 46 companies made campaign contributions. But the 483 who did gave an average of $5,953, compared with an average of $4,202 in 1968.

The compilation showed that 54 individuals contributed $10,000 or more. In 1968, only 43 corporate executives had given $5,500 or more.

All 25 companies on the DOD list had officers or directors who contributed to 1972 campaigns.

Sixteen of the companies on the AEC list also had officials who gave, including the four companies that were duplicated on the DOD or NASA lists.

All companies except one on the NASA list had officials who contributed. The exception was Computing Software Inc. All but six of the top 25 NASA contractors also were among the largest DOD and AEC contractors.

There was no direct correlation between the amount of business a company got from the defense agencies and the size of campaign contributions from the company's officials.

Fund-Raising Dinners

A fund-raising dinner is an effective tool for extracting a hefty check from a well-to-do voter. Where formerly a prospective donor was invited to a dinner and there subjected to give-'em-hell partisan appeals for a contribution or pledge, his gift now is assured in advance by the sale of expensive tickets of admission. President Eisenhower on Jan. 20, 1956, spoke by closed-circuit TV to 53 banquets held simultaneously in 37 states. Ticket sales netted between $4-million and $5-million for the Republican Party.

In the 1960s, techniques for holding political dinners were developed further. President Kennedy's Inaugural Eve Gala in Washington, D.C., grossed $1,250,000. In the administrations of Presidents Kennedy and Lyndon B. Johnson, those who paid $1,000 a plate at major political dinners were known as members of the President's Club. The most profitable form of fund-raising is the $1,000-a-plate political dinner. Overhead on a $1,000-a-plate dinner is approximately 5 per cent to 10 per cent while it can run as high as 50 per cent on a $10-a-plate dinner.

Campaign committees peddle tickets costing from $25 up for other politically oriented meals—breakfast, brunch and lunch. In addition, there are teas, cocktail parties, bean feeds and snack parties. Favorite invitees are Washington lobbyists and representatives of trade associations, as well as friendly corporation executives and labor union officials.

Other Methods

Another way in which candidates and parties raise money is to sell ads in special publications. The Democrats in 1964, for example, published a program booklet called "Toward an Age of Greatness." Large corporations bought advertising space in the booklet at rates approaching those charged by nationally circulated magazines. The Republicans quickly decided to fill their coffers in the same way. Prior to 1966, some corporations not only placed ads in such publications—for up to $15,000 a page—but also deducted the cost as business expenses in their federal tax returns. An act of March 15, 1966, put an end to these deductions, but both parties continue to sell ads.

In seeking campaign contributions from individuals, political committees often resort to the psychologically effective device of seeing to it that prospective donors are solicited by persons whom they will want to please. A prospective donor's best customer, for example, may be sent to ask him for a contribution. The desire of the donor to stand well with the solicitor may transcend, as a motive for giving, any tangible favors hoped for from the victory of a political candidate or his party.

Appointment of millionaire members of the party to office has long been another standard technique for inducing political contributions. Cabinet posts and other high offices in the executive branch, as well as membership on blue-ribbon commissions, are sometimes awarded in recognition of contributions already made or to encourage future contributions.

Wealthy Candidates

One of the best ways for a party to hold down its expenses is to nominate a candidate whose personal wealth is sufficient to absorb many campaign costs. A legislative attempt to limit how much of their own money candidates could spend on their campaigns was ended by a Supreme Court decision of Jan. 30, 1976, which held that such a restriction was unconstitutional. The ruling was thought to open the way for more wealthy candidates for federal office. However, candidates who use their own wealth in campaigning often suffer at the polls from opponents' attacks that they are attempting to buy the election.

Bad Political Debts

Questions have been raised in recent years as to the legality of a long-standing corporation practice which is tantamount to contributing funds to a candidate or a political committee. The practice involves post-election settlement, by a corporation, of campaign debts, especially those incurred by the loser, at less than 100 cents on the dollar. "Winners pay their debts; losers negotiate theirs," according to an election adage. Hotel bills, debts to airlines for candidates' and newsmen's fares, car rental fees, and telephone bills sometimes are paid off by a loser at 25 to 50 cents on the dollar.

Ambassadors and Money

Ambassadors and persons seeking ambassadorships often have made large contributions to presidential campaigns. After his 1972 re-election, President Nixon appointed 13 more non-career ambassadors, eight of whom had donated a minimum of $25,000 each and $706,000 in aggregate to his campaign. This led to charges that the Nixon administration was brokering ambassadorships.

According to the Senate Watergate Committee report, over $1.8-million in presidential campaign contributions was attributable, in whole or in part, to persons holding ambassadorial appointments from Nixon. The report said further that about 30 per cent of all foreign envoy posts were held in July 1974 by non-career appointees. The largest concentration was in Western Europe, where there was also a high concentration of persons contributing $100,000 or more.

While White House officials maintained they told persons seeking ambassadorships that no *quid pro quo* could follow contributions, the Senate Watergate Committee report concluded that "at the very least, a number of persons saw the making of a contribution as a means of obtaining the recognition needed to be actively considered."

A list of nine U.S. ambassadors to Western Europe and their contributions to Nixon's 1972 re-election campaign follows:

Country	Ambassador	Contribution
Great Britain	Walter H. Annenberg	$ 250,000
Switzerland	Shelby Davis	100,000
Luxembourg	Ruth L. Farkas	300,000
Belgium	Leonard K. Firestone	112,600
Netherlands	Kingdon Gould	100,900
Austria	John F. Humes	100,000
France	John N. Irwin II	50,500
France	Arthur K. Watson	300,000
Ireland	John D. Moore	10,442
Total		**$1,324,442**

Source: Congressional Quarterly, *Dollar Politics* (1974), vol. 2, p. 15.

Power of Incumbents

Incumbent members of Congress, Democrats and Republicans alike, have a powerful advantage over their challengers when it comes to raising money for re-election. But when neither major-party candidate is an incumbent, the ability to raise funds evens out.

These were two of the findings of a study on campaign spending conducted by Common Cause, the self-styled citizens' lobby. The results, based on analysis of reports filed by congressional candidates and their campaign committees, were announced on Sept. 13, 1973.

Further data collected by Common Cause on the 1972 House and Senate Campaigns was released on Nov. 30, 1973. At that time Fred Wertheimer, Common Cause legislative director, commented, "In Congress today we have neither a Democratic nor a Republican Party. Rather we have an incumbency party which operates a monopoly."[16]

The 106 candidates who ran for the Senate in the November 1972 elections raised about $27.3-million and spent about $26.4-million, according to Common Cause. Winners of the 33 elections outspent their major-party opponents by about two to one. And incumbents outspent challengers by about the same ratio. The study found that:

- In 19 of 25 races, incumbents outspent challengers.
- In 28 of 33 races, winners outspent losers.
- In all eight races in which there was no incumbent, winners outspent losers.

Similar patterns prevailed in the contests for House seats. The 318 incumbents who had majority-party challengers out-collected and out-spent their opponents by wide margins, but not so wide as in the Senate.

Races without incumbents not only featured a more equal distribution of spending, but a lot more spending in general. Democrats in these House districts spent an average of $90,074, Republicans a nearly identical $90,030. In 52 House districts, incumbents had no major-party challengers in 1972.

Common Cause reported finding a connection between plurality and cost—the closer a race was, the more expensive it was likely to be. House candidates who won with more than 60 per cent of the vote spent an average of less than $55,000. Elections won with less than 55 per cent cost more than $100,000, on the average, not only for the winner but for the loser as well.

Costs of Fund-Raising

No matter how it is done, campaign fund-raising is an expensive proposition. As much as two-thirds of every dollar raised is spent by some political committees for soliciting the funds. In July and August, 1971, Congressional Quarterly examined records in the House Clerk's office and interviewed officials of several political committees to determine the costs of raising money for various types of groups.[17]

The study found that fund-raising costs ranged from as low as 13 per cent for one direct mail effort to 58-65 per cent for comprehensive fund-raising programs. Probably the highest fund-raising costs were reported in 1968 by the United Republicans of America. Candidates supported by the committee received less than 10 per cent of the $473,453 it raised.

Finding the Funds

The 1976 campaign was especially difficult for fund-raising, as candidates and their managers puzzled over new campaign financing laws. Candidates had to spend more time raising money. The problem was especially acute in the presidential campaign, where the largest amounts had to be raised.

"We've done everything," a staff man for one liberal Democratic candidate told Congressional Quarterly. "We've held tennis parties, dinners, cocktail parties, breakfasts, receptions and concerts. We've even passed the hat at dances."[18]

Contributors also were making fund-raising more time consuming in the 1976 elections. They apparently wanted to see who was receiving their money and to take the candidates' measure before making donations.

Douglas L. Bailey, a political consultant in Washington, D.C., said, "The members of a candidate's finance committee have far more difficulty raising dough than the candidate. There's no automatic giving to establishment fund-raisers."[19]

Bailey saw nothing wrong with contributors wanting to personally size up the candidate they are helping to finance. But he and other campaign consultants worried that campaigns might suffer from the time it takes. "Candidates who have to spend most of their time raising money spend proportionately less time reaching voters," said Joseph Napolitan, a campaign consultant from Springfield, Mass. "If I had my choice, I'd like to see candidates spend their time meeting voters, not contributors."[20]

Campaigns and Broadcasting

Regulation of campaign expenditures entails, among other things, decisions on who may compete for purchase of television time and under what conditions such competition may occur. The basic legislation on the subject, Section 315 (a) of the Communications Act of 1934, apparently raised more questions than it answered. Section 315 (a) provided: "If any licensee shall permit any person who is a legally qualified candidate for any public office to use a broadcasting station, he shall afford equal opportunities to all other such candidates for that office in the use of such broadcasting station."

In 1959, Lar Daly, write-in candidate for Mayor of Chicago, made a demand on Chicago television stations which, if complied with, would have provided him with exposure on television without any expenditure on his part. He said that under the Act of 1934 he was entitled to receive as much time on Chicago news broadcasts as was given to Democratic and Republican candidates. He based his demand on a 20-second news shot of Mayor Richard J. Daley, Democratic candidate for re-election, greeting a foreign dignitary, and a one-minute news report on Daley's opening of the March of Dimes campaign. On Feb. 19, 1959, the Federal Communications Commission, in a surprise decision, ruled by a vote of four to three that Daly's demand was justified.

The commission's application of the equal-time provision to news broadcasts aroused a wave of protests. President Eisenhower on March 19, 1959, called the ruling "ridiculous." Congress, by an act of Sept. 14, 1959, nullified the commission's ruling by inserting, at the end of Section 315 (a), the words: "Appearance by a legally qualified candidate on any (1) bona fide newscast, (2) bona fide news interview, (3) bona fide news documentary (if the appearance of the candidate is incidental to the presentation of the subject or subjects covered by the news documentary), or (4) on-the-spot coverage of bona fide news events (including but not limited to political conventions and activities incidental thereto), shall not be deemed to be use of a broadcasting station within the meaning of this subsection."

Equal-Time Provision in the 1960s

The equal-time provision of the Act of 1934 was suspended in part by an act of Aug. 24, 1960, to make possible a series of television debates between the 1960 presidential candidates of the two major parties, John F. Kennedy (D) and Richard M. Nixon (R). Congress also considered but did not enact a proposal to suspend Section 315 (a) for the period of the 1962 congressional campaign.

The Senate and the House in 1964 passed different bills to make possible a television debate between the two major presidential contenders of that year, President Johnson and Sen. Barry Goldwater (R Ariz.). Although a conference committee reconciled the two bills, the measure was allowed to die, because President Johnson did not want to appear with Sen. Goldwater on a basis which implied equality of status for the incumbent and the challenger. Similarly, in 1968 and 1972 there were no debates between Richard M. Nixon and challengers Hubert H. Humphrey and George McGovern. However, in 1976 plans were made in September for a resumption of campaign debates *(see next column)*.

Legislation

In 1970 Congress passed a bill which would have limited spending on political broadcasts by candidates for election to Congress, the presidency and state governorships. The bill also would have made possible televised debates between the major parties' candidates for President by repealing the equal time requirements of the 1934 act. President Nixon vetoed the bill.

The Federal Election Campaign Act of 1971 (PL 92-225) set limits on the amounts candidates could spend for

---

Equal Time, Fairness

The "equal time" provision of the Communications Act of 1934—Section 315(a)—and the "fairness doctrine" of the Federal Communications Commission, although related to the federal regulation of broadcasting, differed significantly in their intent and effect.

The equal time provision required almost mathematical equality in television and radio broadcast treatment of legally qualified candidates for public office. The fairness doctrine, promulgated by the FCC after extensive hearings in 1949, required only fair or balanced treatment of community issues. Congress in 1959 added the fairness standard to Section 315(a) of the Communications Act by providing that broadcast licensees "must operate in the public interest and afford reasonable opportunity for the discussion of conflicting views on controversial issues of public interest."

The key distinction was between individuals, in equal time questions of law, and community issues, in fairness doctrine questions of policy. In no case under existing law or policy was there provision for equal time or fair broadcast treatment of political or social groups, organizations or institutions. That is, no group, organization, institution or individual—except legally qualified political candidates for public office—was guaranteed a right of access to the broadcast media.

Under the fairness doctrine, each licensee was compelled to seek responsible contrasting opinions on public issues once the broadcaster had provided time for raising an issue.

But the licensee was left with full discretion to determine what issues he would raise or permit to be raised on the air, who would be the "responsible spokesman" for opposing views, and at what length and in what context or format those issues would be raised and opposing views aired.

The FCC in 1964 said: "In passing on any complaint (under the fairness doctrine), the commission's role is not to substitute its judgment for that of the licensee as to any...programming decisions, but rather to determine whether the licensee can be said to have acted reasonably and in good faith."

---

broadcasting and other forms of advertising, and restricted the rates to be charged by broadcasters during campaigns. The law retained the 1934 equal time requirements.

In 1973 the Senate approved campaign reform legislation (S 372) which would have repealed the equal time provision, but the House did not act on the bill. The broadcasting industry contended that because Section 315 required broadcasters to make equal time available to all candidates, it discouraged them from making time available to major party candidates.[21]

The limits on broadcast advertising were tested in the 1972 elections and appeared not to have been unreasonable. The Federal Communications Commission reported that presidential candidates spent a total of $14.3-million on radio, television and cable TV advertising in 1972, compared with $28.5-million in the previous presidential election. Senatorial candidates spent $6.4-million in 1972, compared with $16-million in 1970 and $10.4-million in 1968. Broadcast spending in House races increased, however, from $6.1-million in 1970, when the FCC first computed it, to $7.4-million in 1972.[22]

In the Federal Election Campaign Amendments of 1974 (PL 93-443), Congress repealed the media spending limitations of the 1971 law. The Senate-approved bill again would have repealed the equal time provision of the 1934 Federal Communications Act, but House conferees eliminated that from the final legislation.

FCC Reversal, 1976 Debates

The Federal Communications Commission itself revised the equal time provision in a Sept. 25, 1975, decision. By a 5-2 vote, the commission ruled that broadcast news conferences and political debates sponsored by a third party would not be subject to Section 315 requirements. The change exempted from Section 315 press conferences held not only by the President, but by governors, mayors "and any candidates whose press conferences may be considered newsworthy and subject to on-the-spot coverage."[23]

As a result of this change, plans were made in September 1976 for televised debates between President Ford and Democratic challenger Jimmy Carter. The series of three debates as well as one between the vice presidential candidates were sponsored by the League of Women Voters.

The FCC's majority opinion stated: "The undue stifling of broadcast coverage of news events involving candidates for public office has been unfortunate, and we believe that this remedy will go a long way toward ameliorating the paucity of coverage accorded these events during the past 15 years." But a dissenter who called the new ruling a "tragic mistake," Commissioner Benjamin L. Hooks, wrote that "by exempting two popular forms of political weaponry, the press conference and the debate, the delicate balance of egalitarian precepts underlying political 'equal time' has suffered a severe and, perhaps, mortal blow."[24]

The debate was limited to Ford and Carter after a federal district court judge in Washington, D.C., ruled that two other presidential candidates could not participate because they had not gone through proper channels. Eugene J. McCarthy, running as an independent, had asked to be included in the debates. Tom Anderson, the nominee of the American Party, had sought an injunction to prevent the debates from being held. Judge Aubrey Robinson said the two candidates had no right to relief from the court because they had not first sought permission from the Federal Communications Commission (FCC) and the Federal Election Commission.

Two other presidential candidates, Lester Maddox of the American Independent Party and Peter Camejo of the Socialist Workers, asked the FCC to grant them equal time on television. Their request was denied.[25]

Campaign Finance Legislation

Legislation on campaign spending in the United States has had three aims: (1) to limit and regulate donations made to candidates and their campaign committees; (2) to limit and regulate disbursements made by candidates and their committees, and (3) to inform voters of the amounts and sources of the donations and the amounts, purposes and payees of the disbursements. Disclosure was intended to reveal which candidates, if any, were unduly indebted to interest groups, in time to forewarn the voters. But more than a century of legislative attempts to regulate campaign financing resulted in much controversy and minimal control.

Money has been a major issue in American politics since colonial times. In his race for the House of Burgesses in Virginia in 1757, George Washington was accused of campaign irregularities. He was charged with dispensing during his campaign 28 gallons of rum, 50 gallons of rum punch, 34 gallons of wine, 46 gallons of beer and two gallons of cider royal. "Even in those days," noted George Thayer, a historian of American campaign financing, "this was considered a large campaign expenditure, because there were only 391 voters in his district, for an average outlay of more than a quart and a half per person."[26]

Campaign spending was a central issue in the 1832 presidential race, in which President Andrew Jackson and Henry Clay, his Whig opponent, fought over the fate of the United States Bank. During the campaign, the U.S.-chartered but semi-autonomous bank spent heavily to support Clay. The strategy backfired, however. Jackson met the challenge with a strong veto message against legislation renewing the bank's charter, in which he described the bank as a "money monster," and he used it as an effective issue to defeat Clay.

Money played an important role in the victory of Republican William McKinley over populist Democrat William Jennings Bryan in the 1896 presidential election. McKinley's campaign was managed by Marcus A. Hanna, the wealthy Ohio financier and industrialist who turned the art of political fund raising into a system.

The first provision of federal law on campaign financing was incorporated in an act of March 2, 1867, making naval appropriations for the fiscal year 1868. The final section of the act read: "And be it further enacted, That no officer or employee of the government shall require or request any workingman in any navy yard to contribute or pay any money for political purposes, nor shall any workingman be removed or discharged for political opinion; and any officer or employee of the government who shall offend against the provisions of this section shall be dismissed from the service of the United States."

Reports circulated in the following year that at least 75 per cent of the money raised by the Republican Congressional Committee came from federal officeholders. Continuing agitation on this and other aspects of the spoils system in federal employment led to adoption of the Civil Service Reform Act of Jan. 16, 1883, which authorized establishment of Civil Service rules. One of the rules stated

"That no person in the public service is for that reason under any obligation to contribute to any political fund...and that he will not be removed or otherwise prejudiced for refusing to do so." The law made it a crime for any federal employee to solicit campaign funds from another federal employee.

Federal Corrupt Practices Laws

Muckrakers in the early part of the 20th century exposed the influence on government that was exerted by big business through unrestrained spending on behalf of favored candidates. After the 1904 election, a move for federal legislation took shape in the National Publicity Law Association headed by former Rep. Perry Belmont (D N.Y.). President Theodore Roosevelt, in his annual message to Congress on Dec. 5, 1905, proposed that: "All contributions by corporations to any political committee or for any political purpose should be forbidden by law." Roosevelt repeated the proposal in his message of Dec. 3, 1906, suggesting that it be the first item of congressional business.[27]

Tillman Act

In response to the President's urging, Congress on Jan. 26, 1907, passed the Tillman Act, which made it unlawful for a corporation or a national bank to make "a money contribution in connection with any election" of candidates for federal office. Additional regulation of campaign financing was provided in 1910. The new law required every political committee "which shall in the two or more states influence the result or attempt to influence the result of an election at which Representatives in Congress are to be elected" to file with the Clerk of the House of Representatives, within 30 days after the election, the name and address of each contributor of $100 or more, the name and address of each recipient of $10 or more from the committee, and the total amounts that the committee received and disbursed. Individuals who engaged in similar activities outside the framework of committees were also required to submit such reports.

Legislation was passed in 1911 extending the filing requirements to committees influencing senatorial elections and to require filing of financial reports by candidates for the office of either senator or representative. In addition, it required statements to be filed both before and after an election. The most important innovation of the 1911 act was the limitation of the amount that a candidate might spend toward nomination and election: a candidate for the Senate, no more than $10,000 or, if less, the maximum amount permitted in his state; for the House, no more than $5,000 or, if less, the maximum amount permitted in his state.

Corrupt Practices Act

The basic campaign financing law in effect through 1971 was the Federal Corrupt Practices Act, approved Feb. 28, 1925. It limited its restrictions to campaigns for election, in view of the unsettled state at that time of the question whether Congress had power to regulate primary elections. Unless a state law prescribed a smaller amount, the act set the limit of campaign expenditures at (1) $10,000 for a would-be senator and $2,500 for a would-be member of the House; or (2) an amount equal to three cents for each vote cast in the last preceding election for the office sought, but not more than $25,000 for the Senate and $5,000 for the House.

The 1925 act incorporated the existing prohibition of campaign contributions by corporations or national banks, the ban on solicitation of political contributions from federal employees by candidates or other federal employees and the requirement that reports be filed on campaign finances. It prohibited giving or offering money to anyone in exchange for his vote. In amending the provisions of the act of 1907 on contributions, the new law substituted for the word "money" the expression "a gift, subscription, loan, advance, or deposit of money, or anything of value."

The Senate in 1927 barred Senator-elect William S. Vare (R Pa.) from taking his seat after reports indicated that his campaign had cost $785,000. In the same year, the Senate refused to seat Sen.-elect Frank L. Smith (R Ill.). More than 80 per cent of Smith's campaign fund had come from three men who had a direct interest in a decision of the Illinois Commerce Commission, of which Smith continued to be a member throughout the campaign. One of the three donors was Samuel Insull, owner of a controlling interest in a network of utility companies.

In 1934, a case reached the Supreme Court which required the court to rule on, among other things, the constitutionality of the requirement in the 1925 act that lists and amounts of campaign contributions and expenditures be filed publicly. The case, *Burroughs and Cannon v. United States,* involved primarily the applicability of the act to the election of presidential electors. Justice George Sutherland on Jan. 8, 1934, delivered the opinion of the court. Applicability of the act to presidential campaigns was upheld. The decision included the following statement on disclosure: "Congress reached the conclusion that public disclosure of political contributions, together with the names of contributors and other details, would tend to prevent the corrupt use of money to affect elections. The verity of this conclusion reasonably cannot be denied" (290 U.S. 548).

'Clean Politics' and Other Laws

Between the early efforts to regulate spending and the broad reforms of the 1970s, some legislation related to campaign financing had less direct effects than the corrupt practices laws.

Hatch Act

An act of Aug. 2, 1939, commonly called the Hatch Act but also known as the Clean Politics Act, affected campaign financing in only a secondary way. It barred federal employees from active participation in national politics and prohibited collection of political contributions from persons receiving relief funds provided by the federal government. But an amendment to the Hatch Act, approved July 19, 1940, made three significant additions to legislation on campaign financing. It forbade individuals or business concerns doing work for the federal government under contract to contribute to any political committee or candidate. It asserted the right of Congress to regulate primary elections for the nomination of candidates for federal office and made it unlawful for anyone to contribute more than $5,000 "during any calendar year, or in connection with any campaign for nomination or election, to or on behalf of any candidate for an elective federal office." However, the act specifically exempted from this limitation "contributions made to or by a state or local committee." The 1940 amendment also placed a ceiling of $3-million in a calendar year on expenditures by a political committee operating in two or more

states. Legislation in 1943 temporarily, and the Taft-Hartley Act of 1947 permanently, forbade labor unions to contribute to political campaigns from their general funds.

Congress on March 31, 1976, approved legislation to amend the Hatch Act. It would have allowed federal employees to run for federal office and to participate in partisan election campaigns for the first time since enactment of the original Hatch Act. The bill would have permitted workers, except while on federal grounds, to solicit and make political contributions. But President Ford vetoed the bill April 12, saying it would "deny the lessons of history" by "endangering the entire concept of employee independence and freedom from coercion which has been largely successful in preventing undue political influence in government programs or personnel management."[28] The veto was sustained.

Financing of Primary Campaigns

Application of federal laws on campaign financing to primary elections made a complete circuit on the wheel of judicial and legislative fortune. The act of 1911 limiting campaign expenditures in congressional elections covered primaries as well as general elections. However, the Supreme Court in 1921 in *Newberry v. United States* (256 U.S. 232) struck down the application of the law to primaries, on the ground that the power the Constitution gave Congress to regulate the "manner of holding election" did not extend to party primaries and conventions. The Federal Corrupt Practices Act of 1925 exempted primaries from its operation.

The Hatch Act amendments of 1940, as noted, made primaries again subject to federal restrictions on campaign contributions despite the Newberry decision. This new legislation was upheld in 1941, when the Supreme Court handed down its decision in *United States v. Classic et al.* (313 U.S. 299), which reversed the Newberry decision. The *Classic* decision was confirmed by the Supreme Court in 1944 in *Smith v. Allwright* (321 U.S. 649). When the Taft-Hartley Act was adopted in 1947, its prohibition of political contributions by corporations, national banks and labor organizations was phrased so as to cover primaries as well as general elections.

Tax Checkoff

Proponents of governmental subsidization of election campaigns appeared to have won a major victory in 1966. An act approved Nov. 13 of that year authorized any individual paying federal income tax to direct that $1 of the tax due in any year be paid into a Presidential Election Campaign Fund. The fund, to be set up in the U.S. Treasury, was to disburse its receipts, on a proportional basis, among political parties whose presidential candidates had received 5 million or more votes in the preceding presidential election.

However, an act of June 13 of the following year provided that "Funds which become available under the Presidential Election Campaign Fund Act of 1966 shall be appropriated and disbursed only after the adoption by law of guidelines governing their distribution." But Congress failed to adopt any guidelines, so the 1966 act was in effect voided in 1967.

State Laws on Campaign Financing

New York State in 1883 enacted a law prohibiting solicitation of campaign contributions from state employees

State Campaign Financing Laws

State legislatures, feeling the reverberations of the Watergate scandals, responded with a flurry of measures to reform campaign financing laws. Many states, in fact, responded faster than Congress.

The wave of reform began during the 1972 elections, when Washington and Colorado passed "open government" initiatives. In 1973 and 1974, as many as 40 state legislatures enacted 67 measures concerned with limiting campaign contributions and expenditures, and monitoring ethical standards of politicians.

Early in 1976 the reform movement in the states stood as follows:

Campaign Finance Disclosure. Forty-nine of the 50 states had statutes requiring public disclosure of campaign financing. Only North Dakota had no such law. Seven other states did not require disclosure until after the elections had taken place.

Public Financing. Eleven states had some form of tax checkoff or tax add-on (added liability) to help finance elections with public funds. In addition, New Jersey, which had no state income tax at the time, provided matching funds for gubernatorial general elections starting in 1977. Oregon citizens were scheduled to vote on public financing in 1976.

Contribution Limits. Twenty-two states set limits on the amounts of money that individuals could contribute to political campaigns.

Personal Finances. Thirty-eight states required some public officials to disclose their personal finances. In 28 of those 38 states, such laws were either enacted or strengthened in the three years before 1976.

Lobbying Disclosure. All 50 states at least required lobbyists to register. Between November 1972 and 1976, 24 states and the District of Columbia enacted new or stronger lobbying laws.

Open Meetings. From November 1972 to 1976, 27 states adopted or strengthened laws requiring open meetings of public agencies.

Source: Common Cause, March 1976.

and in 1890 required candidates to file sworn financial statements. California in 1893 limited the total amount of money that could be spent on behalf of a candidate and established a list of legitimate campaign expenses. By 1905, some type of regulation of campaign finances was in effect in 14 states. However, Justice Felix Frankfurter, delivering the opinion of the Supreme Court, March 11, 1957, in *United States v. U.A.W.* (352 U.S. 571), said: "These state publicity laws either became dead letters or were found to be futile."

Florida in 1951 adopted a law on campaign financing which often is cited as a model. It requires each candidate to appoint a campaign treasurer and to designate a single bank as the campaign depository. Contributions to the campaign must be deposited within 24 hours of receipt, with deposit slips showing the names and addresses of donors and the amounts contributed by each. Candidates are required to publish periodic reports of campaign expenditures during the campaign, every week in the case of candidates for the U.S. Senate and the governorship and every month in the case of candidates for all other offices.

By 1971, eight states regulated campaign financing by imposing limits on spending by candidates and political committees and by requiring candidates and committees to report receipts and expenditures. Twelve states made some, but not all, of the foregoing requirements. Twenty-one other states had less comprehensive regulations. Nine states—Alaska, Delaware, Georgia, Illinois, Louisiana, Maine, Nevada, Pennsylvania, Rhode Island—had no regulations. Prosecutions for violation of state laws on campaign financing have been rare.

Enforcement and Loopholes

In the six decades from 1907 to 1968, the Tillman Act, the Corrupt Practices Act and other federal laws on campaign financing were rarely enforced. All the campaign regulatory legislation passed through 1925 was largely ignored. Alexander Heard wrote in *The Costs of Democracy* in 1960 that the prohibition in the Federal Corrupt Practices Act of direct purchases of goods or advertising for the benefit of a candidate was "manifestly violated right and left;" that the prohibition of campaign contributions by federal contractors "goes ignored;" and that the prohibition of loans to candidates by banks was "disregarded."[29]

Then, in the late 1960s, Washington's attitude toward enforcement of the Federal Corrupt Practices Act seemed to change. The Nixon administration successfully pressed charges in 1969 against corporations (mostly in California) that had contributed campaign money in 1968.

Another form of violation, failure to report or false reporting under the Corrupt Practices Act, had also been ignored despite the fact that newsmen repeatedly uncovered instances of failure to file reports or the filing of incomplete reports. Attorney General Herbert Brownell in 1954 had stated as the position of the Department of Justice that the initiative in such cases rested with the secretary of the Senate and the clerk of the House, and that policy was continued.

Secretaries of the Senate and clerks of the House for many years winked at violations of the legal requirement that candidates and supporting committees periodically file with them detailed statements of contributions received and disbursements made. The situation changed in 1967 when former Rep. W. Pat Jennings (D Va., 1955-67) was elected clerk of the House. He began sending lists of violations to the Department of Justice for prosecution, but then the department refused to act.

Federal Loopholes

Enforcement efforts could hardly succeed because the federal laws were so flawed. It became common knowledge long ago that the limitations supposedly imposed by campaign financing legislation did not limit, that the prohibitions did not prohibit and that the restrictions did not restrict.

Some loopholes were available to donors. The Corrupt Practices Act required reporting the name and address of every donor of $100 or more to a campaign; a donor could give less than $100 to each of numerous committees supporting his candidate, and the gifts would not be recorded. Members of the same family could legally contribute up to $5,000 each; a wealthy donor could privately subsidize gifts by his relatives to one candidate. Corporations could skirt the prohibition against political contributions by giving bonuses or salary increases to executives in the expectation that they would make corresponding contributions to candidates favored by the corporations. Labor unions could contribute to a candidate or political committee funds collected from members apart from dues. They could also use such funds for nonpartisan registration and voting drives even if the drives were confined to precincts loaded with voters who favored pro-union candidates or to areas where registration was poor for the party they favored.

Other loopholes were available to candidates. The 1925 law referred to candidates' "knowledge or consent" of campaign gifts and expenditures. Thus many candidates, by insisting that all financing be handled by independent committees, could report that they personally received and spent not one cent on their campaigns. In addition, the law applied only to political committees operating in two or more states, and not to those operating in one state only that were not subdivisions of a national committee.

Limits on the expenditures that a political committee could make were evaded by establishing more than one committee and apportioning receipts and expenditures among them so that no one committee exceeded the limit. Since the law limited annual spending by a political committee to $3-million, the major parties formed committees under various names, each of which was free to spend up to $3-million.

Loopholes in State Laws

A law on campaign finances adopted in Massachusetts in 1962 was hailed as uncommonly tough. It limited the number of committees supporting a candidate to three. The law also required that each committee have a bank account, that the bank report money deposited in the account or paid out from it, and that names and addresses of donors of more than $25, and the addresses of persons whose bills were paid, be made public. Despite the supposed stringency of the law, when Edward M. Kennedy in 1964 reported expenditures of $100,292.45 for his successful bid for the Democratic nomination for the U.S. Senate, newspapers estimated that his staff, billboard, television and other expenses amounted to 10 times that sum.

Some state laws exempt from the ceilings and reporting requirements money spent directly on publicity, such as the costs of television and radio spots, advertisements in newspapers and handbills and booklets. Exemptions apply in other states to renting of halls for meetings, hiring of publicity agents and conveyance of voters to and from the polls. Some states require reports from candidates but not committees, or reports on receipts but not expenditures. Places where reports are to be filed, such as the headquarters of the candidate's party, or the place "where the candidate resides," often constitute obstruction rather than promotion of disclosure.

Reform in the 1970s

Government officials, political scientists, public interest organizations and others made dozens of proposals aimed at plugging loopholes in campaign statutes, curtailing inflation of campaign costs, and reducing the threats to democratic ideals that arise from the financial demands of campaigning. Many proposals came from practicing politicians, in and out of Congress. But for decades no action was taken.

Perennial discussions about reforming campaign financing began coming to a head as the 1970s approached. Both sessions of the 91st Congress (1969-70) showed signs of movement. However, only one bill, which concerned allocation of broadcasting time, was passed by both the House and Senate. It was vetoed.

The need for new legislation on campaign financing was acknowledged on all sides when the 92nd Congress convened in 1971. Within five years, Congress passed four major laws which changed the ways in which political campaigns for national office are financed and conducted. Stunned by the campaign abuses that came to light during the Watergate scandals, state governments and the courts also moved to alter the methods of campaign financing.

Tax Checkoff Campaign Fund

After a bitter partisan debate dominated by the approaching 1972 presidential election campaign, Congress on Dec. 8, 1971, approved legislation to establish a federal fund from public tax revenues to finance presidential election campaigns. The measure was initially adopted by the Senate as a non-germane amendment to the Revenue Act of 1971 (PL 92-178) reducing business and individual taxes to stimulate the economy.

A similar plan was cleared by Congress in 1966 but was rendered inoperative in 1967.

As approved by Congress, however, the campaign funding plan was to become effective in time for the 1976 election. House-Senate conferees, faced with a threat by President Nixon to veto the bill, delayed the effective date of the campaign financing provision until after 1972.

At the insistence of House conferees, the conference committee set up to iron out differences between House and Senate versions of the bill also revised the Senate amendment by requiring Congress annually to appropriate to the campaign fund the money designated by federal taxpayers as contributions to presidential campaigns. Citizens first had an opportunity to contribute to the fund on their 1972 federal income tax returns, filed in 1973.

Despite his continued opposition to the campaign funding provision, the President signed the bill Dec. 10. Nixon reportedly planned to leave further challenges to the plan to congressional action or the courts.

Had the plan gone into effect before the 1972 election, about $20.4-million of federal funds would have been made available to each of the major party candidates. About $6.3-million would have been available for Democratic Gov. George C. Wallace (Ala.) running for President as a third-party candidate.

The plan gave each taxpayer the option starting in 1973 of designating $1 of his annual federal income tax payment for use by the presidential candidate of the eligible political party of his choice or for a general campaign fund to be divided among eligible presidential candidates.

Democrats, whose party was $9-million in debt following the 1968 presidential election, said the voluntary tax checkoff was needed to free presidential candidates from obligation to wealthy contributors to their election campaigns.

Republicans, whose party treasury was well stocked, charged that the plan was a device to rescue the Democratic Party from financial difficulty and assure a Wallace candidacy in 1972 that would lessen President Nixon's re-election chances.

Provisions. Officially called the Presidential Election Campaign Fund Act, the 1971 law (PL 92-178) included the following major campaign financing provisions:

● Allowed a tax credit of $12.50 ($25 for a married couple) or, alternatively, a deduction against income of $50 ($100 for a married couple) for political contributions to candidates for local, state or federal office.

● Allowed taxpayers to designate on their federal income tax returns $1 of their tax payment as a contribution to the presidential and vice presidential candidates of the political party of their choice, beginning with the 1972 taxable year.

● As an alternative, allowed taxpayers to contribute to a general fund for all eligible presidential and vice presidential candidates by authorizing $1 of their annual income tax payment to be placed in such a fund.

● Authorized to be distributed to the candidates of each major party (one which obtained 25 per cent of the votes cast in the previous presidential election) an amount equal to 15 cents multiplied by the number of U.S. residents age 18 and over.

● Established a formula for allocating public campaign funds to candidates of minor parties whose candidates received 5 per cent or more but less than 25 per cent of the previous presidential election vote.

● Authorized payments after the election to reimburse the campaign expenses of a new party whose candidate received enough votes to be eligible or of an existing minor party whose candidate increased its vote to the qualifying level.

● Prohibited major party candidates who chose public financing of their election campaign from accepting private campaign contributions unless their shares of funds contributed through the income tax check-off procedure fell short of the amounts to which they were entitled.

● Prohibited a major party candidate who chose public financing and all campaign committees authorized by the candidate from spending more than the mount to which the candidate was entitled under the contributions formula.

● Provided penalties of $5,000 or one year in prison, or both, for candidates or campaign committees which spent more on a campaign than the amounts they received from the campaign fund or which accepted private contributions when sufficient public funds were available.

● Provided penalties of $10,000 or five years in prison, or both, for candidates or campaign committees which used public campaign funds for unauthorized expenses, gave or accepted kickbacks or illegal payments involving public campaign funds or knowingly furnished false information to the Comptroller General.

Campaign Fund Status. At first, relatively few taxpayers bothered to designate their $1 payments for the presidential campaign fund. But participation increased as more people became aware of the fund, as the checkoff feature was displayed more prominently on income tax forms, and as the 1976 presidential campaign drew closer. The Internal Revenue Service reported that payments were authorized on 23.9 per cent of the 1974 tax forms, higher than any previous year. But 25.9 per cent of the 1975 forms tabulated through July 1976 designated payments to the fund.

Although participation was not as high as proponents of public-supported elections may have hoped, the fund grew steadily. The fund received $4-million for the 1972 tax year, $26.2-million for 1973, $31.8-million for 1974, and $33.4-million for 1975 (tabulated through July 1976)—for a total of $95.4-million. The Federal Election Commission reported

in September 1976 that it had disbursed $24.1-million in matching funds to 15 presidential candidates and $3.9-million combined for the Democratic and Republican national conventions. The two nominees, President Ford and Jimmy Carter, were slated to receive $21.8-million each for the 1976 general election campaign.

1971-1976 Election Law Changes

The income tax checkoff and public financing of presidential campaigns was the beginning of extensive election law reforms that were to be passed over the following five years.

Laws passed in 1971 (PL 92-225), 1974 (PL 93-443) and 1976 (PL 94-283) placed limits on contributions, imposed some expenditure limits, required public disclosure of campaign financing details and set up a federal commission to enforce the law.

Provisions. The major provisions of the three laws dealing with candidates and committees, reporting, contributions, expenditures, publication and broadcast notices, the Federal Election Commission and compliance and penalties are compared in tabular form beginning on page 553. *(For contribution limits, see box p. 75)*

Immediately following are highlights of action on the three laws and summaries of important sections of each law.

1971 Federal Election Law

The first major reform following the tax checkoff law went into effect early in 1972 with enactment of the Federal Election Campaign Act of 1971 (PL 92-225). The law placed a ceiling on expenditures by candidates for President, Vice President, the Senate or the House, and required full disclosure of campaign contributions and expenditures. The law went into effect April 7, 1972, 60 days after it was signed by the President.

The heart of the new law was the spending ceiling of 10 cents per eligible voter for all forms of media advertising—radio and television time, newspapers, magazines, billboards and automatic telephone equipment.

Attempts at reform began early in the 92nd Congress when numerous bills to reform election campaigning were introduced in the House and the Senate. President Nixon was committed to a major overhaul of campaign practices. In October 1970, he had vetoed a bill to limit broadcast spending by candidates for President, Congress and governor. The bill set ceilings on general election campaign broadcast spending by candidates at seven cents per vote cast in the previous election. It also repealed the equal time provision of the 1934 Communications Act for presidential and vice presidential candidates.

In vetoing the bill, Nixon said it would have discriminated against broadcasters, would have given an unfair advantage to incumbents and would not have provided much needed overall campaign reform.[30]

Pressure for Reform. The 1968 and 1970 federal election campaigns saw a skyrocketing of political campaign spending by both major parties. There also was a profusion of affluent candidates which made political spending a major campaign issue in itself. By 1971, after Nixon's veto of the first reform bill, members came under considerable pressure to pass a bill that would be applicable to the 1972 presidential and congressional elections. Even as the proposals were being introduced, potential candidates from both major parties were collecting and spending sizable amounts to finance campaign organizations in preparation for the elections.

Proponents of reform, cognizant of the partisan considerations that could have threatened any revision of campaign laws, worked to avoid writing a law that would favor any political party or candidate. Republicans, aware of the relatively healthy financial condition of their party in 1971, were eager to protect their coffers; Democrats did not want to jeopardize their large contributions from organized labor.

The reform thrust was also pushed by various groups outside Congress, including the National Committee for an Effective Congress, the chief pressure group, the self-styled citizens' lobby Common Cause, labor unions and some media organizations.

Key Provisions. The Federal Election Campaign Act of 1971 (PL 92-225) was the first major election reform law to be passed since the Federal Corrupt Practices Act of 1925. Major provisions included the following:

● Limited the amount that could be spent by federal candidates for advertising time in communications media to 10 cents per eligible voter, or $50,000, whichever was greater. Included in the definition of "communications media" were radio and television broadcasting stations, newspapers, magazines, billboards and automatic telephone equipment. Of the total amount permitted to be spent in a campaign, up to 60 per cent could be used for broadcast advertising time.

● Defined "election" to mean any general, special, primary or runoff election, nominating convention or caucus, delegate selection primary, presidential preference primary or constitutional convention.

● Prohibited promises of employment or other political rewards or benefits by any candidate in exchange for political support, and prohibited contracts between candidates and any federal department or agency.

● Placed a ceiling on contributions by any candidate or his immediate family to his own campaign of $50,000 for President or Vice President, $35,000 for senator, and $25,000 for representative.

● Required all political committees that anticipated receipts in excess of $1,000 during the calendar year to file a statement of organization with the appropriate federal supervisory officer, which was to include the names of all principal officers, the scope of the committee, the names of all candidates the committee supported and other information as required by law.

● Stipulated that the appropriate federal supervisory officer to oversee election campaign practices, reporting and disclosure was the clerk of the House for House candidates, the secretary of the Senate for Senate candidates and the comptroller general of the General Accounting Office (GAO) for presidential candidates.

● Required each political committee to report any individual expenditure of more than $100 and any expenditures of more than $100 in the aggregate during the calendar year.

● Required disclosure of all contributions to any committee or candidate in excess of $100, including a detailed report with the name and address of the contributor and the date the contribution was made.

● Required candidates and committees to file reports of contributions and expenditures on the 10th day of March, June and September of every year, on the 15th and fifth days preceding the date on which an election was held and on the 31st day of January. Any contribution of $5,000 or more was to be reported within 48 hours after its receipt.

● Required reporting of the names, addresses and occupations of any lender and endorser of any loan in excess of $100 as well as the date and amount of such loans.

● Required reporting of the total proceeds from the sales of tickets to all fund-raising events, mass collections made at such events and sales of political campaign materials.

● Required any person who made any contribution in excess of $100, other than through a political committee or directly to the candidate, to report such contribution to the appropriate supervisory officer.

● Prohibited any contribution to a candidate or committee by one person in the name of another person.

Loopholes in the Act of 1971

The 1972 presidential and congressional elections highlighted some major failures of the new spending law. A loophole that existed previously that was not satisfactorily corrected was the "pass-through" political contribution. This occurs when a donor gives a sum of money to another person, committee or organization who in turn hands over the money, according to the wishes of the original donor, to a candidate for public office.

Although the pass-through tactic was prohibited under PL 92-225 in 1971, a loophole was created which allowed an organization such as a social club, which was not established primarily to influence the outcome of an election, to use some of its dues for such purposes. If the organization contributed to a particular candidate an amount exceeding $1,000, it would have to report the total amount, but the names of the contributors would be shielded from public view. There was no requirement in the law to force such an organization to disclose the names of its members who had paid the dues which eventually became the political donation.

Another loophole was the loose definition of the word "candidate" in Title I of the law establishing media spending limitations for candidates. The language was construed in such a way as to permit persons to accept contributions and to spend money to aid their own prospects for public office and still not come under the law's spending ceiling for political advertising of 10 cents per eligible voter. The definition, moreover, was narrower than that contained in Titles II and III of the same law or that used by the Federal Communications Commission in dealing with requests for political broadcast time. Thus the Title I definition permitted unlimited spending during a time when a person might be a candidate in every way but name. Presidential candidates, for example, in recent years had made a habit of running unannounced for long periods before making an official announcement of candidacy, sometimes almost up to the eve of the first presidential primary.

A continuing tax loophole that was not plugged was the exemption from federal gift taxes of political contributions under $3,000. It was evident from the 1972 campaigns that many persons had contributed substantially more than this amount to a single candidate—while avoiding the gift tax —by making more than one donation under $3,000 to numerous political committees working on behalf of the same candidate.

A big loophole that showed up during 1972 was in the use of loans to candidates. While the law provided that all debts had to be reported until they were terminated, it was silent on the means by which such loans were to be paid off. Thus a supporter of a particular candidate could forgive a debt to him or require only a token payment on the loan, and the report that was later made public would indicate only that the debt had been terminated. The source of the loan would not have to be named.

A related loophole involved the provision limiting the amount that a candidate or his immediate family could contribute to his own campaign. The restriction did not apply to relatives of the family, and there was no regulation against a member of a family giving the maximum contribution allowed and, in addition, making a loan to the candidate.

A serious flaw according to many observers was the failure of Congress to approve an independent election campaign commission to monitor and enforce the law, particularly Title I setting spending limits. Under the arrangement finally agreed to in PL 92-225, the clerk of the House was responsible for overseeing House elections, the secretary of the Senate for Senate elections and the comptroller general of the GAO for presidential elections.

One of the defects of this procedure was the way in which the Justice Department was given responsibility for prosecuting any violations brought to its attention by the House or Senate overseers or by the comptroller general. While Justice was required to act in any civil case, the language of the law allowed the department complete discretion in deciding whether or not to prosecute in criminal cases.

It was reported that during the 1972 campaigns the department had only one full-time attorney supervising enforcement of the act.

Enforcement was further impeded by another provision in the law requiring periodic reporting of contributions and expenditures. According to many members of Congress, the frequency required for the filing of these reports during election campaigns by all political committees of candidates—required for both primary and general elections—created monumental bookkeeping chores for the candidates. Correspondingly, the mammoth number of reports filed with the House clerk, the Senate secretary and the comptroller general made closer scrutiny practically impossible.

Under the law, only contributions "in excess of $100" had to be reported and thus made public. Some members felt this language went counter to the intent of the act to open up the election process because it shielded from public view substantial sums donated in amounts of $100 and less.

Efforts to Amend 1971 Act

The Senate in 1972 refused to consider a bill passed earlier by the House to modify a provision of the Federal Election Campaign Act of 1971 prohibiting corporations and labor unions having federal government contracts from making direct political contributions to candidates for federal office. The House-passed bill would have allowed these corporations and unions to engage in the same kinds of political activity as those not having government contracts.

The Senate in 1973, motivated in part by the Watergate scandals, twice voted to tighten federal laws on financing of political campaigns. Portions of the legislation were opposed by House members responsible for initiating such legislation, and House action went no further than the hearings stage.

However, the failure of campaign reform legislation in 1973 did not mean that it was dead in the second session. Soon after Congress reconvened following its Christmas recess, the Senate Rules and Administration Committee began work on a comprehensive public financing bill. Many

---

T. R. and the 1974 Law

The 1974 campaign financing law works against the stability of minor parties by allowing a presidential candidate who qualifies for public financing in one election to take the money with him if he switches parties in the next election.

If the new law had been in effect in 1912, for example, Theodore Roosevelt, the Progressive Party candidate that year, would have become eligible for full public financing in 1916, because he polled 27 per cent of the vote with his "Bull Moose" campaign. Winning more than 25 per cent would have given him major-party status.

In the same election, the Republican Party, under whose banner Roosevelt had served as President from 1901 until 1909, collected only 23 per cent of the vote and thus would have been a minor party in 1916 and would have had only partial public financing.

But if Roosevelt had rejoined the Republicans and been their candidate in 1916, they would have taken the full public funding away from the Progressives.

---

reforms which the Senate had passed previously were incorporated in the new legislation.

1974 Campaign Act Amendments

Almost two and a half years after it passed the Federal Election Campaign Act of 1971 that was a factor in breaking open the Watergate scandal, Congress, reacting to presidential campaign abuses, enacted another landmark campaign reform bill that substantially overhauled the existing system of financing election campaigns. Technically the 1974 law (PL 93-443) was a set of amendments to the 1971 legislation, but in fact it was the most comprehensive of the three campaign reform laws passed in the early 1970s.

The new measure, which President Ford signed into law Oct. 15, established the first spending limits ever for candidates in presidential primary and general elections and in primary campaigns for the House and Senate. It set new expenditure ceilings for general election campaigns for Congress to replace the limits established by the 1925 Federal Corrupt Practices Act that were never effectively enforced and were repealed in the 1971 law. Further changes were made in 1976. (See table p. 75)

The 1974 law also introduced the first use of public money to pay for political campaign costs by providing for optional public financing in presidential general election campaigns and establishing federal matching grants to cover up to 45 per cent of the cost of presidential primary campaigns. The final bill did not contain Senate-passed provisions for partial public financing of congressional campaigns.

Major Provisions. The major sections of PL 93-443 established contribution and expenditure limits and created a Federal Election Commission to enforce the law. The expenditure, contribution and other provisions were affected by a 1976 Supreme Court decision and subsequently revised by Congress. These and other major provisions are compared in tabular form beginning on page 81. Immediately below are details of the law's public financing and disclosure provisions.

Public Financing. PL 93-443 made the following provisions for public financing:

● Presidential general elections—voluntary public financing. Major party candidates would automatically qualify for full funding before the campaign. Minor party and independent candidates would be eligible to receive a proportion of full funding based on past or current votes received. If a candidate opted for full public funding, no private contributions would be permitted.

● Presidential nominating conventions—optional public funding. Major parties would automatically qualify. Minor parties would be eligible for lesser amounts based on their proportion of votes received in a past or current election.

● Presidential primaries—matching public funds of up to $5-million per candidate after meeting fund-raising requirement of $100,000 raised in amounts of at least $5,000 in each of 20 states or more. Only the first $250 of individual private contributions would be matched. The matching funds were to be divided among the candidates as quickly as possible. In allocating the money, the order in which the candidates qualified would be taken into account. Only private gifts raised after Jan. 1, 1975, would qualify for matching for the 1976 election. No federal payments would be made before January 1976.

● All federal money for public funding of campaigns would come from the Presidential Election Campaign Fund. Money received from the federal income tax dollar checkoff would be automatically appropriated to the fund.

Disclosure. PL 93-443 made the following stipulations for disclosure and reporting dates:

● Required each candidate to establish one central campaign committee through which all contributions and expenditures on behalf of a candidate must be reported. Required designation of specific bank depositories of campaign funds.

● Required full reports of contributions and expenditures to be filed with the Federal Election Commission 10 days before and 30 days after every election, and within 10 days of the close of each quarter unless the committee received or expended less than $1,000 in that quarter. A year-end report was due in non-election years.

● Required that contributions of $1,000 or more received within the last 15 days before an election be reported to the commission within 48 hours.

● Prohibited contributions in the name of another.

● Treated loans as contributions. Required a cosigner or guarantor for each $1,000 of outstanding obligation.

● Required every person who spent or contributed over $100 other than to or through a candidate or political committee to report.

● Permitted government contractors, unions and corporations to maintain separate, segregated political funds. (Formerly all contributions by government contractors were prohibited.)

Enforcement, Penalties. The 1974 law set up a Federal Election Commission to enforce the law and spelled out detailed and stringent penalties. However, the Supreme Court in 1976 *(see following section)* declared the method of appointing commissioners unconstitutional. Congress then rewrote the commission appointment procedures and in the process made many other changes in the law. Major changes, including those involving enforcement and penalties, are summarized in the text beginning on page 74.

1976 Supreme Court Decision

As soon as the Campaign Act Amendments of 1974 took effect, the law was challenged in court. Several plaintiffs filed suit against PL 93-443 on Jan. 2, 1975.

The plaintiffs included Sen. James L. Buckley (Cons-R N.Y.), former Sen. Eugene J. McCarthy (D Minn. 1959-71), the New York Civil Liberties Union and *Human Events,* a conservative publication.

Their basic arguments were that the law's new limits on campaign contributions and expenditures curbed the freedom of contributors and candidates to express themselves in the political marketplace and that the public financing provisions discriminated against minor parties and lesser-known candidates in favor of the major parties and better-known candidates.

The U.S. Court of Appeals for the District of Columbia on Aug. 14, 1975, upheld all of the law's major provisions, thus setting the stage for Supreme Court action.

The Supreme Court handed down its ruling *(Buckley v. Valeo)* on Jan. 30, 1976, in an unsigned 137-page opinion. In five separate, signed opinions, several justices concurred with and dissented from separate issues in the case.

In its decision, the court upheld the provisions of PL 93-443 that:

● Set limits on how much individuals and political committees may contribute to candidates.

● Provided for the public financing of presidential primary and general election campaigns.

● Required the disclosure of campaign contributions of more than $100 and campaign expenditures of more than $10.

But the court overturned other features of the law, ruling that the campaign spending limits were unconstitutional violations of the First Amendment guarantee of free expression. For presidential candidates who accepted federal matching funds, however, the ceiling on expenditures remained intact. The court also struck down the method for selecting members of the Federal Election Commission, the agency established to oversee and enforce the 1974 law.

"A restriction on the amount of money a person or group can spend on political communication during a campaign necessarily reduces the quantity of expression," the court stated, "by restricting the number of issues discussed, the depth of their exploration and the size of the audience reached. This is because virtually every means of communicating ideas in today's mass society requires the expenditure of money." Only Justice Byron R. White dissented on this point; he would have upheld the limitations.

Although the court acknowledged that both contribution limits and spending limits had First Amendment implications, it distinguished between the two by saying that the act's "expenditure ceilings impose significantly more severe restrictions on protected freedom of political expression and association than do its limitations on financial contributions."

The court removed all the limits imposed on political spending and, by so doing, weakened the effect of the contribution ceilings. The law had placed spending limits on House, Senate and presidential campaigns and on party nominating conventions. To plug a loophole in the contribution limits, it also placed a $1,000 annual limit on how much an individual could spend independently on behalf of a candidate.

The independent expenditure ceiling, the opinion said, was a clear violation of the First Amendment. "While the...ceiling thus fails to serve any substantial government interest in stemming the reality or appearance of corruption in the electoral process, it heavily burdens core First Amendment expression," the court wrote. "...Advocacy of the election or defeat of candidates for federal office is no less entitled to protection under the First Amendment than the discussion of political policy generally or advocacy of the passage or defeat of legislation."

The court struck down the limits on how much of their own money candidates could spend on their campaigns. The law had set a $25,000 limit on House candidates, $35,000 on Senate candidates and $50,000 on presidential candidates. "The candidate, no less than any other person, has a First Amendment right to engage in the discussion of public issues and vigorously and tirelessly to advocate his own election and the election of other candidates," the opinion said.

The ruling made it possible for a wealthy candidate to finance his own campaign and thus to avoid the limits on how much others could give him. That aspect did not concern the court, which wrote that "the use of personal funds reduces the candidate's dependence on outside contributions and thereby counteracts the coercive pressures and attendant risks of abuse to which the act's contribution limitations are directed."

Associate Justice Byron R. White dissented on expenditure limits. Rejecting the argument that money is speech, he wrote that there are "many expensive campaign activities that are not themselves communicative or remotely related to speech." Furthermore, he wrote, the expenditure and contribution limits are integral to the spending limit, "lessening the chance that the contribution ceiling will be violated."

Associate Justice Thurgood Marshall rejected the court's reasoning in striking down the limit on how much candidates may spend on their own campaigns. "It would appear to follow," he said, "that the candidate with a substantial personal fortune at his disposal is off to a significant 'head start.' " Moreover, he added, keeping the limitations on contributions but not on spending "put[s] a premium on a candidate's personal wealth."

Federal Election Commission. The court held unanimously that the Federal Election Commission was unconstitutional. The court said the method of appointment of commissioners violated the Constitution's separation-of-powers and appointments clauses because some members were named by congressional officials but exercised executive powers.

The justices refused to accept the argument that the commission, because it oversaw congressional as well as presidential elections, could have congressionally appointed members. "We see no reason to believe that the authority of Congress over federal election practices is of such a wholly different nature from the other grants of authority to Congress that it may be employed in such a manner as to offend well established constitutional restrictions stemming from the separation of powers," the court wrote.

According to the decision, the commission may exercise only those powers Congress is allowed to delegate to congressional committees—investigating and information-gathering. Only if the commission's members were appointed by the President, as required under the Constitution's appointments clause, could the commission carry out the administrative and enforcement responsibilities the law originally gave it, the court ruled.

That last action put Congress on the spot, because the justices stayed their ruling for 30 days—until Feb. 29—to give the House and Senate time to "reconstitute the commission by law or adopt other valid enforcement mechanisms." As things developed, Congress took much longer than 30 days to act, and instead of merely reconstituting the commission it passed a whole new campaign financing law.

Supporters and opponents of the 1974 law hailed the court's ruling, with each side claiming victory. John Gardner, chairman of Common Cause, called the decision a triumph "for all those who have worked so hard to clean up politics in this country. The fat cats won't be able to buy elections or politicians any more." Sen. Buckley said the court "struck a major blow for the forces of freedom" by allowing unchecked political spending. But Buckley added that the court had left standing "a clearly unworkable set of ground rules" that Congress would have to revise.

Campaign Act Amendments of 1976

The court decision forced Congress to return to campaign finance legislation for the fourth time in five years. The 1976 election campaign was already underway, but the court said that the Federal Election Commission could not continue to disburse public funds to presidential candidates as long as some commission members were congressional appointees.

Congress did not begin its work until late February. The court extended the original Feb. 29 deadline until March 22, but the extra three weeks still did not give Congress the time members wanted to revise the law. One result was that for two months after March 22 the presidential candidates did not receive the federal matching funds they had expected.

President Ford had wanted only a simple reconstitution of the commission, but Congress insisted on going much further and writing an extensive new campaign finance law. The new law, arrived at after much maneuvering and arguing between Democrats and Republicans, closed old loopholes in existing law and opened new ones, depending on the point of view of the observer.

In its basic provision, the law (PL 94-283), signed by the President May 11, reconstituted the Federal Election Commission as a six-member panel appointed by the President and confirmed by the Senate.

Commission members could not engage in outside business activities. The commission was given exclusive

---

Unchanged Provisions

The Federal Election Campaign Act amendments of 1976 (PL 94-283) did not change the following provisions of the 1974 campaign finance legislation:

● The public financing provisions for presidential campaigns.

● Spending limits for the prenomination and general election campaigns of presidential candidates accepting public funds.

● The prohibition against political contributions by foreign nationals, earmarked contributions and cash contributions of more than $100.

● The dates by which campaign finance reports have to be filed with the election commission.

● The 30-legislative-day time period for Congress to disapprove election commission regulations.

Limits on Campaign Contributions

This table shows the limits on campaign contributions for federal elections. The figures are those in effect following the 1976 amendments to the 1971 and 1974 financing laws.

Contribution from:	To candidate or his/her authorized committee	**To national party committees[5] (per calendar year)[6]	**To any other committee (per calendar year)[6]	Total contributions (per calendar year)[7]
Individual	$1,000 per election[3]	$20,000	$5,000	$25,000
Multicandidate committee[1]	$5,000 per election	$15,000	$5,000	No limit
Party committee	$1,000 or $5,000[4] per election	No limit	$5,000	No limit
Republican or Democratic senatorial campaign committee,[2] or the national party committee, or a combination of both**	$17,500 to Senate candidate per calendar year[6] in which candidate seeks election	Not applicable	Not applicable	Not applicable
Any other committee	$1,000 per election	$20,000	$5,000	No limit

1. A multicandidate committee is any committee with more than 50 contributors which has been registered for at least six months and, with the exception of state party committees, has made contributions to five or more federal candidates.
2. Republican and Democratic senatorial campaign committees are subject to all other limits applicable to a multicandidate committee.
3. Each of the following elections is considered a separate election: primary election, general election, run-off election, special election, and party caucus or convention which, instead of a primary, has authority to select the nominee.
4. Limit depends on whether or not party committee is a multicandidate committee.
** See footnote 6.

5. For purposes of this limit, national party committees include a party's national committee, the Republican and Democratic Senate and House campaign committees and any other committee established by the party's national committee, provided they are not authorized by any candidate.
6. In 1976 only, and solely in the case of contribution limits established in the 1976 amendments (those indicated by double asterisk), the calendar year extends from May 11 (date of enactment of the act) through Dec. 31, 1976.
7. Calendar year extends from Jan. 1 through Dec. 31, 1976. Individual contributions made or earmarked before or after 1976 to influence the 1976 election of a specific candidate are counted as if made during 1976.

Source: Federal Election Commission.

authority to prosecute civil violations of the campaign finance law and was vested with jurisdiction over violations formerly covered only in the criminal code, thus strengthening its power to enforce the law.

A major controversy that delayed enactment was the insistence of organized labor that corporate fund-raising activity through political action committees be curtailed. Labor won some but not all of its goal. The final law permitted company committees to seek contributions only from stockholders, executives and administrative personnel and their families. It restricted union political action committees to soliciting contributions from union members and their families. However, twice a year, union and corporate political action committees were permitted to seek campaign contributions by mail only from all employees. Contributions would have to remain anonymous and would be received by an independent third party that would keep records but pass the money to the committees.

The final bill also included provisions restricting the commission's use of advisory opinions and giving Congress the power to veto discrete sections of commission regulations. President Ford objected particularly to the latter provision. He said the provision "not only circumvents the original intent of campaign reform but, in my opinion, violates the Constitution." He directed the Justice Department to challenge the constitutionality of the provision in court.

The final bill also contained another provision prompted by the Supreme Court decision. In addition to finding the make-up of the election commission unconstitutional, the court had thrown out the 1974 law's limitations on independent political expenditures as a clear violation of the First Amendment. Members of Congress feared that the ruling would open a major new loophole. As a result, they included a provision in the new bill requiring that political committees and individuals making independent political expenditures of more than $100 to advocate the defeat or election of a candidate swear that the expenditures were not made in collusion with the candidate.

Other Major Provisions. The 1976 legislation also revised contribution limits *(see table above)* and contained these other important provisions:

● Required an affirmative vote of four members for the commission to issue regulations and advisory opinions and initiate civil actions and investigations.

● Required labor unions, corporations and membership organizations to report expenditures of over $2,000 per election for communications to their stockholders or members advocating the election or defeat of a clearly identified candidate. The costs of communications to members or stockholders on issues would not have to be reported.

● Required that candidates and political committees keep records of contributions of $50 or more. The 1974 law required records of contributions of $10 or more.

● Required that independent expenditures of $1,000 or more made within 15 days of an election be reported within 24 hours.

● Limited the commission to issuing advisory opinions only for specific fact situations. Advisory opinions could not be used to spell out commission policy. Advisory opinions were not to be considered as precedents unless an activity was "indistinguishable in all its material aspects" from an activity already covered by an advisory opinion.

● Permitted the commission to initiate investigations only after it received a properly verified complaint or had reason to believe, based on information it obtained in the normal course of its duties, that a violation had occurred or was about to occur. The commission was barred from relying on anonymous complaints to institute investigations.

● Required the commission to rely initially on conciliation to deal with alleged campaign law violations before going to court.

● Restricted the proliferation of membership organization, corporate and union political action committees. All political action committees established by a company or an international union would be treated as a single committee for contribution purposes. The contributions of political action committees of a company or union would be limited to no more than $5,000 overall to the same candidate in any election.

● Raised the limit on honoraria members of Congress and federal employees may receive to $2,000 per individual event and a total of $25,000 a year from $1,000 per individual event and a total of $15,000 a year. The $25,000 limit was a net amount; booking agents' fees, travel expenditures, subsistence and expenses for an aide or a spouse to accompany the speaker could be deducted.

● Provided for a one-year jail sentence and a fine of up to $25,000 or three times the amount of the contribution or expenditure involved in the violation, whichever was greater, if an individual was convicted of knowingly committing a campaign law violation that involved more than $1,000.

● Provided for civil penalties of fines of $5,000 or an amount equal to the contribution or expenditure involved in the violation, whichever was greater. For violations knowingly committed, the fine would be $10,000 or an amount equal to twice the amount involved in the violation, whichever was greater. The fines could be imposed by the courts or by the commission in conciliation agreements. The 1974 law included penalties for civil violations of a $1,000 fine and/or a one-year prison sentence.

● Limited spending by presidential candidates to no more than $50,000 of their own, or their family's money, on their campaigns, if they accepted public financing.

● Cut off federal campaign subsidies to a presidential candidate who won less than 10 per cent of the vote in two consecutive presidential primaries in which he ran.

Commission Reconstituted. The President appointed six members of the new commission in May soon after signing the legislation. The commission was formally reconsituted May 21 and tax funds began to flow to candidates for the presidency soon after.

Impact of Interest Groups on 1976 Elections

Labor and liberal backers of Democratic candidates had the most to celebrate Nov. 2, 1976.

In a year of low overall voter turnout in most areas outside of the South, organized labor's efforts to bring out the union vote in such key states as Ohio, Pennsylvania and New York clearly saved Jimmy Carter from defeat. The same efforts contributed to a relatively easy sweep of the congressional races by the Democrats, keeping the heavy Democratic majorities in both the House and Senate largely intact.

"We put out our biggest effort ever," said a spokesman for the AFL-CIO's Committee on Political Education (COPE), noting that it paid off with the election of COPE's choices in 19 Senate races and 258 House races—as well as Jimmy Carter.

In the House, relatively few seats changed hands, and incumbents in both parties proved difficult to beat. Labor and liberal groups were especially pleased with the high proportion of Democratic freshmen who survived; all but three of the 76 first-term Democrats were re-elected, despite a determined drive by conservative and business-related interest groups to unseat them. Even several liberal freshmen in normally conservative districts—such as Martha Keys (D Kan.) and Bob Carr (D Mich.)—won by larger than expected margins after closely fought campaigns.

On balance, though, the Senate results left interest groups on each side of the political spectrum only partly satisfied. Democrats with strong labor and liberal support picked up seats in Maryland, Tennessee, New York, Hawaii and Arizona, while the losing candidates had solid backing from business and conservative interests.

Higher Contributions

Ironically, interest groups—particularly those associated with business and conservative interests—could owe much of their prominence in the 1976 elections to the new campaign finance law.

By limiting individual contributions to $1,000 per election, the law almost certainly encouraged wealthy donors to give more heavily to multi-candidate political action committees than they had in the past. As amended in May 1976, the 1974 law placed ceilings of $5,000 per election on individucal contributions to the committees, which then could give up to $5,000 per candidate per race (primary, general and special elections).

According to Common Cause, the self-styled citizens' lobby, 1,041 interest group committees had registered with the Federal Election Commission by Sept. 1—more than twice the number in operation for the 1974 congressional elections. Corporations and trade associations were responsible for most of this proliferation, but labor committees expanded modestly as well.

As a result, contributions from interest group committees to congressional races nearly doubled between 1974 and 1976. For the first time, business-related groups appeared to be outspending labor committees; by October 1, business, professional and agricultural groups already had put $7.5-million into the 1976 campaigns—compared with $5.8-million from their labor counterparts. Business interests also directed more money toward Democratic incumbents than they had in previous elections, reflecting greater pragmatism and less ideological uniformity in their candidate choices. *(Box, p. 77)*

Eleven of the 20 House candidates to receive the most money from labor groups were freshman Democrats, and all won re-election. Fifteen out of 20 of the leading recipients of business, professional and agricultural groups' contributions were successful.

In the Senate, nine out of the 15 candidates receiving the most financial support from labor won, compared with six out of the top 15 business recipients.[31]

Interest-Group Contributions to Congressional Campaigns

From January 1, 1975, through September 30, 1976, congressional candidates received about $14.9-million from registered special interest groups. More than half of this amount—or about $7.5-million—came from committees identified with business, professional or agricultural interests. During the same time period, labor groups contributed $5.8-million.

The House and Senate candidates receiving the most interest-group money from labor and business sources are shown below. The ordering of the top recipients in each category is based on amounts contributed as of October 1.

Labor Groups

Senate

1.	*Harrison A. Williams Jr. (D N.J.)	$125,525
2.	*Vance Hartke (D Ind.)	122,350
3.	*John V. Tunney (D Calif.)	119,273
4.	*Hubert H. Humphrey (D Minn.)	113,821
5.	William J. Green (D Pa.)	108,515
6.	Paul S. Sarbanes (D Md.)	103,150
7.	Howard M. Metzenbaum (D Ohio)	80,423
8.	Elmo R. Zumwalt Jr. (D Va.)	77,030
9.	Daniel P. Moynihan (D N.Y.)	73,833
10.	James R. Sasser (D Tenn.)	73,675
11.	*Frank E. Moss (D Utah)	71,075
12.	Donald W. Riegle Jr. (D Mich.)	70,135
13.	*Edward M. Kennedy (D Mass.)	62,350
14.	*Joseph M. Montoya (D N.M.)	57,200
15.	Dennis DeConcini (D Ariz.)	45,200

House

1.	Jim Mattox (D Texas 5th)	$ 43,500
2.	*Martin A. Russo (D Ill. 3rd)	37,750
3.	*Thomas L. Ashley (D Ohio 9th)	34,050
4.	*Michael T. Blouin (D Iowa 2nd)	30,175
5.	*Floyd Fithian (D Ind. 2nd)	29,800
6.	*John H. Dent (D Pa. 21st)	29,750
7.	*Les AuCoin (D Ore. 1st)	29,740
8.	*Leo C. Zeferetti (D N.Y. 15th)	29,433
9.	*Lloyd Meeds (D Wash. 2nd)	28,850
10.	*Robert W. Edgar (D Pa. 7th)	28,160
11.	Lanny Davis (D Md. 8th)	28,027
12.	*William Lehman (D Fla. 13th)	27,800
13.	*Mark W. Hannaford (D Calif. 34th)	27,150
14.	*Charles J. Carney (D Ohio 19th)	26,850
15.	*Edward Mezvinsky (D Iowa 1st)	26,700
16.	*John L. Burton (D Calif. 5th)	26,650
17.	*James J. Blanchard (D Mich. 18th)	26,375
18.	*Martha Keys (D Kan. 2nd)	26,310
19.	*Thomas J. Downey (D N.Y. 2nd)	26,175
20.	*James J. Florio (D N.J. 1st)	26,150

Business, Professional, Agricultural Groups

Senate

1.	*Lloyd Bentsen (D Texas)	$131,839
2.	*Robert Taft Jr. (R Ohio)	131,690
3.	*Vance Hartke (D Ind.)	96,350
4.	*Bill Brock (R Tenn.)	90,755
5.	*J. Glenn Beall Jr. (R Md.)	85,245
6.	*James L. Buckley (Cons-R N.Y.)	71,885
7.	*Harry F. Byrd Jr. (Ind Va.)	70,549
8.	*Harrison A. Williams Jr. (D N.J.)	69,723
9.	Richard Lugar (R Ind.)	64,593
10.	Marvin L. Esch (R Mich.)	64,138
11.	John Y. McCollister (R Neb.)	56,575
12.	S. I. Hayakawa (R Calif.)	52,697
13.	*John V. Tunney (D Calif.)	45,427
14.	Sam Steiger (R Ariz.)	45,148
15.	John C. Danforth (R Mo.)	42,170

House

1.	*John J. Rhodes (R Ariz. 1st)	$ 70,450
2.	*Samuel L. Devine (R Ohio 12th)	45,300
3.	*Ron Paul (R Texas 22nd)	41,150
4.	*Donald D. Clancy (R Ohio 2nd)	40,950
5.	*Jerry M. Patterson (D Calif. 38th)	39,405
6.	*Carroll Hubbard Jr. (D Ky. 1st)	38,550
7.	*John J. McFall (D Calif. 14th)	35,425
8.	*John W. Jenrette Jr. (D S.C. 6th)	34,600
9.	*Jim Wright (D Texas 12th)	32,905
10.	*Joe D. Waggonner Jr. (D La. 4th)	31,100
11.	*Robert Krueger (D Texas 21st)	31,100
12.	*Gene Taylor (R Mo. 7th)	30,050
13.	*Ted Risenhoover (D Okla. 2nd)	30,000
14.	*Richard Kelly (R Fla. 5th)	29,850
15.	David G. Crane (R Ind. 6th)	29,400
16.	*Jim Santini (D Nev. AL)	29,300
17.	*M. G. (Gene) Snyder (R Ky. 4th)	29,075
18.	*Don H. Clausen (R Calif. 2nd)	29,025
19.	*Albert W. Johnson (R Pa. 23rd)	28,850
20.	Morgan Maxfield (D Mo. 6th)	28,270

* Indicates incumbent.
† Includes interest group contributions to Bentsen's campaign for the Democratic presidential nomination, as well as to his Senate race.

SOURCE: Common Cause, based on reports filed with the Federal Election Commission.

Footnotes

1. Congressional Quarterly, *Dollar Politics* (1974), vol. 2, p. iv.

2. Congressional Quarterly, *Dollar Politics* (1971), vol. 1, p. 1.

3. David W. Adamany and George E. Agree, *Political Money: A Strategy for Campaign Financing in America* (Johns Hopkins University Press, 1975), p. 19.

4. *Dollar Politics,* vol. 1, p. 1 and *Dollar Politics,* vol. 2, p. 60.

5. Adamany and Agree, *Political Money,* pp. 19-20.

6. *Ibid.,* pp. 20-21.

7. *Dollar Politics,* vol. 1, p. 12.

8. *Ibid.,* p. 13.

9. *Ibid.*

10. *Ibid.,* p. 11.

11. Congressional Quarterly, *Weekly Report,* March 13, 1976, p. 554.

12. *Dollar Politics,* vol. 1, p. 5.

13. *Ibid.*

14. *Dollar Politics,* vol. 2, p. 55.

15. *Ibid.,* pp. 83-84.

16. *Ibid.,* pp. 73-75.

17. *Dollar Politics,* vol. 1, pp. 4-5.

18. Congressional Quarterly, *Weekly Report,* March 13, 1976, p. 555.

19. *Ibid.*

20. *Ibid.*

21. Congressional Quarterly, *1973 Almanac,* p. 750.

22. *Dollar Politics,* vol. 2, pp. 61-62.

23. Congressional Quarterly, *Weekly Report,* Oct. 4, 1975, p. 2131.

24. *Ibid.*

25. Congressional Quarterly, *Weekly Report,* Sept. 25, 1976, p. 2597.

26. George Thayer, *Who Shakes the Money Tree?* (Simon and Schuster, 1973), p. 25.

27. Yorick Blumenfeld and Bruce Freed, "Campaign Spending in Europe and America," *Editorial Research Reports,* Oct. 11, 1974, p. 776.

28. Congressional Quarterly, *Weekly Report,* April 17, 1976, p. 902.

29. Cited in Blumenfeld and Freed, "Campaign Spending," *Editorial Research Reports,* p. 777.

30. Congressional Quarterly, *Congress and the Nation, 1969-1972,* vol. 3, p. 397.

31. Congressional Quarterly, *Weekly Report,* Nov. 6, 1976, p. 3136.

Selected Bibliography

Books

Adamany, David W. and Agree, George E. *Political Money: A Strategy for Campaign Financing in America.* Baltimore: Johns Hopkins University Press, 1975.

The American Bar Association. Special Committee on Election Reform. *Symposium on Campaign Financing Regulation.* Tiburon, Calif.: April 25-27, 1975.

Alexander, Herbert E. *Financing the 1960 Election.* Princeton: Citizens' Research Foundation, 1962.

_____. *Financing the 1964 Election.* Princeton: Citizens' Research Foundation, 1968.

_____. *Financing the 1968 Election.* Lexington, Mass.: D.C. Heath, 1971.

_____. *Financing the 1972 Election.* Lexington, Mass.: D.C. Heath, 1976.

_____. *Financing Politics.* Washington: Congressional Quarterly Press, 1976.

_____. *Political Financing.* Minneapolis: Burgess Publishing Co., 1972.

_____. *Money, Politics and Public Reporting.* Princeton: Citizens' Research Foundation, 1960.

_____. *Money in Politics.* Washington: Public Affairs Press, 1972.

_____. *Regulation of Political Finance.* Published jointly by Institute of Governmental Studies, Berkeley and Citizens' Research Foundation, Princeton, 1966.

_____, ed. *Studies in Money in Politics.* 2 vols. Princeton: Citizens' Research Foundation, 1965-1970.

Boyd, James. *Above the Law.* New York: New American Library, 1968.

Committee for Economic Development. Research and Policy Committee. *Financing a Better Election System.* New York, 1968.

Congressional Quarterly. *Dollar Politics.* Vol. I (1971), Vol. II (1974). Washington.

Domhoff, G. William. *Fat Cats and Democrats: The Role of the Big Rich in the Party of the Common Man.* Englewood Cliffs, N.J.: Prentice-Hall, 1972.

Dunn, Delmer D. *Financing Presidential Campaigns.* Washington: The Brookings Institution, 1972.

Felknor, Bruce L. *Dirty Politics.* New York: Norton, 1966.

Heard, Alexander. *The Costs of Democracy.* Chapel Hill: University of North Carolina Press, 1960.

McCarthy, Max. *Elections for Sale.* Boston: Houghton Mifflin, 1972.

Nichols, David. *Financing Elections: The Politics of an American Ruling Class.* New York: New Viewpoints, 1974.

1972 Congressional Finances. 10 vols. Prepared by the Campaign Finance Monitoring Project, Common Cause. Washington: 1974.

1972 Federal Campaign Finances: Interest Groups and Political Parties. 2 vols. Prepared by Campaign Monitoring Project, Common Cause. Washington, 1974.

1974 Congressional Campaign Finances. 5 vols. Prepared by Campaign Monitoring Project, Common Cause. Washington, 1976.

Overacker, Louise. *Money in Elections.* New York: Macmillan, 1932.

Peabody, Robert L. *To Enact a Law: Congress and Campaign Financing.* New York: Praeger, 1972.

Shannon, Jasper B. *Money and Politics.* New York: Random House, 1959.

Stinnett, Ronald F. *Democrats, Dinners, & Dollars.* Introduction by Hubert H. Humphrey. Ames: Iowa State University Press, 1967.

Thayer, George. *Who Shakes the Money Tree?* New York: Simon and Schuster, 1973.

Twentieth Century Fund. Commission on Campaign Costs in the Electronic Era. *Voters' Time; Report.* New York, 1969.

_____. Task Force on Financing Congressional Campaigns. *Electing Congress; The Financial Dilemma; Report* (and) *Background Paper* by David L. Rosenbloom. New York, 1970.

Articles

Adamany, David. "Election Campaign Financing: the 1974 Reforms." *Political Science Quarterly,* Summer, 1975, pp. 201-20.

_____. "Sources of Money: An Overview." *Annals of the American Academy of Political and Social Science,* May 1976, pp. 17-32.

Alexander, Herbert E., "Financing American Politics." *Political Quarterly,* October/December 1974, pp. 439-48.

_____, ed. "Political Finance: Reform and Reality; Symposium." *Annals of the American Academy of Political and Social Science,* May 1976, pp. 1-149.

_____, et al. "The High Costs of TV Campaigns." *Television Quarterly,* Winter 1966, pp. 47-65.

Berry, Jeffrey M. "Congress and Public Policy: A Study of the Federal Election Campaign Act of 1971." *Harvard Journal on Legislation,* February 1973, p. 331.

Biden, Joseph R. Jr. "Public Financing of Elections: Legislative Proposals and Constitutional Questions." *Northwestern University Law Review,* March/April 1974, pp. 1-70.

Boeckel, Richard. "Excessive Expenditures in Election Campaigns." *Editorial Research Reports,* 1926, vol. 2. pp. 636-58.

"Campaign Spending in the 1968 Elections." Congressional Quarterly, *Weekly Report,* Dec. 5, 1969, Part 1, pp. 2433-61.

Dawson, P. A. and Zinser, J. E. "Political Finance and Participation in Congressional Elections." *Annals of the American Academy of Political and Social Science,* May 1976, pp. 59-73.

Dean, E. Joseph. "Undisclosed Earmarking: Violation of the Federal Election Campaign Act of 1971." *Harvard Journal on Legislation,* February 1973, p. 175.

"The Federal Election Campaign Act of 1971: Reform of the Political Process?" *Georgetown Law Review,* May 1972, p. 1309.

Heard, Alexander. "Political Financing." *International Encyclopedia of the Social Sciences* (Macmillan, 1968, 17 vols.), Vol. 12, pp. 235-44.

Lambert, Jeremiah D. "Corporate Political Spending and Campaign Finance." *New York University Law Review,* December 1965, pp. 1033-78.

Lobel, Martin. "Federal Control of Campaign Contributions." *Minnesota Law Review,* 1966-67, pp. 1-62.

"Loophole Legislation—State Campaign Finance Laws." *University of Pennsylvania Law Review,* April 1967, pp. 983-1006.

Macdonald, George P. "Union Political Involvement and Reform of Campaign Financing Regulation." *Prospectus; A Journal of Law Reform,* April 1969, pp. 347-70.

Rauh, Joseph L. Jr. "Legality of Union Political Expenditures." *Southern California Law Review,* Winter 1961, pp. 152-64.

Sterling, Carleton W. "Control of Campaign Spending: The Reformers Paradox." *American Bar Association Journal,* October 1973, p. 1148.

Walters, Robert. "Campaign Spending from Loopholes." *National Journal Reports,* Jan. 11, 1975, p. 67.

Government Documents

U.S. Congress. House. Committee on House Administration. *Election Reform Act of 1966; Hearings on H.R. 15317 and related Bills.* 89th Cong., 2nd sess., 1966.

_____. *Federal Election Campaign Act of 1971.* H. Rept. 92-752, conference report on S. 382. 92nd Cong., 1st sess., 1971.

U.S. Congress. House. Committee on Standards of Official Conduct. *Report Under the Authority of H. Res. 1031.* H. Rept. 91-1803. 91st Cong., 2nd sess., 1970.

_____. *Campaign Finances; Hearings on H. Res. 1031, Regulation of Lobbying and Management of Campaign Money.* 92nd Cong., 1st sess., 1971.

U.S. Congress. House. Special Committee to Investigate Campaign Expenditures. *Reports.* H. Rept. 88-1946, 88th Cong., 2nd sess., 1964; H. Rept. 89-2348, 89th Cong., 2nd sess., 1966; H. Rept. 91-2, 91st Cong., 1st sess., 1968; Committee Print, 92nd Cong., 1st sess., 1970; H. Rept. 93-1 and 93-286, 93rd Cong., 1st sess., 1973.

U.S. Congress. Senate. Committee on Finance. *Political Campaign Financing Proposals; Hearings on Various Proposals for Financing Political Campaigns.* 90th Cong., 1st sess., 1967.

_____. *Report on Honest Elections Act of 1967.* S. Rept. 90-714. 90th Cong., 1st sess., 1967.

U.S. Congress. Senate. Committee on Rules and Administration. *Election Law Guidebook 1976.* S. Doc. 94-216. 94th Cong., 2nd sess., 1976.

_____. *Federal Election Campaign Act of 1973, Report.* S. Rept. 93-310 to accompany S. 372. 93rd Cong., 1st sess., 1973.

_____. *Hearings Before the Subcommittee on Privileges and Elections on Proposed Amendments to and Improvements in the Federal Election Laws.* 3 parts. 87th Cong., 1st sess., 1961.

_____. *Hearings on 1956 Presidential and Senatorial Campaign Contributions and Practices.* 84th Cong., 2nd sess., 1956.

U.S. Congress. Senate. Select Committee on Presidential Campaign Activities. *Final Report.* S. Rept. 93-981, 93rd Cong., 2nd sess., 1974.

U.S. Congress. Senate. Office of the Secretary. *Report on Audits, Field Investigations, Complaints and Referrals in Connection with the Election of the U.S. Senate.* Washington: Government Printing Office, 19__.

U.S. Federal Election Commission. *Federal Election Campaign Laws.* Washington: Government Printing Office, 1976.

U.S. Library of Congress. American Law Division. *Analysis of Federal and State Campaign Finance Law: Summaries,* 1976.

Major Campaign Finance Law Provisions

Source: Federal Election Commission.

The material below gives major provisions of the campaign finance laws passed in 1971, 1974 and 1976. The material is presented in a form to show the major changes made by each law. The material does not include provisions on public financing of presidential elections or nominating conventions *(see text pp. 70, 73);* in addition, the sum-

mary below does not include many detailed provisions relating to the fundamental disclosure, reporting, contribution and enforcement sections of the law that are summarized.

Column 2 (1971/1974 provisions) highlights the law in effect prior to the 1976 amendments. Column 3 (1976 amendments) highlights the changes made by the 1976 law.

SUBJECT	1971/1974 PROVISIONS	1976 AMENDMENTS
1) CANDIDATES AND COMMITTEES		
(A) ORGANIZATION Principal Campaign Committee Support	Could not support any other candidate.	Now may provide "occasional, isolated, or incidental" support of another candidate.
(B) REGISTRATION		(No change)
(C) RECORD-KEEPING Records of contributions	Had to be kept for contributions over $10.	Now only requires record-keeping of contributions over $50. Note: No change, however, in requirement that donors who contribute over $100 in the aggregate be identified in the reports where committee has knowledge of such aggregated contributions.
Campaign depositories	Candidate had to have "a" checking account for deposit of any contributions.	Now may also maintain "such other accounts" as desired (including checking accounts, savings accounts, or certificates of deposit).
(D) REPORTING Filing with Principal Campaign Committee	Every committee supporting a candidate had to file its report with that candidate's Principal Campaign Committee.	New law clarifies that only committees authorized by a candidate to raise contributions or make expenditures must file with the Principal Campaign Committee.
Treasurer's "best efforts"	(No provision)	Committee treasurers and candidates who show they have used "best efforts" to obtain and submit all required information shall be deemed in compliance with the law.
Waiver of quarterly report filing	Quarterly reports waived for any quarter in which $1,000 is not received or spent. (Except for end-of-year report due in January regardless of amount).	In addition, in non-election year, candidates and committees authorized by candidates do not have to file reports in quarters when combined contributions and expenditures do not exceed $5,000 (except for end-of-year report due in January regardless of amount).
Internal communications	(No provision)	Adds new requirement that membership organizations (including labor organizations or corporations) must report their expenditures for all communications primarily devoted to express advocacy of the election or defeat of a clearly identified candidate, when the total actual cost of such communications relating to all candidates in an election exceeds $2,000.
(2) CONTRIBUTIONS		
(A) CONTRIBUTION LIMITS (i) FROM AN INDIVIDUAL To a candidate or that candidate's authorized committee(s)	$1,000 per election.	Same.
To national political party committees	No limit (except $25,000 limit on total contributions per year).	$20,000 per year.
To any other political committee	No limit (except $25,000 limit on total contributions per year).	$5,000 per year.
Total aggregate contributions per year.	$25,000 per year.	Same.

SUBJECT	1971/1974 PROVISIONS	1976 AMENDMENTS
(ii) FROM A POLITICAL COMMITTEE QUALIFYING AS A "MULTI-CANDIDATE COMMITTEE"* (See definition p. 557)		
To a candidate or that candidate's authorized committee(s)	$5,000 per election.	Same.
To national political party committees	No limit.	$15,000 per year.
To any other political committee	No limit.	$5,000 per year.
Total aggregate contributions per year	No limit.	Same.
(iii) FROM ANY OTHER POLITICAL COMMITTEE OR ORGANIZATION		
To a candidate or that candidate's authorized committee(s)	$1,000 per election.	Same.
To national political party committees	No limit.	$20,000 per year.
To any other political committee	No limit.	$5,000 per year.
Total aggregate contributions per year	No limit.	Same.

(iv) SPECIAL EXCEPTIONS ADDED TO THE 1976 AMENDMENTS

Senate Elections: The Republican or Democratic Senatorial Campaign Committee, or the National Committee of a political party, or any combination of such committees may contribute not more than $17,500 in an election year to a Senate candidate.

Party Committee Limits: No limits on "transfers" between political committees of the same political party.

Subsidiary Committee Limits: For purposes of applying contribution limits, all political committees (including corporate or union separate segregated funds) established, financed, maintained or controlled by the same organization (such as subsidiaries, divisions, local units, etc.) are treated as a single political committee for purposes of contribution limits.

NOTE: There is an exception to this "single political committee" rule for political parties. Contributions by a single national political party committee and by a single state political party committee are not treated as one committee for purposes of applying the contribution limits.

(B) CONTRIBUTION DEFINITIONS

SUBJECT	1971/1974 PROVISIONS	1976 AMENDMENTS
"Contract"	Defined as "a contract, promise, or agreement, express or implied."	Now only defined as a "written" contract. Also the words "express or implied" were deleted.
Legal or accounting services	(No provision)	Not counted as "contribution" so long as lawyer/accountant is paid by his or her regular employer and does not engage in general campaign activities. But amounts paid or incurred must be reported.
$500 exemption	Costs to an individual, up to $500, of sale of food or beverage by a vendor at cost.	$500 exemption for vendor applies to a person (including committees, corporations, groups, etc.), not just an individual.

(3) EXPENDITURES
(A) EXPENDITURE LIMITS

SUBJECT	1971/1974 PROVISIONS	1976 AMENDMENTS
Candidate personal spending limits from own funds	Presidential, $50,000; Senate, $35,000; House, $25,000.	No limits except for presidential candidates accepting public funds, which remain the same.
Campaign spending limits	Presidential: primary, $10-million; general, $20-million. Senate: primary, greater of 8¢ per voter or $100,000; general, greater of 12¢ per voter or $150,000. House: $70,000 each election. Annual cost-of-living increase in spending limits. Exemption of fund-raising costs up to 20% of the spending limits.	No limits except for presidential candidates accepting public funds, which remain the same.

SUBJECT	1971/1974 PROVISIONS	1976 AMENDMENTS
(B) EXPENDITURE DEFINITIONS		
Legal or accounting services	(No provision)	Not counted as "expenditure" so long as lawyer/accountant is paid by his or her regular employer and does not engage in general campaign activities. But amounts paid or incurred must be reported.
(4) INDEPENDENT EXPENDITURES		
Definition	An expenditure "relative to a clearly identified candidate...advocating the election or defeat of a clearly identified candidate."	Changed to refer to expenditures "expressly" advocating a candidate. To be "independent" an expenditure also cannot involve any "cooperation," "consultation," or be in "concert" with or "be at the request or suggestion of" any candidate or candidate's agent. An expenditure made with any such involvement with a candidate is a "contribution" subject to contribution limits.
Independent spending limit	$1,000 per candidate per election.	No limit.
Reports:		
(i) Filed by individuals	Reports of independent expenditures over $100 on dates political committees file, but reports need not be cumulative.	Basically same reporting requirements, except the language "need not be cumulative" is stricken. Additional language added that must file the same information required of contributors over $100, and the same information required of political committees. Must also report name(s) of candidate(s) independently supported or opposed, and state "under penalty of perjury" whether there was any cooperation, etc., with any candidate. Must report any "independent expenditure" of $1,000 or more within 24 hours if made within 15 days of an election.
(ii) Filed by political committees	No special requirement. Same reports required of any political committee.	Basically same, except must also report name(s) of candidate(s) independently supported or opposed, and state "under penalty of perjury" whether there was any cooperation, etc., with any candidate. Must report any "independent expenditure" of $1,000 or more within 24 hours if made within 15 days of an election.
(5) PUBLICATION/BROADCAST NOTICES		
(A) Unauthorized literature or advertisements	Must contain statement that unauthorized by candidate, and that candidate not responsible.	These two sections (A) and (B) are replaced by a single new section covering communications "expressly advocating the election or defeat of a clearly identified candidate" through use of media, direct mail, or any advertisements. In such cases, the communication must either:
(B) Pamphlets or advertisements	Must state who is responsible, and list names of officers for any organization.	(1) if authorized, state the name of the candidate or candidate's agent who authorized the communication, or (2) if unauthorized, state that the communication is unauthorized, identify who "made or financed" it, and list the name(s) of any affiliated or connected organization.
(C) Fund-raising solicitation	There is no change in the requirement that any fund-raising solicitation (whether authorized or unauthorized) contain a statement that reports are filed with, and available for purchase from, the FEC.	
(6) MISCELLANEOUS PROVISIONS		
Definition of "election"	Included any political party caucus or convention "held" to nominate a candidate.	**Changed to include those which have "authority to"** nominate a candidate.
FEC indexes	———	FEC required to compile 2 new indexes: (1) Independent expenditures made on behalf of each candidate; (2) All political committees supporting more than one candidate, including the dates they qualify for the "multicandidate committee" contribution levels.

SUBJECT	1971/1974 PROVISIONS	1976 AMENDMENTS
Honorariums	Federal officeholders or officers limited to $15,000 per year, and $1,000 per "appearance, speech, or article." Exemption for recipient's actual travel and subsistence.	Limits increased to $25,000 per year and $2,000 per honorarium. Travel and subsistence exemption extended to spouse or one aide. Additional exemption added for agent or booking fees. Honorariums exempt from definition of "contribution" to a candidate.
Issue-oriented organization report	Reports required by an organization making any reference to a candidate, including voting record lists, issue-oriented comments, etc.	Deleted.
(7) FEDERAL ELECTION COMMISSION		
Appointment	6 Commissioners, 2 each appointed by President, Senate and House. Staggered terms every year. 6-year terms.	6 Commissioners, all appointed by the President. Confirmed by the Senate with 6-year terms staggered every 2 years (so terms expire in non-election years).
Authority to prescribe regulations	Only for Title 2 disclosure provisions. No authority to prescribe regulations for Title 18 limitations provisions.	Since all the provisions of the FECA formerly codified in Title 18 are now included in Title 2, FEC now has authority to prescribe regulations for all provisions of the act.
Advisory opinions **Who may request**	Any federal officeholder, any federal candidate, or any political committee.	Also, the national committee of any political party.
Scope	Must relate to specific transaction or activity of requestor.	Basically same, but language now reads that advisory opinions must relate to the "application" of a general rule of law in the act or regulations to a specific factual situation.
Immunity	Person receiving advisory opinion and acting in good faith reliance on it "presumed to be in compliance" with the law. Limited to person asking and receiving advisory opinion.	Basically same, but language now reads that such person "shall not...be subject to any sanction" of the law. Extended to any person involved in same transaction, or in another transaction "indistinguishable in all its material aspects."
(8) COMPLIANCE PROCEDURES		
Authority	FEC had "primary" civil jurisdiction authority.	Now has "exclusive" primary civil jurisdiction authority.
Form of complaints	(No provision)	Now must be in writing, signed and sworn, notarized, and subject to false reporting laws. FEC may not act solely on basis of an anonymous complaint.
FEC investigation	Any complaint filed.	Only if FEC "has reason to believe" violation has been committed.
Rights of person complained against	Right to request hearing concerning any complaint.	Hearings eliminated, but when FEC investigates (see above), right to demonstrate that no action should be taken.
Voluntary compliance	FEC to utilize "informal means of conference, conciliation or persuasion" to settle cases.	Basically same, except minimum of 30 days (or half the number of days before an election) to use informal methods. Cases to be settled by adoption of "conciliation agreement." Civil penalties can be included in conciliation agreement involving "knowing and willful violations."
Civil actions	FEC authority to seek civil action in court, or ask Justice Department to seek civil relief.	Now sole FEC authority.
Referral of cases to Justice Department	If apparent violation of a Title 18 provision (see (9), below), or if FEC unable to correct a violation of Title 2 provision (see (9)).	Now only if FEC determines there is probable cause of a knowing and willful violation, and if the violation involves contributions or expenditures aggregating $1,000 or more.
Confidentiality	FEC barred from making any information public about any investigation without consent of subject of investigation.	Same. However, new provision requires FEC after investigation to make public any conciliation agreement, any attempt at conciliation, and any determination that no violation has occurred.

SUBJECT	1971/1974 PROVISIONS	1976 AMENDMENTS
FEC inaction	(No provision)	Right to appeal to U.S. district court for FEC failure to act on complaint within 90 days or for FEC dismissal of a complaint.
Court enforcement	No specific language, except referral to Justice Department.	FEC has authority to seek court enforcement of a conciliation agreement, or of a court order.
(9) PENALTIES STRUCTURE **Title 2 reporting and disclosure provisions**	A fine up to $1,000; or 1 year prison; or both.	For any violation, a fine up to the greater of $5,000 or the amount of any contribution or expenditure involved; (or in the case of a knowing and willful violation, a fine up to the greater of $10,000 or twice the amount of any contribution or expenditure involved).
Limitations sections codified in the 1971/1974 Provisions in Title 18, and re-codified in the 1976 Amendments in Title 2	A fine up to $25,000; 1 or 5 years prison (depending on the section); or both.	Same as above for any violation, except: For knowing and willful violations of contribution and expenditure provisions aggregating $1,000 or more, a fine up to the greater of $25,000 or 300% of any amount involved; or 1 year prison; or both. Exceptions: (i) these additional penalties apply to violations over $250 for: corporate/union provisions $100 cash contribution limit prohibition of contributions in the name of another. (ii) these additional penalties apply to violations of any amount for misrepresentation of campaign authority.

---

*Definition of "Multicandidate Committee"—A political committee meeting all of the following three conditions: (1) has been registered under the act for six months; (2) has received contributions from more than 50 persons; (3) has made contributions to five or more federal candidates. A state political party committee need only meet (1) and (2). Note: There is no change in these conditions from the 1971/1974 provisions, but the special term "multicandidate committee" was added in the 1976 amendments.

Seating and Disciplining of Members

In laying down the authority of Congress to seat, unseat and punish its members, the Constitutional Convention of 1787 drew inspiration from its favorite concept, that of checks and balances. The Constitution, while empowering Congress to pass judgment on the qualifications of members, put bounds on that power by listing certain mandatory qualifications. In carrying out the concept of a balance of power among the branches of the federal government, the judicial branch has been called on at various times to interpret the authority of Congress under the constitutional clauses on membership qualifications and on punishment of members' misconduct.

The power of Congress to determine whether a member-elect fulfills the requirements for service as a national legislator has come into conflict, over the years, with the right of voters in each state to decide who shall represent them. When Congress has ruled on disputed elections, the uncertain citizenship of a member-elect, or other questions of competence, senators or representatives from all over the country have decided whether a state may or may not be represented in Washington by a person certified by the state as the choice of its electorate.

Although Congress has acted often to determine the winner in contested elections, it has rejected the clear choice of the voters, for lack of the requisite qualifications, in fewer than 20 cases since 1789. Congress has shown like restraint in exercise of its constitutional right to punish or expel members for disorderly or improper conduct. Seven senators, 18 representatives and one territorial delegate have been formally censured by their colleagues for misconduct. Expulsions have numbered 15 in the Senate and three in the House.

Constitutional Provisions

The authority of Congress to judge the qualifications of members and to punish those who behave improperly rests on two clauses in Article I of the Constitution. The first is Clause 1 of Article I, Section 5, which reads in part: "Each House shall be the Judge of the Elections, Returns and Qualifications of its own members...." This clause would appear to give each house carte blanche in the validation of elections and the seating of members-elect. However, the election of members of Congress is regulated elsewhere in Article I and in the Seventeenth Amendment. In addition, the Constitution specifically lists the qualifications required for membership in Congress.

The second clause on seating, unseating, and punishment of members is Clause 2 of Article I, Section 5, reading: "Each House may determine the Rules of its Proceedings, punish its Members for disorderly Behavior, and, with the Concurrence of two thirds, expel a Member." The original draft of this clause did not include the words "with the concurrence of two thirds." When the clause was considered in the Constitutional Convention, Aug. 10, 1787, James Madison of Virginia said that the right of expulsion was "too important to be exercised by a bare majority of a quorum, and in emergencies might be dangerously abused."[1] He therefore proposed requiring a two-thirds vote for expulsion.

Gouverneur Morris of Pennsylvania opposed Madison's proposal. He said: "This power may be safely trusted to a majority. To require more may produce abuses on the side of the minority. A few men from fractious motives may keep in a member who ought to be expelled."[2] But Edmund Randolph and George Mason of Virginia and Daniel Carroll of Maryland spoke in support of Madison's proposal, and it was adopted by a vote of 10 states in favor, one (Pennsylvania) divided and none opposed.

Judicial Interpretations

Litigation on the seating and disciplining of members of Congress reached the Supreme Court in the latter part of the 19th century in suits pivoting mainly on legalistic questions such as the power of Congress to subpoena witnesses when considering the qualifications of members. These suits afforded the court an opportunity to indicate bases upon which to judge the qualifications of members and to suggest the scope of punishment that may be imposed on members. In cases argued during the present century, the court has ruled more directly on the nature of the power of Congress to exclude members-elect and to punish or expel sitting members.

Application of the constitutional clause on judgment of the qualifications of members-elect has raised more questions of interpretation than has use of the authority to punish members. Perhaps the most serious of the issues involved in these cases has been whether exclusion of a member-elect deprives a state unwarrantedly, even for a short time, of its constitutionally guaranteed representation in Congress. The court ruled on this question in a case based on the 1926 contested election to the Senate of William S. Vare of Pennsylvania. It said that exclusion in such a case did not violate a state's rights. But the right of a state to send to Congress anyone it chooses, if he has the constitutionally listed qualifications and is legally elected, was upheld by the court in a 1969 case in which it reversed the exclusion of Adam Clayton Powell Jr. (D N.Y.) from the House of Representatives. *(Details, p. 92)*

Right to Compel Testimony, Imprison Members

The Supreme Court, in its 1880-81 term, handed down a decision which did not involve the seat or good standing of a member of either house of Congress but which specified a form of punishment which the House of Representatives might impose on a member guilty of misconduct. The case stemmed from an order by the House, March 14, 1876, for the arrest and detention of Hallett Kilbourn, a business broker in the District of Columbia, who had refused to produce papers needed in a House investigation of the bankruptcy of Jay Cooke and Co. Kilbourn brought suit, contending that punishment of an individual in his situation was not included in the powers allotted to Congress by the Constitution.

The year in which the House ordered Kilbourn's arrest was notable for financial scandals allegedly involving House members. Although the bankruptcy of the Cooke firm raised questions about the conduct of officers in an executive department rather than members of Congress, charges which arose in 1876 over trading in Union Pacific Railroad bonds and maneuverings of the Credit Mobilier affected several House members, including Speaker James G. Blaine (R Maine). The *Kilbourn* case therefore proceeded in an atmosphere of suspicion about the financial dealings of House members.

Justice Samuel F. Miller delivered the opinion of the Supreme Court in *Kilbourn v. Thompson* (103 U.S. 168). The court ruled that the House had exceeded its jurisdiction in investigating the Cooke bankruptcy and, thus, denied the right of the House to imprison Kilbourn for refusing to testify.

The court then went on to discuss the circumstances under which the House could use imprisonment and compel testimony. Speaking in the context of calls for punishment of members accused of unethical financial involvement in the businesses under investigation, it said:

● "The Constitution expressly empowers each House to punish its own members for disorderly behavior. We see no reason to doubt that this punishment may in a proper case be imprisonment."

● "Each House is by the Constitution made the judge of the election and qualifications of its members. In deciding on these it has an undoubted right to examine witnesses and inspect papers, subject to the usual rights of witnesses in such cases; and it may be that a witness would be subject to like punishment at the hands of the body engaged in trying a contested election, for refusing to testify, that he would if the case were pending before a court of judicature."

Although the *Kilbourn* case established the right of each house of Congress to compel testimony, that right was nevertheless challenged in a subsequent case which centered on legislation enacted prior to the *Kilbourn* case. That legislation, enacted in 1857 and amended in 1862, required witnesses to answer summonses and respond to questions on "any matter" before either chamber or any congressional committee.[3] Interpretation of the words "any matter" as used in the legislation came into play in an investigation of stock deals of senators charged with corruption in regard to tariff legislation.

Elverton R. Chapman, a New York stockbroker, was indicted Oct. 1, 1894, for violating the 1857 and 1862 statutes by refusing to answer questions about the accounts of the senators under question. Chapman's lawyers contended that the statutes were unconstitutional and that the Senate had no right to demand answers to questions about the accounts. The case reached the Supreme Court on appeal. Chief Justice Melville W. Fuller on April 19, 1897, delivered the opinion of the court, which reaffirmed the right of either chamber to compel testimony in matters which were within that chamber's jurisdiction. The opinion also defined the circumstances under which either chamber might expel a member. The court said:

"Nor will it do to hold that the Senate had no jurisdiction to pursue the particular inquiry because the preamble and resolutions did not specify that the proceedings were taken for the purpose of censure or expulsion, if certain facts were disclosed by the investigation. The matter was within the range of the constitutional powers of the Senate. The resolutions adequately indicated that the transactions referred to were deemed by the Senate reprehensible and deserving of condemnation and punishment. The right to expel extends to all cases where the offense is such as in the judgment of the Senate is inconsistent with the trust and duty of a member" (*In re Chapman*, 166 U.S. 661).

Question of Automatic Expulsion

The reference to expulsion in the court's opinion of 1897 was supplemented in an opinion handed down in 1906 interpreting an act of Congress approved June 11, 1864. The act provided that any senator or representative found guilty of illegally receiving compensation for services rendered in connection with a claim, contract or other proceeding before a government agency "shall...be rendered forever thereafter incapable of holding any office...under the government of the United States."[4] Sen. Joseph R. Burton (R Kan.) had been convicted on a charge of illegally receiving such compensation, and the question of his right to retain his seat in the Senate consequently arose. Burton's lawyers contended that the 1864 law violated the constitutional right of the Senate to decide on expulsion of its members.

Justice John M. Harlan, delivering the court's opinion on May 21, 1906, said: "The final judgment of conviction did not operate, *ipso facto*, to vacate the seat of the convicted senator nor compel the Senate to expel him or to regard him as expelled by force alone of the judgment" (*Burton v. United States*, 202 U.S. 344). On the following day, the Senate asked its Committee on Privileges and Elections to report what options remained and what further action, if any, should be taken in relation to Burton's seat. Burton resigned on June 4, 1906, before the committee had prepared a report.

Exclusion for Misconduct in Primary Election

Misconduct, not by sitting members of Congress, but by a member-elect was the problem in the next major case requiring the Supreme Court to rule on the power of Congress to judge its members' qualifications. This case grew out of the Federal Corrupt Practices Act of June 25, 1910, as amended Aug. 19, 1911. The two laws limited the amount of money that a candidate for Congress could spend on his campaign.

Truman H. Newberry and 16 others were found guilty of conspiring to violate the corrupt practices legislation in the Democratic senatorial primary election of Aug. 27, 1918, in Michigan. Newberry's opponent in the primary was Henry Ford. The conviction was appealed up to the Supreme Court. Here, the issue was whether Congress, despite its lack of express authority to regulate primary elections, might exercise some control over them through its right to pass judgment on its members' qualifications.

In *Newberry v. United States* (256 U.S. 232), the court took a restrictive view of that right. It decided, May 2, 1921, that Congress did not have power to control in any way a state's party primaries or conventions for designating candidates for the Senate or the House. A concurring opinion by Justice Mahlon Pitney, in which Justices Louis D. Brandeis and John H. Clarke joined, went beyond the inapplicability of the Corrupt Practices Act to primaries. On the right of Congress to exclude Newberry, Pitney said: "I am unable to see how, in right reason, it can be held that one of the houses of Congress, on the just exercise of its power, may exclude an elected member for securing by bribery his nomination at the primary, if the regulation by law of his conduct at the primary is beyond the constitutional power of Congress itself."

The concurring opinion made the additional point that neither house, in judging the qualifications of its members, is authorized to set up standards having the effect of legislation.

Twenty years after the *Newberry* decision, the Supreme Court reversed itself on the right of Congress to legislate on primary elections. Justice Harlan F. Stone on May 26, 1941, delivered the opinion of the court in *United States v. Classic.* He said that the power to regulate national elections, assigned by the Constitution to Congress, "includes the authority to regulate primary elections when, as in this case, they are a step in the exercise by the people of their choice of representatives in Congress" (313 U.S. 299).

Right to Subpoena Ballot Boxes

Investigative powers inherent in the right of each house of Congress to judge the qualifications of its members, although passed on by the Supreme Court in the *Kilbourn* and *Chapman* cases, came up again as an unsettled question following the senatorial election of Nov. 2, 1926, in Pennsylvania. William S. Vare, Republican, was declared the winner of the election over William B. Wilson, Democrat. But in view of reports of corruption in the election, the Senate established a committee consisting of James A. Reed (D Mo.) and others to investigate the Pennsylvania election campaign. Reed and his committee filed a suit aimed at compelling local officials to produce ballot boxes for inspection. The ballot boxes were produced, but the question of the committee's right to sue remained open.

The question reached the Supreme Court in *Reed et al. v. County Commissioners of Delaware County, Pa.* (277 U.S. 376). Lawyers for the committee contended that its right to sue was derived from "powers of inquiry auxiliary to the power to judge the elections, returns, and qualifications of the members of the Senate, or auxiliary to the power to legislate for the regulation of the times and manner of holding senatorial elections." The court's opinion, delivered May 28, 1928, by Justice Pierce Butler, reaffirmed the right of each house of Congress to "secure information upon which to decide concerning elections" but ruled that the

---

Constitutional Qualifications for Membership in Congress

● A senator must be at least 30 years old and have been a citizen of the United States not less than nine years (Article I, Section 3, Clause 3).

● A representative must be at least 25 years old and have been a citizen not less than seven years (Article I, Section 2, Clause 2).

● Every member of Congress must be, when elected, an inhabitant of the state that he is to represent (Article I, Section 2, Clause 2, and Section 3, Clause 3).

● No one may be a member of Congress who holds any other "Office under the United States" (Article I, Section 6, Clause 2).

● No person may be a senator or a representative who, having previously taken an oath as a member of Congress to support the Constitution, has engaged in rebellion against the United States or given aid or comfort to its enemies, unless Congress has removed such disability by a two-thirds vote of both houses (Fourteenth Amendment, Section 3).

---

wording of the resolution setting up the Reed committee did not give it the right to sue. The Senate on Dec. 6, 1929, denied Vare his seat.

Denial of State Representation

Not until 1929 was the Supreme Court required to rule on the question whether a house of Congress, in excluding a member-elect, deprives a state, though only temporarily, of its right to representation. Presented for decision was a case involving that question in only a secondary way, but the court took the occasion to state its view on the question. The case arose because Thomas W. Cunningham, member of a William S. Vare-for-Senator organization, refused to answer a Senate committee's questions on the organization's funds. On March 22, 1928, the Senate adopted a resolution ordering Cunningham to be taken into custody. He petitioned for a writ of habeas corpus, contending that the Senate had exceeded its powers.

The case was appealed to the Supreme Court as *Barry et al. v. United States ex rel. Cunningham* (279 U.S. 597). In an opinion delivered by Justice George Sutherland on May 27, 1929, the court ruled that the Senate had not exceeded its jurisdiction in investigating Vare's election and confirmed its right to examine witnesses during the investigation.

The court referred to the contention that the power which the Constitution conferred on the Senate was the power of judging the elections, returns and qualifications of its members and that, the Senate having refused to seat Vare, he was not a member. "When a candidate is elected to either house, he of course is elected a member of the body; and when that body determines, upon presentation of his credentials, without first giving him his seat, that the election is void, there would seem to be no real substance in the claim that the election of a 'member' has not been adjudged. To hold otherwise would be to interpret the word 'member' with a strictness in no way required by the obvious purpose of the constitutional provisions,...which, so far as the present case is concerned, was to vest the Senate with the authority to exclude persons asserting membership, who either had not been elected or, what amounts to the same thing, had been elected by resort to fraud, bribery, corruption, or other sinister methods having the effect of vitiating the election."

The court then made a pronouncement on the most important issue presented in the case, although the issue was not central to the situation affecting Cunningham: "Nor is there merit in the suggestion that the effect of the refusal of the Senate to seat Vare pending investigation was to deprive the state of its equal representation in the Senate. The equal representation clause is found in Article V, which authorizes and regulates amendments to the Constitution, 'provided,...that no state, without its consent, shall be deprived of its equal suffrage in the Senate.' This constitutes a limitation upon the power of amendment and has nothing to do with a situation such as the one here presented. The temporary deprivation of equal representation which results from the refusal of the Senate to seat a member pending inquiry as to his election or qualifications is the necessary consequence of the exercise of a constitutional power, and no more deprives the state of its 'equal suffrage' in the constitutional sense than would a vote of the Senate vacating the seat of a sitting member or a vote of expulsion."

The Vare case was significant for one other question answered by the Supreme Court: whether Congress, in judging election cases, was violating the principle of separation of powers by exercising a judicial function. The court said that the Constitution, by authorizing Congress to be the judge of its members' qualifications, conferred on each house "certain powers which are not legislative but judicial in character," including the power "to render a judgment which is beyond the authority of any other tribunal to review."

Additional Qualifications for Membership

The Supreme Court in 1969, while pointing to the right of either house to expel a member for any kind of misconduct, limited the grounds on which a member-elect might be excluded to those specifically listed in the Constitution. Adam Clayton Powell Jr. (D N.Y.), whose exclusion gave rise to the case, was elected to the House of Representatives in 1944 and every two years thereafter. When the 90th Congress in 1967 denied Powell the seat to which he had been re-elected in 1966, on the ground that he had misappropriated public funds, Powell and 13 voters in his district brought suit against the officers of the House. *(Details of Powell case, p. 92)*

The central legal issues in the Powell suit were:

● Could the House add to the Constitution's three qualifications for House membership? The three were that the member be at least 25 years old, have been a U.S. citizen for at least seven years and be, when elected, an inhabitant of the state from which he was elected.

● Could the courts properly examine the actions of the House in such cases, order the House not to add to the Constitution's qualifications, and enforce this order?

U.S. District Judge George L. Hart Jr. ruled April 7, 1967, that he had no jurisdiction in the case and dismissed the suit.

The U.S. Court of Appeals for the District of Columbia on Feb. 28, 1968, affirmed the action of the lower court in dismissing the suit. The Court of Appeals stated that the case involved a political question, which, if decided, would constitute a violation of the separation of powers and produce an embarrassing confrontation between Congress and the courts.

Powell appealed the case to the Supreme Court where it was entered on the docket as *Adam Clayton Powell Jr. et al., Petitioners, v. John W. McCormack et al.* (395 U.S. 486). While the case was pending, the 91st Congress seated Powell, who had been re-elected again in 1968, but the court felt that the issues that had been raised, including Powell's claim for back pay, required settlement. By a 7-1 decision on June 16, 1969, the Supreme Court reversed the lower court. Chief Justice Earl Warren, delivering the opinion of the court, ruled that the House had improperly excluded Powell, a duly elected representative who met the constitutional requirements of age, residence and citizenship.

"In judging the qualifications of its members Congress is limited to the standing qualifications prescribed in the Constitution. Respondents (McCormack et al.) concede that Powell met these.... Therefore, we hold that, since Adam Clayton Powell Jr. was duly elected...and was not ineligible to serve under any provision of the Constitution, the House was without power to exclude him from its membership," Warren wrote.

In response to the question whether the court had jurisdiction over the matter, the court pointed out that the suit had been brought against the Speaker of the House, the majority and minority leaders, the ranking members of the committee that investigated Powell, and three functionaries of the House who had withheld his pay and denied him such perquisites as an office and staff. The Supreme Court held that under the speech or debate clause of the Constitution, the five members of Congress were immune from prosecution but that the three employees were liable for action. The court ruling was limited to the case at hand. No ruling was made on the power of a house of Congress to exclude or expel a properly elected member.

A claim for back pay was remanded to the U.S. District Court for the District of Columbia for further proceedings but was dismissed by Judge George L. Hart Jr. May 14, 1971, when Powell failed to press the matter.

Seating of Members-Elect

The Constitution provides in Article VI that senators and representatives "shall be bound by Oath or Affirmation, to support this Constitution." Congress in implementing that provision, has enacted laws, adopted rules and made ad hoc decisions. These determinations not only prescribed the form of the oath and procedures for administering it, but also settled such questions as whether a member whose right to his seat is disputed should take an oath before the dispute is settled or only after it has been settled in his favor. The ad hoc decisions have gone sometimes one way and sometimes another.

The oath of office of members of Congress was worded as follows by an Act of June 1, 1789: "I, A B, do solemnly swear (or affirm) that I will support the Constitution of the United States."[5] In the light of Civil War experience, this language was expanded by an Act of July 11, 1868, to read: "I, A B, do solemnly swear (or affirm) that I will support and defend the Constitution of the United States against all enemies, foreign and domestic; that I will bear true faith and allegiance to the same; that I take this obligation freely, without any mental reservation or purpose of evasion; and that I will well and faithfully discharge the duties of the office on which I am about to enter. So help me God."[6]

Before the first meeting of each Congress, the secretary of the Senate and the clerk of the next preceding House of Representatives compile lists of members-elect on the basis of certifications signed by the state governors and secretaries of state. At the first meeting of each house in the new Congress, the presiding officer (the Speaker in the House and the Vice President in the Senate) administers the oath orally in the form of a question beginning "Do you solemnly swear (or affirm)...?" and the answer by each new member is "I do." New members chosen by the states between regular elections are similarly sworn in when they take their seats.

The number of new members who are sworn in together has varied. In the Senate, the oath was administered in some Congresses to groups of four and in later Congresses to all new members at once; since 1927, the oath again has been administered to groups of four. In the House, the oath was administered for many years by state delegations; since 1929, to all new members at once.

Challenge Procedure

The right of a member-elect to take the oath of office and be seated may be challenged by an already seated member or by a private individual or group. A member-elect whose title to his seat is questioned presents himself in the usual way for the purpose of taking an oath. The presiding officer then, either on his own authority or, more often, on the basis of a motion, may ask the individual to stand aside while the oath is administered to other members-elect. Sometimes, instead, a member-elect is permitted to take the oath of office without prejudice, and a resolution calling for investigation of his right to the seat is introduced later.

If a member-elect has stood aside while others were sworn in, he nevertheless may be accorded the privilege of the floor. The House in particular has accorded to election contestants the privilege of speaking in behalf of their right to be seated. House Rule 33, which lists those who may be "admitted to the Hall of the House," includes "contestants in election cases during the pendency of their cases in the House." The Senate rule on admission to the floor does not address those involved in election contests. Traditionally, however, contestants have been granted the right to be present during consideration of their cases.

The question whether a claimant to a seat in Congress is entitled to it is usually referred to a committee. Sometimes, a select committee is established for this purpose; at other times, the question is referred to the Senate or House Committee on Administration or another standing committee. Often, the committee assigned such a question conducts hearings. The committee, in reporting its findings, usually presents a draft resolution incorporating its recommendations.

Controversies Over Qualifications

Whether Congress, or either house of Congress, had power to set up qualifications for membership beyond those listed by the Constitution, or power to overlook the lack of one of the constitutional requirements, was a question answered sometimes in the affirmative and sometimes in the negative. Until the Supreme Court gave a negative answer in the *Powell* case, Congress had acted from time to time as if it was entitled to add qualifications as well as to wink at failure to fulfill a stated qualification.

Alexander Hamilton initiated discussion of the question. In No. 60 of *The Federalist*, he wrote: "The qualifications of the persons who may...be chosen are defined and fixed in the Constitution, and are unalterable by the legislature."[7]

However, later authorities, including a committee of the House appointed in 1900 to consider the seating of a Mormon who had been convicted for polygamy, contended that the Constitutional Convention intended to empower Congress to add to the listed qualification. The committee concluded that if the Constitutional Convention had meant to limit the qualifications to those listed in the Constitution, it would have phrased them in the affirmative. They maintained, for example, that the framers would have written: "Every member of the House of Representatives shall be of the age of 25 years at least," rather than deliberately setting on the supposedly more flexible negative phrasing: "No person shall be a Representative who shall not have attained to the age of twenty-five years."

The question of qualifications was widely discussed over an extended period of time and Congress faced a dilemma on the matter. If it adhered rigidly to the constitutional list of requirements, it would be obligated to seat individuals regarded as obnoxious. If it excluded such individuals, it would be open to the charge of exceeding its powers. The issue first came to a head at the start of the Civil War.

The two houses added a qualification for membership in 1862. An act approved July 2 of that year, known as the "Ironclad Oath Law" or the "Test Oath Law," required members of the House and Senate to swear, before taking the oath of office, that they had never voluntarily borne arms against the United States or aided, recognized, or supported a jurisdiction hostile to the United States. This law remained in effect until the Fourteenth Amendment was ratified in 1868. Westel W. Willoughby wrote in *The Constitutional Law of the United States* that during the period in which this act was in force, "Congress imposed, in effect, a disqualification for membership in either of its houses which was not imposed by the Constitution."

At the same time, Willoughby pointed out: "Though neither house may formally impose qualifications additional to those mentioned in the Constitution, or waive those that are mentioned, they may, in practice, do either of these things. That is to say, in case these constitutional provisions are disregarded or added to by either of the houses of Congress, there is no judicial means of overruling their action."[8] The Supreme Court found otherwise in the *Powell* case. *(p. 92)*

Cases Occurring in the Senate

Only three senators-elect have been denied seats for lack of the requisite qualifications:

(1) Albert Gallatin, born in Geneva, became a citizen of the United States in 1785. When elected to the Senate by the Pennsylvania Legislature in 1793, he had not been a citizen nine years as required by the Constitution. He contended, however, that every man who had taken part in the Revolution was a citizen according to the law of reason and nature. The Senate on Feb. 28, 1794, adopted the following resolution by a vote of 14 yeas to 12 nays: "Resolved, That the election of Albert Gallatin to be a Senator of the United States was void, he not having been a citizen of the United States the term of years required as a qualification to be a Senator of the United States."[9]

(2) James Shields, a native of Ireland, was elected a senator from Illinois in 1848. When he appeared, March 5, 1849, to take his seat, at a special session of the Senate, the question of whether he had been a citizen the required

Senate Cases Involving Qualifications for Membership

Congress	Session	Year	Member-elect	Grounds	Disposition
3rd	1st	1793	Albert Gallatin (D Pa.)	Citizenship	*Excluded*
11th	1st	1809	Stanley Griswold (D Ohio)	Residence	Admitted
28th	1st	1844	John M. Niles (D Conn.)	Sanity	Admitted
31st	Special Senate	1849	James Shields (D Ill.)	Citizenship	*Excluded*
37th	2nd	1861	Benjamin Stark (D Ore.)	Loyalty	Admitted
40th	1st	1867	Phillip F. Thomas (D Md.)	Loyalty	*Excluded*
41st	2nd	1870	Hiram R. Revels (R Miss.)	Citizenship	Admitted
41st	2nd	1870	Adelbert Ames (R Miss.)	Residence	Admitted
59th	2nd	1907	Reed Smoot (R Utah)	Mormonism	Admitted*
69th	2nd	1926	Arthur R. Gould (R Maine)	Character	Admitted
74th	1st	1935	Rush D. Holt (D W.Va.)	Age	Admitted
75th	1st	1937	George L. Berry (D Tenn.)	Character	Admitted
77th	2nd	1942	William Langer (R N.D.)	Character	Admitted*
80th	1st	1947	Theodore G. Bilbo (D Miss.)	Character	Died before Senate acted

*Senate decided that a two-thirds majority, as in expulsion cases, would be required for exclusion. The resolution proposing exclusion did not receive a two-thirds majority.

Source: U.S. Senate, Committee on Rules and Administration, Subcommittee on Privileges and Elections, *Senate Election, Expulsion and Censure Cases from 1793 to 1972*, compiled by Richard D. Hupman, S. Doc. 92-7, 92nd Cong. 1st sess., 1972.

number of years was raised. Shields had been naturalized Oct. 21, 1840, and would not be a citizen until Oct. 20, 1849. Although Shields was seated on March 6, the Senate on March 15 adopted a resolution declaring his election void on the ground of insufficient years of citizenship. Shields then was elected to fill the vacancy thus created and was allowed to serve from Oct. 27, 1849.

(3) Philip F. Thomas of Maryland had given $100 to his son when the son entered the military service of the Confederacy. When Thomas was elected a U.S. senator by the Maryland Legislature in 1866, he was charged with being disloyal for giving aid and comfort to the enemy. The Senate voted 27 to 20 to exclude Thomas.

Exclusion proceedings based on the age qualification for senators were avoided, in two cases, by different means. When Henry Clay (D-R Ky.) arrived in Washington to take his seat, he lacked five months of the required 30 years. The Senate tacitly ignored this fact, and he was sworn in, Nov. 19, 1806. Rush D. Holt (D W.Va.) also had not reached the age of 30 when the time came for him to enter the Senate in 1935. He delayed the presentation of his credentials until his 30th birthday and was then admitted. The Senate later rejected, 62-17, a proposal to declare Holt's election invalid on the ground of age.

Exclusion Cases Rejected. Several cases in which exclusion proceedings were begun and failed are noteworthy. John M. Niles, elected to the Senate by the Connecticut Legislature in 1842, was unable to take his seat, owing to severe illness, when the 28th Congress first convened in December 1843. Because Niles showed signs of mental strain when he first appeared with his credentials in April 1844, the Senate appointed a committee to consider his case. After interviewing him, it reported that it was "satisfied that Mr. Niles is at this time laboring under mental and physical debility, but is not of unsound mind in the technical sense of that phrase; the faculties of his mind are subject to the control of his will; and there is no sufficient reason why he be not qualified and permitted to take his seat as a member of the Senate."[10] The Senate on May 16, 1844, accepted the committee's conclusion, and Niles took his seat.

Hiram R. Revels (R Miss.), a former slave, was elected to the Senate in 1870. He was challenged on the ground that he had not become a citizen until 1868, when the Fourteenth Amendment was ratified. The Senate ruled that the amendment made Revels retroactively a citizen, and the oath was administered to him.

On Feb. 23, 1903, Reed Smoot (R Utah) presented his credentials as a senator-elect. A group of Utah citizens opposed his seating on the ground that as a Mormon he favored polygamy and opposed the separation of church and state. The Senate administered the oath to Smoot on a tentative basis on March 4, 1903. The senator's eligibility was then studied by the Committee on Privileges and Elections, which on June 11, 1906, reported a resolution which would have declared Smoot not entitled to his seat. Sen. Philander C. Knox (R Pa.) contended Feb. 14, 1907, that Smoot's case involved expulsion rather than exclusion and therefore required a two-thirds vote: "There is no question as to Sen. Smoot's possessing the qualifications prescribed by the Constitution, and therefore we cannot deprive him of his seat by a majority vote."[11]

Knox's amendment requiring a two-thirds vote was agreed to as a first step. But an amendment to expel Smoot failed on a 27-43 vote. Then the exclusion resolution, with Knox's amendment, also failed, 28-42.

When Arthur R. Gould (R Maine) was elected to the Senate in 1926, various colleagues made an issue of the fact that some 14 years earlier he had been accused of involvement in bribery. Vice President Charles G. Dawes ruled out of order a resolution which would have prevented Gould from being sworn in. Gould later voted for a resolution, which was adopted, directing the Committee on Privileges and Elections to look into his case. In the committee's hearings on the matter, Gould contended that the attempt to deny him his seat contravened the right of Maine's citizens to send to Washington a senator of their choice. The committee on March 4, 1927, reported that Gould's alleged part in the bribery case had not been proved. He was later reimbursed by the Senate for the expenses he had incurred in defending himself before the committee.

In 1941, the right of William Langer (R N.D.) to a seat in the Senate was challenged. Opponents cited alleged misconduct on Langer's part during his service as governor of North Dakota and in other posts in that state's government. When an investigating committee recommended that Langer be excluded, the Senate added a two-thirds requirement, as it had done in the case of Reed Smoot, and then on March 27, 1942, voted down the proposed resolution.

The most recent exclusion case involving a senator-elect arose in January 1947, when Theodore G. Bilbo (D Miss.) presented himself for swearing in. Bilbo had been accused of fraud, violence in preventing blacks from voting, and other offenses. He was asked to stand aside when other senators-elect took the oath. In August 1947, before the question of his right to his seat had been settled, Bilbo died.

Cases Occurring in the House

Ten members-elect have been excluded from the House of Representatives on the ground that they were not qualified to serve. John Bailey of Massachusetts was the first to be excluded. He was challenged on the ground that he was not a resident of the district that he purported to represent. The House, by a resolution of March 18, 1824, declared that Bailey was not entitled to his seat. He returned home, was elected to fill the vacancy created by his exclusion, and was seated Dec. 13, 1824.

In 1867, southern states elected to Congress four citizens whom the House found to be tainted with acts of disloyalty during the Civil War. They were John Y. Brown and John D. Young of Kentucky; W. D. Simpson of South Carolina; and John A. Wimpy of Georgia. The Kentuckians were Democrats; the two others, independents. All four were excluded.

South Carolina had another representative-elect excluded three years later. Benjamin F. Whittemore, a Republican, was censured by the House in 1870 for selling appointments to the U.S. Military Academy and resigned on Feb. 24 of that year. When Whittemore was re-elected to the same Congress, Rep. John A. Logan (D Ill.) discussed his case on the House floor: "It is said that the constituency has the right to elect such member as they deem proper. I say no. We cannot say that he shall be of a certain politics, or of a certain religion, or anything of that kind; but, Sir, we have the right to say that he shall not be a man of infamous character."[12] The House on June 21, 1870, excluded Whittemore by a vote of 130 to 76.

The House based two exclusions on polygamy. George Q. Cannon was elected in 1872 as a delegate from Utah Territory. In the first and second sessions of the 43rd Congress, the question of his eligibility was raised and was settled in his favor. Cannon served in the House until 1881 without being challenged, but in 1882 the issue arose again. The House, taking account both of Cannon's practice of polygamy and of doubts about the validity of his election, declared the seat vacant, in effect excluding Cannon.

In 1900, members of the House questioned the right of Brigham H. Roberts, elected as a representative from Utah, to take his seat. Roberts had been found guilty some years earlier of violating an 1882 law which prohibited polygamy. This was the case, mentioned earlier, in which an investigating committee argued that the Founding Fathers had not foreclosed the right of Congress to establish qualifications for membership other than those mentioned in the Constitution. The House refused to seat Roberts. There were 268 votes for exclusion, 50 against.

In the 20th century, only Victor L. Berger, Wisconsin Socialist, and Adam Clayton Powell Jr., New York Democrat, have been excluded from the House. Berger had been convicted in 1919 of violating the Espionage Act of June 15, 1917, by publishing anti-war statements. While an appeal was pending, he was elected to the 66th Congress. By resolution of the House, Nov. 10, 1919, Berger was declared "not entitled to take the oath of office as a representative."[13] He was re-elected during the same Congress and excluded again on Jan. 10, 1920. But after the Supreme Court had reversed Berger's conviction, he was elected to the House three more times, in 1922, 1924 and 1926, and was seated without question.

Cases in which House proceedings on exclusion ended in admission of the representative-elect evoked various memorable exchanges on the floor. An example is the case of John C. Conner (D Texas), who was accused of having whipped black soldiers under his command in 1868 and of having boasted in 1869 that he would escape conviction by a military court by bribing witnesses. Rep. James A. Garfield (R Ohio), speaking in the House on March 31, 1870, raised a constitutional question on this case: "Allow me to ask...if anything in the Constitution of the United States...forbids that a 'moral monster' shall be elected to Congress?"[14] Rep. Ebon C. Ingersoll (R Ill.) replied: "I believe the people may elect a moral monster to Congress if they see fit, but I believe that Congress has a right to exclude that moral monster from a seat if they see fit."[15] A resolution allowing Conner to take his seat was adopted the same day.

The Powell Case

One of the stormiest episodes in congressional history was the precedent-shattering case of Rep. Adam Clayton Powell Jr. It was Powell's exclusion from the House that resulted in the Supreme Court ruling that Congress could not add to the constitutional qualifications for membership in Congress. In 1937, Powell succeeded his father as pastor of the Abyssinian Baptist Church in Harlem, one of the largest congregations in the country. The new pastor was elected to the 79th Congress in 1944 with the nomination of both the Democratic and Republican Parties. He took his seat with the Democrats, was re-elected regularly by large majorities, served as chairman of the House Committee on Education and Labor from 1961 to 1967, and was considered by many observers the most powerful black in the United States. Throughout his legislative career, he retained his pastorate.

Court Suits

Powell's downfall was brought on in part by his flamboyant personality and his apparent disregard for the law. On the eve of Powell's 1952 re-election bid, he was informed by the Internal Revenue Service that he had underestimated his 1945 income tax by $2,749. A federal grand

House Cases Involving Qualifications for Membership

Congress	Session	Year	Member-elect	Grounds	Disposition
1st	1st	1789	William L. Smith (Fed S.C.)	Citizenship	Admitted
10th	1st	1807	Philip B. Key (Fed Md.)	Residence	Admitted
10th	1st	1807	William McCreery (— Md.)	Residence	Admitted
18th	1st	1823	Gabriel Richard (Ind Mich. Terr.)	Citizenship	Admitted
18th	1st	1823	John Bailey (Ind Mass.)	Residence	*Excluded*
18th	1st	1823	John Forsyth (D Ga.)	Residence	Admitted
27th	1st	1841	David Levy (R Fla. Terr.)	Citizenship	Admitted
36th	1st	1859	John Y. Brown (D Ky.)	Age	Admitted
40th	1st	1867	William H. Hooper (D Utah Terr.)	Mormonism	Admitted
40th	1st	1867	Lawrence S. Trimble (D Ky.)	Loyalty	Admitted
40th	1st	1867	John Y. Brown (D Ky.)	Loyalty	*Excluded*
40th	1st	1867	John D. Young (D Ky.)	Loyalty	*Excluded*
40th	1st	1867	Roderick R. Butler (R Tenn.)	Loyalty	Admitted
40th	1st	1867	John A. Wimpy (Ind Ga.)	Loyalty	*Excluded*
40th	1st	1867	W. D. Simpson (Ind S.C.)	Loyalty	*Excluded*
41st	1st	1869	John M. Rice (D Ky.)	Loyalty	Admitted
41st	2nd	1870	Lewis McKenzie (Unionist Va.)	Loyalty	Admitted
41st	2nd	1870	George W. Booker (Conservative Va.)	Loyalty	Admitted
41st	2nd	1870	Benjamin F. Whittemore (R S.C.)	Malfeasance	*Excluded*
41st	2nd	1870	John C. Conner (D Texas)	Misconduct	Admitted
43rd	1st	1873	George Q. Cannon (R Utah Terr.)	Mormonism	Admitted
43rd	2nd	1874	George Q. Cannon (R Utah Terr.)	Polygamy	Admitted
47th	1st	1881	John S. Barbour (D Va.)	Residence	Admitted
47th	1st	1882	George Q. Cannon (R Utah Terr.)	Polygamy	Seat vacated[1]
50th	1st	1887	James B. White (R Ind.)	Citizenship	Admitted
56th	1st	1899	Robert W. Wilcox (Ind Hawaii Terr.)	Bigamy, treason	Admitted
56th	1st	1900	Brigham H. Roberts (D Utah)	Polygamy	*Excluded*
59th	1st	1905	Anthony Michalek (R Ill.)	Citizenship	Admitted
66th	1st	1919	Victor L. Berger (Socialist Wis.)	Sedition	*Excluded*
66th	2nd	1920	Victor L. Berger (Socialist Wis.)	Sedition	*Excluded*
69th	1st	1926	John W. Langley (R Ky.)	Criminal misconduct	Resigned
70th	1st	1927	James M. Beck (R Pa.)	Residence	Admitted
71st	1st	1929	Ruth B. Owen (D Fla.)	Citizenship	Admitted
90th	1st	1967	Adam C. Powell Jr. (D N.Y.)	Misconduct	*Excluded*[2]

1. Discussions of polygamy and an election contest led to a declaration that the seat was vacant.
2. Supreme Court June 16, 1969, ruled that the House had improperly excluded Powell.

Sources: Hinds and Cannon, *Precedents of the House of Representatives of the United States,* 11 vols. (1935-41); Joint Committee on Congressional Operations, *House of Representatives Exclusion, Censure and Expulsion Cases from 1789 to 1973,* committee print, 93rd Cong., 1st sess., 1973.

jury indicted him in 1958 on a charge of tax evasion. In the ensuing trial, held in 1960, the jury was unable to reach a verdict. The case was dismissed the following year, but the IRS continued to dun Powell. In 1966, he paid $27,833.17 in back taxes and penalties.

The Harlem representative became involved in civil litigation after he had said, in a television interview in 1960, that Esther James, a widow in his district, was a "bag woman," or graft collector, for New York City policemen. James sued Powell for libel. He was ordered by the court to pay her an amount set originally at $211,739 and reduced, on appeal, to $46,500. That sum plus court costs was paid in 1965-67, in part by Powell directly and in part by a record company from royalties on Powell's record "Keep the Faith, Baby."

A second civil case against Powell was instituted by James in 1964 on the basis of an allegation that the representative had fraudulently transferred property to avoid paying the original libel judgment. In this case, a jury awarded James $350,000. That amount was reduced later to $155,785, including $100,000 in punitive damages. The New York Court of Appeals in 1967 eliminated the punitive damages. Powell, after further delays, ultimately paid the remainder. Meanwhile, he had been held in contempt of court on four occasions.

Committee Revolt

In 1966, Powell also ran into trouble from the members of his Education and Labor Committee. That committee had reported a bill authorizing President Johnson's anti-poverty program. Powell favored the legislation but, by long absences and for personal reasons, he delayed bringing it up for floor debate. Angered by the delay, Powell's Democratic colleagues on the committee moved to strip him of most of his basic powers as committee chairman. By a vote of 27 to 1, the committee Sept. 22, 1966, adopted new rules, one of which provided that if the chairman failed to bring a bill to the floor, one of the six subcommittee chairmen could do so.

The House Democratic Caucus on Jan. 9, 1967, removed Powell from the chairmanship of the Committee on Education and Labor for the duration of the 90th Congress. This was the first time since 1925 that a committee chairman had been deposed in either house of Congress. Powell, who attended the caucus, called the action "a lynching, northern style."[16] A day later, Powell was embroiled in a challenge to his seat in the House.

Exclusion Proceedings

In the 1950s and the early 1960s, Powell repeatedly went on costly pleasure trips at government expense. In addition, he incurred criticism for taking a staff member, Corinne A. Huff, on many trips to Bimini Island in the Bahamas. Out of government funds, he paid his wife $20,578 a year as a clerk while she lived in Puerto Rico. The Special Contracts Subcommittee of the House Committee on Administration on Jan. 3, 1967, recommended that Mrs. Powell be dropped from the payroll, as was done soon thereafter.

But Powell's apparent misuse of public funds and his continued legal problems in New York had generated much furor among the public and members of Congress, and on Jan. 10, 1967, the House took up the question of whether Powell should be seated.

A resolution submitted by Morris K. Udall (D Ariz.) proposed that Powell be sworn in, pending the result of a 60-day investigation of his conduct by a select committee. Udall contended that stripping Powell of his chairmanship was punishment enough, since his malfeasance was based on his misuse of that position. But the resolution was rejected on a 126-305 vote.

The House then adopted a resolution, offered by Minority Leader Gerald R. Ford (R Mich.), which denied Powell his seat pending an investigation. The vote was 363 to 65.

House Judiciary Committee Chairman Emanuel Celler (D N.Y.) was chairman of the select committee appointed to investigate Powell's qualifications for his seat. The committee conducted hearings beginning Feb. 8, 1967. Its report, submitted Feb. 23, included a recommendation, unprecedented in congressional history, that Powell be fined. The committee proposed that he be sworn in; that his seniority be based on the date of his swearing in; that he be censured for "gross misconduct" through misuse of funds of the Committee on Education and Labor, refusal to pay the judgment against him, and noncooperation with House investigating committees; and that he be fined $40,000, to be paid to the clerk of the House in the form of a monthly deduction of $1,000 from Powell's salary, in order to "offset any civil liability of Mr. Powell to the United States."[17]

The House on March 1, 1967, rejected the committee's proposals and adopted instead a resolution excluding Powell from the 90th Congress—the first exclusion since Victor L. Berger was barred in 1919 and 1920. On the select committee's proposals, the vote was 202 in favor, 222 against; on the exclusion resolution, 307 in favor, 116 against.

As in his ouster from his committee chairmanship, Powell ascribed his downfall to racism. That racial feeling played a part in the vote to exclude Powell seemed probable. Rep. Celler said on television and on the House floor that he saw "an element of racism in the vote."[18] Arlen

J. Large, a Washington correspondent, wrote in the *Wall Street Journal*, March 22, 1967: "Disclaimers of race as a factor in Mr. Powell's exclusion don't jibe with the nearly solid anti-Powell votes of southern congressmen, reflecting the bitterly worded letters from white voters back home."

Suit Filed

In his appearances before the select committee, Powell responded only to questions relating to the constitutional requirements for House membership—his age, citizenship and inhabitancy. These were the only questions that the House could properly inquire into, Powell and his lawyers claimed. Upon his exclusion by the House, Powell filed suit. The case eventually reached the Supreme Court, which on June 16, 1969, ruled that the House had improperly excluded Powell, a duly elected representative who met the constitutional requirements for membership.

Powell Seated

Meanwhile, New York State conducted a special election April 11, 1967, in Powell's Harlem district to fill the vacancy. Powell entered his name as a candidate but was unable to return to New York City to campaign without being arrested for contempt. Nevertheless, he was elected with 86 per cent of the vote. Powell, however, did not apply to the House to be seated but remained at his vacation retreat on Bimini, waiting the outcome of his lawsuit against the exclusion.

On April 5, 1968, Powell returned to his district where he was arrested and then released because the litigation in which he was involved was under appeal. In the general election of 1968, he again became a candidate for a seat in Congress and once more was victorious at the polls. The 91st Congress on Jan. 3, 1969, ended his two-year exile. Powell was sworn in and seated but subjected to loss of seniority and fined $25,000. In the voting on the resolution imposing these penalties, there were 254 yeas, 158 nays.

Although he had won the right to be seated, Powell rarely attended Congress, preferring instead his retreat in Bimini. In 1970 Charles B. Rangel successfully challenged Powell in the Democratic primary and went on to win the general election. Powell died in Miami, Fla., April 4, 1972.

Contested Elections

Decentralization of control over elections in the United States may have strengthened participatory democracy, but it has led frequently to controversy over election results. Losing candidates and their supporters believe in many cases that more voters were on their side than the official count showed. Floyd M. Riddick wrote in *The United States Congress; Organization and Procedure:* "Seldom if ever has a Congress organized without some losing candidate for a seat in either the Senate or House contesting the right of the member-elect to be senator or representative, as the case might be, as a result of the election in which the losing candidate participated."[19]

To avert partisanship in settling election disputes involving members of the House, an act of 1798 established procedures to be followed in handling contested cases; by its own terms the act expired in 1804. A law approved Feb. 19, 1851, renewed the effort to give the proceedings in contested elections of House members a judicial rather than partisan character, and amendments in 1873 and 1875 improved the procedure for taking testimony in such cases. But despite these efforts, fidelity to party determined the outcome in a large majority of the cases.

The Federal Contested Election Act of 1969 superseded the earlier legislation. The new law, which again applied only to House contests, prescribed procedures for instituting a challenge and presenting testimony, but it did not establish criteria to govern decisions. It was more restrictive than the 1798 and 1851 laws in providing that only candidates listed on the ballot or bona fide write-in candidates might contest election results. Previously, anyone having an interest in a congressional election could initiate proceedings by filing a petition.

Senators were chosen by state legislatures until the adoption in 1913 of the Seventeenth Amendment to the Constitution which provided for direct popular elections. Before then, contested senatorial elections often involved accusations of corruption in the legislatures. Neither before nor after 1913 did Congress enact any law on contested Senate elections comparable to the legislation on contested elections in the House.

It is generally agreed that since 1789, the number of contested elections in the House and Senate has run into the hundreds. An exact number is difficult to ascertain because students of the subject disagree on what constitutes a contested election. George B. Galloway of the Legislative Reference Service stated in 1953 that there had been 136 election contests in the Senate from 1789 to 1952. John T. Dempsey, in an unpublished 1956 University of Michigan doctoral dissertation, counted only 125 in the Senate from 1789 to 1955. [It appears that Galloway included, and Dempsey excluded, contested appointments made by state governors to fill seats vacated by death or otherwise.] In these same time periods, Galloway counted 541 House election contests while Dempsey put the number at 546.

Senate Cases

An illustrative 19th century election contest was that of Henry A. Du Pont (R Del.), who was excluded from the Senate because he had not been duly elected by the Delaware Legislature. Delaware law stated that 15 votes would be sufficient to elect a U.S. senator if the legislature consisted of 29 members; 16 votes, if it consisted of 30 members. Du Pont, in an election held in 1895, received 15 votes, but there was a question whether the legislature consisted of 29 or 30 members. Du Pont admitted that 30 votes had been cast, but he contended that one of the votes had been cast by a person who had no right to participate, because he had succeeded to the governorship through the death of the incumbent. The Senate on May 15, 1895, decided, by a vote of 31 to 30, that Du Pont was not entitled to the seat.

The more important 20th century cases have included those of Lorimer and Vare. William Lorimer (R Ill.) was elected a senator by the Illinois Legislature and took his seat in the Senate on June 18, 1909. In May 1910, he requested that the Committee on Privileges and Elections examine allegations made in the press that bribery and corruption had entered into his election. Following an investigation, the Senate on March 1, 1911, rejected a proposed resolution declaring that Lorimer had not been "duly and legally elected."[20] The vote was 40 for adoption of the resolution, 46 against.

The case, however, was reopened in the next Congress and the first decision reversed. A specially appointed committee took further testimony. While the committee majority favored dropping the charges, the minority proposed adoption of a resolution declaring Lorimer's election invalid on the ground of corruption. On June 13, 1912, the Senate adopted the resolution, 55-28.

Corruption was also the crux of the case of William S. Vare. During the primaries in Pennsylvania in 1926, newspapers charged that persons favoring Vare as the Republican nominee for senator were engaging in corrupt practices. Vare won the primary contest and the November election. The Senate meanwhile, on May 19, 1926, had appointed a committee to investigate Pennsylvania's senatorial primaries and the fall election. Following the election, Vare's Democratic rival, ex-Secretary of Labor William B. Wilson, charged that Vare had won through corruption. When Congress met, Vare was asked to stand aside while other senators-elect were sworn in.

Proceedings in Vare's case dragged on for two years, during which time Vare became seriously ill. The Senate received a series of reports on the case, including the report of a special committee, Feb. 22, 1929, asserting that Vare, owing to his excessive use of money to get nominated and elected, was not entitled to a seat in the Senate. Not until December 1929 did the Senate take final action on the matter. On Dec. 5, the Senate Committee on Privileges and Elections reported that Vare had received a plurality of the legal votes cast in the election. But the Senate on the following day voted 58-22 to deny Vare a seat. At the same time, it concluded by a vote of 66 to 15 that Wilson had not been elected. Subsequently, the governor of Pennsylvania appointed Joseph R. Grundy to the vacant Senate seat.

Wyman-Durkin Contest. The closest Senate election since popular voting for the Senate was instituted in 1913 occurred Nov. 5, 1974, in New Hampshire where Republican Louis C. Wyman led Democrat John A. Durkin by only two votes.

The election resulted in a prolonged dispute in the Senate covering seven months and 41 roll-call votes, and ending when the Senate reached a compromise and for the first time declared a vacancy due to its inability to decide an election contest.[21]

The dispute began when final unofficial returns gave Wyman a 355-vote margin over Durkin. A recount then found Durkin the winner by 10 votes. The state ballot commission examined the recount and found Wyman the winner by two votes.

Durkin filed a petition of contest with the Senate Dec. 27, 1974, challenging Wyman's right to the seat and defending the validity of his own recount victory. Wyman Jan. 5, 1975, filed a petition in the Senate urging that Durkin's petition be dismissed. He also asked that the seat be declared vacant which would open the way for a new election in New Hampshire. Wyman and his supporters feared that Durkin would win if the Senate, with its 61-38 Democratic majority, reviewed the ballot commission findings as the Democratic candidate requested.

The first skirmish occurred soon after the Senate convened. On Jan. 28, the Senate turned aside Republican attempts to temporarily seat Wyman and to declare the seat vacant and voted, 58-34, to send the dispute to the Senate Rules and Administration Committee. The Senate thus accepted the arguments of Senate Majority Leader Mike Mansfield (D Mont.) and Rules Chairman Howard W. Cannon (D Nev.), who cited the constitutional provision that each house of Congress should be the judge of its own elections and said the Rules Committee should at least try to determine who won before calling for a new election.

Democrats also said that the conflicting rulings of the New Hampshire authorities precluded seating either of the contestants, even though Wyman had the most recent certification. Republicans claimed that precedent dictated temporary seating of Wyman, without prejudice to Durkin's challenge. But the motion to temporarily seat Wyman failed on a 34-58 vote, while a motion to declare the seat vacant lost, 39-53.

The Rules Committee agreed to examine and recount the ballots in dispute. By April 25 nearly 1,000 ballots had been examined. But the committee failed to agree on 27 of the ballots, splitting on 4 to 4 tie votes. Tie votes also occurred on eight legal and procedural issues. The eight issues and 27 ballots were sent to the Senate floor to be resolved.

Floor consideration of the disputed election began June 12 with a second attempt by the Republicans to declare the seat vacant. The motion was defeated, 43-55, and a filibuster by Republicans and several southern Democrats supporting the Republican position began. An unprecedented six attempts were made to invoke cloture (shut off debate) but they all failed to obtain the required sixty votes. An attempt to settle one of the eight disputed issues in Wyman's favor July 15 was defeated on a 44-49 vote. After this loss, the Republicans charged that a Democratic "steamroller" was in operation and refused to allow a vote on any other issue.

The Senate began to spend less and less time each day on the New Hampshire dispute and returned to debate on substantive legislation. But neither side appeared ready to compromise. In the absence of any definitive Senate action, public pressure mounted for a vacancy to be declared and a new election held.

Finally, Durkin relented and asked for a new election. Durkin's change of mind came as a complete surprise to the Senate Democratic leadership, but there was a general feeling of relief that the impasse at last had been broken. The Senate June 30 voted 71-21 to declare the seat vacant as of Aug. 8.

Durkin won the special Sept. 16 election with 53.6 per cent of the vote and was sworn in Sept. 18, 1975.

Bellmon Challenged. A second case occurring during the 94th Congress proved the exception to the norm that a member of the minority party cannot win an election contest. Republican incumbent Henry Bellmon had been certified the victor of the November 1974 Oklahoma Senate election by 3,835 votes and was seated by the Senate in January 1975 pending the outcome of a challenge. The Democratic candidate, former Rep. Ed Edmondson, charged that the absence of a straight-ticket lever on voting machines in Tulsa County and confusing voter instructions cost him sufficient votes to have changed the outcome.

The Senate Rules and Administration Committee Dec. 15, 1975, declared that it could not decide which of the two candidates had won the election and sent the dispute to the floor. Under the committee resolution, the Senate could vote to dismiss the challenge, which would confirm Bellmon in office, or it could declare the seat vacant, as it ultimately did in the Wyman-Durkin contest.

After three days of debate, the Senate settled the issue by voting March 4, 1976, to seat Bellmon.[22]

House Cases

George F. Hoar (R Mass.), who served in both houses, wrote in his *Autobiography of Seventy Years* in 1903:

"Whenever there is a plausible reason for making a contest, the dominant party in the House almost always awards the seat to the man of its own side."[23] Thomas B. Reed (R Maine) went further than Hoar's "almost always." In an article on contested elections published in the *North American Review* in 1890, while he was Speaker of the House, Reed wrote: "Probably there is not an instance on record where the minority was increased by the decision of contested cases."[24] While preparing to write a history of the House of Representatives, De Alva Alexander found, in 1906, that up to that time only three persons not of the dominant party had obtained seats in that chamber through the settlement of some hundreds of election contests.

William F. Willoughby asserted in *Principles of Legislative Organization and Administration* in 1934 that "The whole history of the handling of election contests by the House has constituted one of the major scandals of our political system."[25] Willoughby noted that after enactment of the 1851 law on procedures for adjudicating elections, "for many years the House made little or no pretense of settling election contests on any basis of equity, political considerations in practically all cases determining the decision reached." In 1955, John T. Dempsey, a doctoral candidate at the University of Michigan, made a case-by-case examination of the 546 contested election cases he had counted in the House. He found that only on 47 occasions, less than 10 per cent of the total, did the controlling party award a contested seat to a member of the minority party.

Mississippi Dispute. Perhaps the most dramatic election dispute which the House has settled in recent years was that of the Mississippi Five in 1965. The governor of Mississippi certified the election to the House in 1964 of four Democrats and one Republican. The Democrats were Thomas G. Abernethy, William M. Colmer, Jamie L. Whitten and John B. Williams; the Republican was Prentiss Walker. Their right to be seated in the House was contested by a biracial group, the Mississippi Freedom Democratic Party (M.F.D.P.), formed originally to challenge the seating of all-white delegates from the state to the 1964 Democratic National Convention. This group, when unsuccessful in getting its candidates on the 1964 congressional election ballot, conducted a rump election in which Annie Devine, Virginia Gray and Fannie L. Hamer were the winners.[26]

The three women, when they sought entrance to the House floor, were barred. However, Speaker John W. McCormack (D Mass.) asked the regular Mississippi representatives-elect to stand aside while the other members of the House were sworn in. Rep. William F. Ryan (D N.Y.), sponsor of the challenge, contended that the regular congressional election in Mississippi was invalid because blacks had been systematically prevented from voting. A resolution to seat the regular Mississippi delegation was adopted on Jan. 4, 1965, by a voice vote.

The M.F.D.P. on May 16, 1965, filed a brief and petition, with 600 depositions, citing officially inspired harassment of black voters in Mississippi and the admission by state officials of participation in prevention of black voting. The House Committee on Administration on Sept. 15 reported, by a vote of 15 to 9, a proposed resolution rejecting the petition, partly because the contestants had not availed themselves of the proper legal steps and because alleged voting discrimination had been made moot by the Voting Rights Act of 1965. The full House approved the resolution Sept. 17 by a vote of 228 to 143.

Assault on Charles Sumner, 1856

Sen. Charles Sumner (R Mass.), in a speech on the Senate floor, May 20, 1856, denounced in scathing language supporters of the Kansas-Nebraska Act of 1854, which repealed the Missouri Compromise of 1820 and permitted the two new territories to decide whether slavery would be allowed there. Two days later, while Sumner was seated at his desk on the Senate floor after the day's session had ended, he heard his name called. Looking up, he saw a tall stranger, who berated him for his speech and then struck him on the head repeatedly with a heavy walking stick, which was broken by the blows. Sumner fell bleeding and unconscious to the floor. He was absent from the Senate, because of the injuries suffered in the assault, for three and a half years, until Dec. 5, 1859.

The attacker was Rep. Preston S. Brooks (State Rights Dem. S.C.), nephew of one of those whom Sumner had excoriated—Sen. A. P. Butler (State Rights Dem. S.C.). Expulsion proceedings against Brooks failed, on a strictly party vote. He resigned his House seat, July 15, 1856, but was elected to fill the vacancy caused by his resignation.

Rep. Laurence M. Keitt (D S.C.) was censured by the House on July 15, 1856, for having known of Brooks' intention to assault Sumner, for having taken no action to discourage or prevent the assault, and for having been "present on one or more occasions to witness the same." Keitt resigned, July 16, 1856, and was elected to fill the vacancy caused by his resignation. A resolution similar to the one censuring Keitt but directed against Rep. Henry A. Edmundson (D Va.) had failed of adoption, July 15, 1856.

Discipline

For offenses of sufficient gravity, each house of Congress punishes its members by expulsion or censure. Of the two, censure is milder, requiring a simple majority vote while expulsion requires a two-thirds majority vote. Censure also has the advantage of not depriving constituents of their elected senators or representatives. Grounds for disciplining members usually consist of a member's action during service in Congress. Both houses have distrusted their power to punish a member for offenses committed prior to an election and they also have been shy about punishing misdeeds committed during a previous Congress.

For minor transgressions of the rules, the presiding officer of either house may call a member to order, without a formal move to censure. For example, on Jan. 14, 1955, Sen. Russell B. Long (D La.), while presiding over the Senate, called Sen. Joseph R. McCarthy (R Wis.) to order when McCarthy questioned the motives of some senators who had voted with him for a resolution continuing an investigation of Communists in government. Long said: "The statement of the junior senator from Wisconsin was that other senators were insincere. In making that statement, the senator from Wisconsin spoke contrary to the rules of the Senate.... He must take his seat."[27] Later on the same day, Long again called McCarthy to order.

In recent years, Congress has turned to other methods when it wants to discipline members but yet wants to avoid the strong measure of censure or expulsion. These methods have included denial of the member's right to vote, fines, stripping of chairmanships and reprimand.

Expulsion

Fifteen senators have been expelled, one in 1797 and 14 during the Civil War. Expulsion proceedings in the Senate have been instituted 12 times since the Civil War, always without success. In the House, only three members have been expelled, all of them in 1861. Of the five expulsion cases in the House since the Civil War, all were changed to censure cases, and the accused members were censured. Conspiracy against a foreign country (the 1797 case in the Senate) and support of a rebellion (the Civil War cases of 14 senators and three representatives) have been the only grounds on which a senator or representative has been expelled. In a few cases, a senator or representative escaped expulsion by resigning.

Grounds for Expulsion

In the successful expulsion cases, the grounds were conspiracy or disloyalty. The unsuccessful cases were concerned with the killing of a representative in a duel, the assaulting of a senator or a representative, treasonable or offensive utterances, sedition, corruption and Mormonism.

Prior Offenses. The most important question raised about the validity of grounds for expulsion has been whether a member of either house may be expelled for offenses committed prior to his election. John Quincy Adams, while serving in the Senate, submitted a committee report which affirmed the right of the Senate to expel a member for pre-election conduct that came to light after he had taken his seat. The case was that of John Smith (D Ohio), who allegedly had been connected with Aaron Burr's conspiracy to separate several of the western states from the Union. Adams' committee, in its report of Dec. 31, 1807, said: "When a man whom his fellow citizens have honored with their confidence on the pledge of a spotless reputation has degraded himself by the commission of infamous crimes, which become suddenly and unexpectedly revealed to the world, defective, indeed, would be that institution which should be impotent to discard from its bosom the contagion of such a member."[28]

The expulsion case against Smith was lost by a single vote on April 9, 1808, when 19 yeas, not enough to make up the required two-thirds, were cast for expulsion, against 10 nays. Later Congresses which debated proposals to unseat members repeatedly took up the question whether acts committed prior to the member's election furnished legitimate grounds for expulsion.

Incompatible Office. The Constitution, in Article I, Section 6, provides: "...no Person holding any Office under the United States, shall be a Member of either House during his Continuance in Office." When a senator or representative has accepted appointment to another "Office under the United States," he has jeopardized but not always lost his privilege of remaining in Congress, depending on the type of office he accepted and the attitude of the house in which he was serving. If he lost his post in Congress by accepting another office, he is not considered to have been expelled; his seat is treated as having been vacated.

The first of two significant cases in which this provision resulted in a sitting member's loss of his seat was that of

Cases of Expulsion in the Senate

Congress	Session	Year	Member	Grounds	Disposition
5th	2nd	1797	William Blount (Ind Tenn.)	Anti-Spanish conspiracy	*Expelled*
10th	1st	1808	John Smith (D Ohio)	Disloyalty	Not expelled
35th	1st	1858	Henry M. Rice (D Minn.)	Corruption	Not expelled
37th	1st	1861	James M. Mason (D Va.)	Support of rebellion	*Expelled*
37th	1st	1861	Robert M. Hunter (D Va.)	Support of rebellion	*Expelled*
37th	1st	1861	Thomas L. Clingman (D N.C.)	Support of rebellion	*Expelled*
37th	1st	1861	Thomas Bragg (D N.C.)	Support of rebellion	*Expelled*
37th	1st	1861	James Chestnut Jr. (State Rights S.C.)	Support of rebellion	*Expelled*
37th	1st	1861	Alfred O. P. Nicholson (D Tenn.)	Support of rebellion	*Expelled*
37th	1st	1861	William K. Sebastian (D Ark.)	Support of rebellion	*Expelled*[1]
37th	1st	1861	Charles B. Mitchel (D Ark.)	Support of rebellion	*Expelled*
37th	1st	1861	John Hemphill (State Rights Dem. Texas)	Support of rebellion	*Expelled*
37th	1st	1861	Louis T. Wigfall[2] (D Texas)	Support of rebellion	Not expelled
37th	1st	1861	Louis T. Wigfall (D Texas)	Support of rebellion	*Expelled*
37th	1st	1861	John C. Breckinridge (D Ky.)	Support of rebellion	*Expelled*
37th	1st	1861	Lazarus W. Powell (D Ky.)	Support of rebellion	Not expelled
37th	2nd	1862	Trusten Polk (D Mo.)	Support of rebellion	*Expelled*
37th	2nd	1862	Jesse D. Bright (D Ind.)	Support of rebellion	*Expelled*
37th	2nd	1862	Waldo P. Johnson (D Mo.)	Support of rebellion	*Expelled*
37th	2nd	1862	James F. Simmons (Whig R.I.)	Corruption	Not expelled
42nd	3rd	1873	James W. Patterson (R N.H.)	Corruption	Not expelled
53rd	1st	1893	William N. Roach (D N.D.)	Embezzlement	Not expelled
58th	3rd	1905	John H. Mitchell (R Ore.)	Corruption	Not expelled
59th	2nd	1907	Reed Smoot (R Utah)	Mormonism	Not expelled
65th	3rd	1919	Robert M. La Follette (R Wis.)	Disloyalty	Not expelled
73rd	2nd	1934	John H. Overton (D La.)	Corruption	Not expelled
73rd	2nd	1934	Huey P. Long (D La.)	Corruption	Not expelled
77th	2nd	1942	William Langer (R N.D.)	Corruption	Not expelled

1. The Senate reversed its decision on Sebastian's expulsion March 3, 1877. Sebastian had died in 1865 but his children were paid an amount equal to his Senate salary between the time of his expulsion and the date of his death.

2. The Senate took no action on an initial resolution expelling Wigfall because he represented a state that had seceded from the Union; three months later he was expelled for supporting the Confederacy.

Source: U.S. Senate, Committee on Rules and Administration, Subcommittee on Privileges and Elections, *Senate Election, Expulsion and Censure Cases from 1793 to 1972*, compiled by Richard D. Hupman, S. Doc. 92-7, 92nd Cong., 1st sess., 1972.

Rep. John P. Van Ness (D N.Y.), who in the recess between the first and second sessions of the Seventh Congress was appointed a major in the District of Columbia militia. When the question of the compatibility of holding both that office and a seat in Congress was brought up, Van Ness argued that the pertinent provision of the Constitution was intended to apply only to civil offices, and he pointed out that his militia post carried no pay. On Jan. 11, 1803, however, the House, by a vote of 88 to 0, declared that Van Ness had forfeited his right to his House seat.

The second case was that of Rep. Samuel Hammond (Ind Ga.), who in October 1804 accepted an Army commission as colonel commandant for the District of Louisiana. On Feb. 2, 1805, the House declared the seat vacant.

In a similar situation which arose in 1846, the sitting representative involved, Edward D. Baker (Whig Ill.), resigned before the House had received a report on the matter from the Committee on Elections. Although the case was moot, the committee felt impelled to raise a hypothetical question. In its report of Feb. 21, 1847, the committee asked: "Now, suppose that every member of Congress were a colonel in the Army...and the President, who is by the Constitution the Commander in Chief of that Army, should come into the Halls of Congress and order each individual member to retire immediately...to his post in the Army, what would become of Congress?"[29]

War Service of Members. Cases arising in the Civil War and subsequent wars in which members of Congress served in the armed forces generally did not result in vacating of their seats. In the war with Spain, a House committee appointed to investigate the question reported on Feb. 21, 1899: "It cannot be contended that every position held by a member of Congress is an office within the meaning of the Constitution, even though the term office may usually be applied to many of these positions."[30] The committee cited as an example the position of official escort representative at the funeral of a public figure. To come under the constitutional prohibition, the committee said, a position "must not be merely transient, occasional, or incidental."[31]

The committee recommended adoption of a resolution declaring vacant the seats of four representatives who had

Cases of Expulsion in the House

Congress	Session	Year	Member	Grounds	Disposition
5th	2nd	1798	Matthew Lyon (Anti-Fed Vt.)	Assault on representative	Not expelled
5th	2nd	1798	Roger Griswold (Fed Conn.)	Assault on representative	Not expelled
5th	3rd	1799	Matthew Lyon (Anti-Fed Vt.)	Sedition	Not expelled
25th	2nd	1838	William J. Graves (Whig Ky.)	Killing of representative in duel	Not expelled
25th	3rd	1839	Alexander Duncan (Whig Ohio)	Offensive publication	Not expelled
34th	1st	1856	Preston S. Brooks (State Rights Dem. S.C.)	Assault on senator	Not expelled
34th	3rd	1857	Orsamus B. Matteson (Whig N.Y.)	Corruption	Not expelled
34th	3rd	1857	William A. Gilbert (— N.Y.)	Corruption	Not expelled
34th	3rd	1857	William W. Welch (American Conn.)	Corruption	Not expelled
34th	3rd	1857	Francis S. Edwards (— N.Y.)	Corruption	Not expelled
35th	1st	1858	Orsamus B. Matteson (Whig N.Y.)	Corruption	Not expelled*
37th	1st	1861	John B. Clark (D Mo.)	Support of rebellion	*Expelled*
37th	1st	1861	Henry C. Burnett (D Ky.)	Support of rebellion	*Expelled*
37th	1st	1861	John W. Reid (D Mo.)	Support of rebellion	*Expelled*
38th	1st	1864	Alexander Long (D Ohio)	Treasonable utterance	Not expelled*
38th	1st	1864	Benjamin G. Harris (D Md.)	Treasonable utterance	Not expelled*
39th	1st	1866	Lovell H. Rousseau (R Ky.)	Assault on representative	Not expelled*
41st	2nd	1870	Benjamin F. Whittemore (R S.C.)	Corruption	Not expelled*
41st	2nd	1870	Roderick R. Butler (R Tenn.)	Corruption	Not expelled*
42nd	3rd	1873	Oakes Ames (R Mass.)	Corruption	Not expelled*
42nd	3rd	1873	James Brooks (D N.Y.)	Corruption	Not expelled*
43rd	2nd	1875	John Y. Brown (D Ky.)	Insult to representative	Not expelled*
44th	1st	1875	William S. King (R Minn.)	Corruption	Not expelled
44th	1st	1875	John G. Schumaker (D N.Y.)	Corruption	Not expelled
48th	1st	1884	William P. Kellogg (R La.)	Corruption	Not expelled
67th	1st	1921	Thomas L. Blanton (D Texas)	Abuse of leave to print	Not expelled*

* Censured after expulsion move failed or was withdrawn.

Sources: Hinds and Cannon, *Precedents of the House of Representatives of the United States,* 11 vols. (1935-41); Joint Committee on Congressional Operations, *House of Representatives Exclusion, Censure and Expulsion Cases from 1789 to 1973,* committee print, 93rd Cong., 1st sess., 1973.

accepted commissions in the Army to serve in the war with Spain. "No mere patriotic sentiment," it said, "should be permitted to override the plain language of the fundamental written law."[32] On March 2, 1899, the House, by a vote of 77 yeas and 163 nays, declined to consider the proposed resolution.

Members of both houses have been appointed to serve as commissioners to negotiate peace and arbitrate disputes, as members of "blue ribbon" boards of inquiry, and so forth, without losing their seats in Congress. The House in 1919 authorized members who had been absent on military service to be paid their salaries minus the amount they were paid for military service. Judge Gerhard A. Gesell of the U.S. District Court for the District of Columbia ruled April 2, 1971, that the 117 members who held commissions in military reserve units were violating the incompatible-office clause of the Constitution. The decision was appealed all the way to the Supreme Court which ruled June 25, 1974, that the plaintiffs—present and former members of the reserves opposed to the Vietnam War—did not have legal standing to make the challenge. (*Schlesinger v. Reservists Committee to Stop the War,* 418 U.S. 208)

Civil War Cases

After the Senate's expulsion of William Blount (Ind Tenn.) in 1797 for conspiracy to incite members of two In-

dian tribes to attack Spanish Florida and Louisiana, the only successful expulsion cases were those resulting from the Civil War. On Jan. 21, 1861, Jefferson Davis (D Miss.), like a number of other southern senators before and after that date, announced his support of secession and withdrew from the Senate. On March 14, 1861, ten days after Lincoln's inauguration, the Senate adopted a resolution ordering that inasmuch as the seats of these southerners had "become vacant, ...the Secretary be directed to omit their names respectively from the roll."[33] Although Davis and the five other southern senators had left voluntarily, they had not formally resigned. Hence the Senate's action bore some resemblance to expulsion.

Senate Expulsions. On a single day, July 11, 1861, the Senate actually expelled 10 members, two each from Arkansas, North Carolina, Texas and Virginia, and one each from South Carolina and Tennessee, for failure to appear in their seats and for participation in secession. The vote was 32 in favor of expulsion, 10 against. Sen. John C. Breckinridge (D Ky.), who had been Vice President of the United States from 1857 to 1861, was expelled Dec. 4, 1861, by the following resolution: "Whereas John C. Breckinridge, a member of this body from the State of Kentucky, has joined the enemies of his country, and is now in arms against the Government he had sworn to support: Therefore, Resolved, That said John C. Breckinridge, the traitor, be, and he hereby is, expelled from the Senate."[34] On this resolution the vote was 37 to 0.

Of the 10 expulsions voted by the Senate on July 11, 1861, one was later annulled. In 1877, the Committee on Privileges and Elections reviewed the expulsion of Sen. William K. Sebastian (D Ark.), decided that the Senate had a right to reverse its earlier action, and recommended such reversal. The Senate on March 3, 1877, adopted the committee's recommendation, which was based on its findings that the charges made against Sebastian in 1861 were "occasioned by want of information, and by the overruling excitement of a period of great public danger."[35] Sebastian had remained loyal to the Union throughout the war.

In 1862, the Senate expelled three senators, all for disloyalty to the government—Missouri Democrats Trusten Polk and Waldo P. Johnson and Indiana Democrat Jesse D. Bright. Polk was accused of stating in a widely published letter his hopes that Missouri would secede from the Union. Johnson reportedly held similar feelings and furthermore did not appear to take his Senate seat. Bright was charged with treason for giving an arms salesman a letter of introduction to Confederate President Jefferson Davis.

House Expulsions. On July 13, 1861, the House expelled a member-elect, John B. Clark (D Mo.), who had not yet taken the oath. After a brief debate on Clark's entrance into the Confederate forces, and without referring the case to a committee, the House adopted the expulsion order by slightly more than a two-thirds vote, 94 to 45.

In December of the same year, the House adopted by two-thirds votes the only other expulsions in its history, affecting John W. Reid (D Mo.) and Henry C. Burnett (D Ky.). Reid was expelled for taking up arms against the country; Burnett was expelled for being in open rebellion against the federal government.

More Recent Expulsion Efforts

Sen. Robert M. La Follette (R Wis.) made a speech at St. Paul, Minn., Sept. 20, 1917, decrying American participation in the war in Europe. On the basis of that speech, Minnesota's Public Safety Commission petitioned the Senate to expel La Follette for sedition. The petition was referred to the Committee on Privileges and Elections, which held hearings during a 14-month period. On Dec. 2, 1918, three weeks after the World War I armistice, the committee recommended that the petition be dismissed. The Senate on Jan. 16, 1919, adopted the recommendation by a vote of 50 to 21.

In 1932-34, the two senators from Louisiana, Huey P. Long and John H. Overton, both Democrats, were accused of fraud and corruption in connection with their nomination and election. Resolutions of expulsion were introduced, and the Committee on Privileges and Elections conducted an investigation. Eventually it asked to be discharged from further consideration of the two cases. The Senate complied with this request on June 16, 1934, in effect burying the expulsion resolutions.

Charges of corruption against Sen.-elect William Langer (R N.D.) led to an effort to prevent his serving in the Senate. The effort took the form in part of a proposal to exclude Langer and in part of a proposal to expel him after he had taken the oath. On March 27, 1942, the Senate first rejected a resolution, 37-45, stating that the case did not fall within the constitutional provisions for expulsion. It then rejected, 30-52, a second resolution declaring that Langer was not entitled to his seat in the Senate.

Censure

In the entire history of the Congress, the Senate has censured seven of its members, the House 19. In the Senate, censure proceedings are carried out with a degree of moderation. The alleged offender, for example, is granted the privilege of speaking in his own behalf. The House often has denied that privilege to a representative accused of wrongdoing. In most cases in the House, a censured member is treated like a felon; the Speaker calls him to the bar and makes a solemn pronouncement of censure. For example, Speaker Frederick H. Gillett (R Mass.) on Oct. 27, 1921, directed the sergeant-at-arms to bring to the bar of the House Rep. Thomas L. Blanton (D Texas). The Speaker than made the following statement:

"Mr. Blanton, by a unanimous vote of the House—yeas, 293; nays, none—I have been directed to censure you because, when you had been allowed the courtesy of the House to print a speech which you did not deliver, you inserted in it foul and obscene matter, which you knew you could not have spoken on the floor; and that disgusting matter, which could not have been circulated through the mails in any other publication without violating the law, was transmitted as part of the proceedings of this House to thousands of homes and libraries throughout the country, to be read by men and women, and worst of all by children, whose prurient curiosity it would excite and corrupt. In accordance with the instructions of the House and as its representative, I pronounce upon you its censure."[36]

Censure by the Senate

Timothy Pickering (Fed Mass.) was the first member to be censured by the Senate. In December 1810, he had read aloud in the chamber secret documents relating to the 1803 convention with France for the cession of Louisiana. The Senate on Jan. 2, 1811, adopted the following resolution of censure: "Resolved, That Timothy Pickering, a Senator from the State of Massachusetts, having,...whilst the Senate was in session with open doors, read from his place certain documents confidentially communicated by the President of the United States to the Senate, the injunction of secrecy not having been removed, has, in so doing, committed a violation of the rules of this body."[37] Twenty senators voted for the resolution; seven, against it.

Benjamin Tappan (D Ohio) was similarly censured on May 10, 1844, when the Senate adopted a two-part resolution concerning his release to the press of confidential material relating to a treaty for the annexation of Texas. The first part, adopted 35 to 7, censured Tappan for releasing the documents in "flagrant violation" of the Senate rules. The second, adopted 39 to 3, accepted Tappan's apology and said that no further censure would "be inflicted on him."[38]

Threatened violence was involved in the next censure case in the Senate. On the Senate floor April 7, 1850, Thomas H. Benton (D Mo.) made menacing gestures and advanced toward Henry S. Foote (Unionist Miss.) while Foote was making a speech. Foote drew a pistol from his pocket and cocked it. Before any damage was done, other senators intervened and restored order. A committee appointed to consider the incident said in its report, July 30, that what the two men had done was deplorable. The committee recommended that Foote be censured, but the Senate took no action. This was the only Senate case in

Censure Proceedings in the Senate

Congress	Session	Year	Member	Grounds	Disposition
11th	3rd	1811	Timothy Pickering (Fed Mass.)	Breach of confidence	*Censured*
28th	1st	1844	Benjamin Tappan (D Ohio)	Breach of confidence	*Censured*
31st	1st	1850	Thomas H. Benton (D Mo.)	Disorderly conduct	Not censured
31st	1st	1850	Henry S. Foote (Unionist Miss.)	Disorderly conduct	Not censured
57th	1st	1902	John L. McLaurin (D S.C.)	Assault	*Censured*
57th	1st	1902	Benjamin R. Tillman (D S.C.)	Assault	*Censured*
71st	1st	1929	Hiram Bingham (R Conn.)	Bringing Senate into disrepute	*Censured*
83rd	2nd	1954	Joseph R. McCarthy (R Wis.)	Obstruction of legislative process, insult to senators, etc.	*Censured*
90th	1st	1967	Thomas J. Dodd (D Conn.)	Financial misconduct	*Censured*

Source: U.S. Senate, Committee on Rules and Administration, Subcommittee on Privileges and Elections, *Senate Election, Expulsion and Censure Cases from 1793 to 1972,* compiled by Richard D. Hupman, S. Doc. 92-7, 92nd Cong., 1st sess., 1972.

which an investigating committee's recommendation of censure was not adopted.

More than half a century later, on Feb. 22, 1902, while the Senate was debating Philippine affairs, Sen. Benjamin R. Tillman (D S.C.) made a statement questioning the integrity of Sen. John L. McLaurin (D S.C.). When McLaurin branded it as "a willful, malicious and deliberate lie,"[39] Tillman advanced toward McLaurin, and they engaged in a brief fistfight. After they had been separated, the Senate by a vote of 61 to 0 declared them to be "in contempt of the Senate" and by a voice vote referred the matter to the Committee on Privileges and Elections for a report on any further action that should be taken.

The committee on Feb. 27 reported a resolution declaring it to be the judgment of the Senate that the two men, "for disorderly behavior and flagrant violation of the rules of the Senate..., deserve the censure of the Senate, and they are hereby so censured, for their breach of the privileges and dignity of this body," and provided that after its adoption the previous declaration that the two men were in contempt of the Senate "shall be no longer in force and effect."[40] The Senate adopted the resolution by a vote of 54 to 12, with 22 senators (including the two participants in the affray) not voting.

The censure case of Sen. Hiram Bingham (R Conn.) occurred in 1929 when he placed on the Senate payroll, as a member of his staff, Charles L. Eyanson, a secretary to the president of the Connecticut Manufacturers' Association, to assist him in dealing with tariff legislation.

Sen. George W. Norris (R Neb.) introduced a resolution declaring that Bingham's action was "contrary to good morals and senatorial ethics."[41] During consideration of the resolution on Nov. 4, 1929, the Senate agreed to add language stating that Bingham's actions were "not the result of corrupt motives."[42] The resolution was then adopted by a vote of 54 to 22, with 18 senators (including Bingham) not voting.

McCarthy Case. The sixth member of the Senate to be censured was Joseph R. McCarthy (R Wis.). Proceedings on this case began in the 82nd Congress (1951-52) and were concluded in the 83rd (1953-54). Sen. William Benton (D

Conn.) in August 1951 offered a resolution calling on the Committee on Rules and Administration to investigate, among other things, McCarthy's participation in the defamation of Sen. Millard E. Tydings (D Md.) during the Maryland senatorial campaign, in order to determine whether expulsion proceedings should be instituted against McCarthy. On April 10, 1952, McCarthy submitted a resolution calling for investigation by the same committee of Benton's activities as Assistant Secretary of State, campaign contributions Benton had received, and other matters. Both proposals were referred to the Rules Committee's Privileges and Elections Subcommittee which, after conducting an investigation, submitted an inconclusive report on Jan. 2, 1953.

In the spring of 1954, the Senate Permanent Investigations Subcommittee conducted hearings on mutual accusations of misconduct by McCarthy and Army officials. During the hearings, McCarthy told Army Brig. Gen. Ralph W. Zwicker that he was "not fit to wear that uniform" and implied that Zwicker did not have "the brains of a five-year-old." In June, Sens. Ralph E. Flanders (R Vt.) and Herbert H. Lehman (D N.Y.) introduced resolutions to strip McCarthy of his chairmanship of the Senate Permanent Investigations Subcommittee. Both resolutions were referred to the Rules Committee.

The two resolutions became moot when 73-year-old Flanders on July 30 introduced a resolution censuring McCarthy. Among Flanders' reasons for pressing censure were McCarthy's refusal to testify before a Rules subcommittee in the 1952 Benton-McCarthy exchange of accusations, refusal to repudiate the "frivolous and irresponsible" conduct of Investigations Subcommittee Counsel Roy M. Cohn and consultant G. David Schine on their 1953 subversion-seeking trip to Europe, and "habitual contempt for people."[43] The Senate on Aug. 2 adopted, by a vote of 75 to 12, a proposal to refer Flanders' censure resolution to a select committee. Three days later, Vice President Richard M. Nixon appointed the select committee.

The Select Committee to Study Censure Charges held hearings from Aug. 31 to Sept. 13, 1954. McCarthy, in defending himself before the committee, contended that the

Senate Condemnation of
Joseph R. McCarthy (R Wis.)

Resolution relating to the conduct of the Senator from Wisconsin, Mr. McCarthy. [S. Res. 301, 83rd Cong., 2nd sess., adopted Dec. 2, 1954.]

Section 1. Resolved, that the Senator from Wisconsin, Mr. McCarthy, failed to cooperate with the Subcommittee on Privileges and Elections of the Senate Committee on Rules and Administration in clearing up matters referred to that Subcommittee which concerned his conduct as a Senator and affected the honor of the Senate and, instead, repeatedly abused the Subcommittee and its Members who were trying to carry out assigned duties, thereby obstructing the constitutional processes of the Senate, and that this conduct of the Senator from Wisconsin, Mr. McCarthy, is contrary to Senatorial traditions and is hereby condemned.

Section 2. The Senator from Wisconsin (Mr. McCarthy), in writing to the chairman of the Select Committee to Study Censure Charges (Mr. Watkins) after the Select Committee had issued its report and before the report was presented to the Senate charging three members of the Select Committee with "deliberate deception" and "fraud" for failure to disqualify themselves;

In stating to the press on Nov. 4, 1954, that the special Senate session that was to begin Nov. 8, 1954, was a "lynch party";

In repeatedly describing this special Senate Session as a "lynch bee" in a nationwide television and radio show on Nov. 7, 1954;

In stating to the public press on Nov. 13, 1954, that the chairman of the Select Committee (Mr. Watkins) was guilty of "the most unusual, most cowardly thing I've ever heard of" and stating further: "I expected he would be afraid to answer the questions, but didn't think he'd be stupid enough to make a public statement"; and in characterizing the said Committee as the "unwilling handmaiden," "involuntary agent," and "attorneys-in-fact" of the Communist party and in charging that the said Committee in writing its report "imitated Communist methods—that it distorted, misrepresented, and omitted in its efforts to manufacture a plausible rationalization" in support of its recommendations to the Senate, which characterizations and charges were contained in a statement released to the press and inserted into the Congressional Record of Nov. 10, 1954, acted contrary to Senatorial ethics and tended to bring the Senate into dishonor and disrepute, to obstruct the constitutional processes of the Senate, and to impair its dignity.

And such conduct is hereby condemned.

Senate cannot punish a member for what he did in a previous Congress. The committee rejected that contention and on Sept. 27 submitted a 40,000-word report which included a unanimous recommendation that the Senate adopt a resolution censuring McCarthy. After a recess during the congressional election campaign, the Senate reconvened Nov. 8 to consider the censure proposal. Proceedings in the next few weeks led to modifications of that proposal and

substitution of the word "condemned" for "censured." *(Text of final resolution, this page)*

The Senate adopted the resolution of condemnation on Dec. 2 by a vote of 67 to 22. Republicans split evenly, 22 favoring and 22 opposing the resolution. All 44 Democrats, together with Sen. Wayne Morse (Ind Ore.), voted for the resolution. In January 1955, when control of Congress passed to the Democrats, McCarthy lost his committee and subcommittee chairmanships. His activities thereafter attracted less public attention, and he died May 2, 1957.

Dodd Case. House Speaker Sam Rayburn (D Texas) often said that the ethics of a member of Congress should be judged not by his peers but by the voters at re-election time. By the mid-1960s, it had become clear that neither Congress nor the public felt this was enough. In 1964, the Senate was jolted by adverse publicity over charges that Robert G. (Bobby) Baker had used his office as secretary to the Senate majority to promote his business interests. To allay public misgivings, the Senate on July 24 of that year established a Select Committee on Standards and Conduct with responsibility for investigating "allegations of improper conduct" by senators and Senate employees. In September, however, the Senate assigned jurisdiction over the Baker case to the Rules and Administration Committee. *(Baker case, p. 122)*

The new select committee's first inquiry, begun in 1966, concerned the Dodd case. On Jan. 24, 1966, and later dates, columnists Drew Pearson and Jack Anderson accused Sen. Thomas J. Dodd (D Conn.) of having (1) used for personal expenses funds contributed to him to help meet the costs of his campaign for re-election in 1964, (2) double-billed the government for travel expenses, and (3) improperly exchanged favors with Julius Klein, a public relations representative of West German interests. On the last charge, the columnists said that Dodd had gone to Germany for the purpose of interceding with Chancellor Konrad Adenauer on behalf of Klein's accounts, although the trip was supposedly made on Senate business.

Dodd on Feb. 23, 1966, requested the Select Committee on Standards and Conduct to investigate his relationship with Klein. The committee conducted hearings on all three of the Pearson-Anderson charges in June-July 1966 and March 1967. Dodd testified in his own defense.

● On the first charge, Dodd said he "truly believed" the proceeds from the testimonial dinners "to be donations to me from my friends."[44]

● The second charge, he said, stemmed from "sloppy bookkeeping" by Michael V. O'Hare, who had been an employee of Dodd. O'Hare and other former Dodd employees reportedly had taken documents from Dodd's files and made copies of them available to the committee. In the course of the hearings, Dodd called O'Hare a liar.[45]

● On charge three, Dodd denied that he had been a mere errand boy for Klein on the trip to Europe.

The committee on April 27, 1967, submitted its report on the Dodd case. It recommended that Dodd be censured for spending campaign contributions for personal purposes and for billing seven trips to both the Senate and private organizations. The committee dropped the third charge, saying that while Dodd's relations with Klein were indiscreet, there was not sufficient evidence of wrongdoing.

Voting on the committee's recommendations, June 23, 1967, the Senate censured Dodd on the first charge, by a vote of 92 to 5, but refused by a vote of 45 yeas to 51 nays to censure him on the second charge. The resolution as adopted recorded the judgment of the Senate that Dodd, "for having engaged in a course of conduct...from 1961 to 1965 of exer-

Censure Proceedings in the House

Congress	Session	Year	Member	Grounds	Disposition
5th	2nd	1798	Matthew Lyon (Anti-Fed Vt.)	Assault on representative	Not censured
5th	2nd	1798	Roger Griswold (Fed Conn.)	Assault on representative	Not censured
22nd	1st	1832	William Stanbery (D Ohio)	Insult to Speaker	*Censured*
24th	1st	1836	Sherrod Williams (Whig Ky.)	Insult to Speaker	Not censured
25th	2nd	1838	Henry A. Wise (Tyler Dem. Va.)	Service as second in duel	Not censured
25th	3rd	1839	Alexander Duncan (Whig Ohio)	Offensive publication	Not censured
27th	2nd	1842	John Q. Adams (Whig Mass.)	Treasonable petition	Not censured
27th	2nd	1842	Joshua R. Giddings (Whig Ohio)	Offensive paper	*Censured*
34th	2nd	1856	Henry A. Edmundson (D Va.) ⎱	Complicity in assault	Not censured
34th	2nd	1856	Laurence M. Keitt (D S.C.) ⎰	on senator	*Censured*
35th	1st	1858	Orsamus B. Matteson (Whig N.Y.)	Corruption	*Censured*
36th	1st	1860	George S. Houston (D Ala.)	Insult to representative	Not censured
38th	1st	1864	Alexander Long (D Ohio)	Treasonable utterance	*Censured*
38th	1st	1864	Benjamin G. Harris (D Md.)	Treasonable utterance	*Censured*
39th	1st	1866	John W. Chanler (D N.Y.)	Insult to House	*Censured*
39th	1st	1866	Lovell H. Rousseau (R Ky.)	Assault on representative	*Censured*
40th	1st	1867	John W. Hunter (Ind N.Y.)	Insult to representative	*Censured*
40th	2nd	1868	Fernando Wood (D N.Y.)	Offensive utterance	*Censured*
40th	3rd	1868	E. D. Holbrook[1] (D Idaho)	Offensive utterance	*Censured*
41st	2nd	1870	Benjamin F. Whittemore (R S.C.)	Corruption	*Censured*
41st	2nd	1870	Roderick R. Butler (R Tenn.)	Corruption	*Censured*
41st	2nd	1870	John T. Deweese (D N.C.)	Corruption	*Censured*
42nd	3rd	1873	Oakes Ames (R Mass.)	Corruption	*Censured*
42nd	3rd	1873	James Brooks (D N.Y.)	Corruption	*Censured*
43rd	2nd	1875	John Y. Brown (D Ky.)	Insult to representative	*Censured*[2]
44th	1st	1876	James G. Blaine (R Maine)	Corruption	Not censured
47th	1st	1882	William D. Kelley (R Pa.)	Offensive utterance	Not censured
47th	1st	1882	John D. White (R Ky.)	Offensive utterance	Not censured
47th	2nd	1883	John Van Voorhis (R N.Y.)	Offensive utterance	Not censured
51st	1st	1890	William D. Bynum (D Ind.)	Offensive utterance	*Censured*
67th	1st	1921	Thomas L. Blanton (D Texas)	Abuse of leave to print	*Censured*

1. *Holbrook was a territorial delegate, not a representative.*
2. *The House later rescinded part of the censure resolution against Brown.*

Sources: Hinds and Cannon, *Presidents of the House of Representatives of the United States,* 11 vols. (1935-41); Joint Committee on Congressional Operations, *House of Representatives Exclusion, Censure and Expulsion Cases from 1789 to 1973,* committee print, 93rd Cong., 1st sess., 1973.

cising the influence and favor of his office as a United States Senator...to obtain, and use for his personal benefit, funds from the public through political testimonials and a political campaign, deserves the censure of the Senate; and he is so censured for his conduct, which is contrary to accepted morals, derogates from the public trust expected of a Senator, and tends to bring the Senate into dishonor and disrepute."[46] The preponderance of affirmative votes was the largest in the history of censure proceedings in the Senate.

Dodd declined to seek the Democratic nomination for senator from Connecticut in 1970 but ran in the general election as an independent. He placed third, with 24 per cent of the votes, while the Democratic nominee lost to Republican Lowell P. Weicker Jr., 34 per cent to 42 per cent. Dodd had served four years in the House and 12 years in the Senate. He died May 24, 1971.

Censure by the House

The House in 1789 adopted a rule which, as amended in 1822 and 1880, is still in effect (Rule 14, Section 4). It reads:

"If any member, in speaking or otherwise, transgress the rules of the House, the Speaker shall, or any member may, call him to order; ...and if the case require it, he shall be liable to censure or such punishment as the House may deem proper."[47] The censure clause of this rule has been invoked 31 times, and censure has been voted 19 times, two-thirds of them in the 1860s and 1870s. Grounds for censure have included assault on a fellow member of the House, insult to the Speaker, treasonable utterance, corruption and other offenses. Only once in the 20th century has a representative been censured—Thomas L. Blanton (D Texas) in 1921 for abuse of the leave to print.

The first censure motion in the House was introduced following a physical attack in January 1798 by Rep. Matthew Lyon (Anti-Fed Vt.) on Rep. Roger Griswold (Fed Conn.), who had taunted Lyon on his allegedly poor military record. The censure motion failed. In the following month, Lyon and Griswold engaged in an affray with tongs and cane. Both fracases occurred on the House floor. Following the second incident, a motion was introduced to censure both members. The motion failed.

The first formal censure by the House was imposed in 1832 on William Stanbery (D Ohio) for saying, in objection to a ruling by the chair, "The eyes of the Speaker [Andrew Stevenson (D Va.)] are too frequently turned from the chair you occupy toward the White House."[48] There were 93 votes for censuring Stanbery; 44 were opposed. Censure for unacceptable language or offensive publication was imposed in seven other cases. For example, Rep. John W. Hunter (Ind N.Y.) was censured on Jan. 26, 1867, for saying, about a statement made by a colleague, "So far as I am concerned, it is a base lie."[49] The vote on censure was 77 to 23. One year later, on Jan. 15, 1868, the House by a vote of 114 to 39 censured Rep. Fernando Wood (D N.Y.) for describing a bill on the government of the southern states as "a monstrosity, a measure the most infamous of the many infamous acts of this infamous Congress."[50]

In 1842, censure was considered and rejected in the case of one of the most distinguished representatives in American history, John Quincy Adams, a former President of the United States. Adams had presented to the House, for 46 of his constituents, a petition asking Congress to dissolve the Union and allow the states to go their separate ways. A resolution proposing to censure him for this act was worded so strongly that Adams asserted his right, under the Sixth Amendment to the Constitution, to a trial by jury. He succeeded in putting his opponents on the defensive, and the resolution was not put to a vote.

Rep. Lovell H. Rousseau (R Ky.) during the evening of June 14, 1866, assaulted Rep. Josiah B. Grinnell (R Iowa) with a cane in the portico on the East Front of the Capitol. On the House floor, earlier in the month, Grinnell had imputed cowardice to Rousseau. A committee appointed to report on the case recommended that Rousseau be expelled. That recommendation was rejected, but the House voted on July 17, 1866, that he "be summoned to the bar of this House, and be there publicly reprimanded by the Speaker for his violation of its rights and privileges."[51] The order was carried out July 21, despite Rousseau's announcement that he had sent his resignation to the governor of Kentucky.

Corruption was the basis for censure or proposed censure in a number of cases. The House on Feb. 27, 1873, by a vote of 182 to 36, censured Reps. Oakes Ames (R Mass.) and James Brooks (D N.Y.) for their part in a financial scandal involving Crédit Mobilier stock given to members of Congress. Three years later, Speaker James G. Blaine (R Maine) was accused of involvement in that scandal as well as of receiving excessive payments from the Union Pacific Railroad Co. for bonds sold to the company. Two months before the convention at which Blaine hoped to be chosen the Republican candidate for President, he spoke in the House on the charges against him. By selective reading of a series of allegedly incriminating letters, Blaine managed to confuse the evidence sufficiently to rout the proponents of censure.

In one instance, the House rescinded part of a censure resolution. During debate on a bill in 1875, Rep. John Y. Brown (D Ky.) referred to Rep. Benjamin Butler (R Mass.) as "outlawed in his own home from respectable society; whose name is synonymous with falsehood; and who is the champion, and has been on all occasions, of fraud; who is the apologist of thieves; who is such a prodigy of vice and meanness that to describe him would sicken imagination and exhaust invective."[52]

Brown was censured Feb. 4, 1875, for that insult and for lying to the Speaker in order to continue his insulting

Censure for Dueling Withheld

The killing of one representative by another in a duel in 1838 went uncensured by the House. Rep. Jonathan Cilley (Jackson Dem. Maine) had made statements on the floor reflecting on the character of James W. Webb, prominent editor of a New York City newspaper which was a Whig organ. When Webb sent Cilley a note by the hand of Rep. William J. Graves (Whig Ky.), demanding an explanation of the statements, Cilley refused to receive the note. Further correspondence led to a challenge by Graves and agreement by Cilley to a duel with rifles.

The duel took place on Feb. 24, 1838, on the Marlboro Pike in Maryland, close to the District of Columbia. Graves and Cilley each fired twice, with no result. In the third volley, Cilley was shot fatally in the abdomen. Four days later, the House appointed a committee to investigate the affair. A majority of the committee recommended on April 21 that Graves be expelled from the House and that the seconds in the duel, Rep. Henry A. Wise (Tyler D Va.) and George W. Jones (a member of the Tennessee House of Representatives who served in the national House of Representatives, 1843-59), be censured. One of the minority group on the committee, Rep. Franklin H. Elmore (State Rights Dem S.C.), observed that dueling by members had been frequent and generally had gone unnoticed by the House. A motion to lay the committee's report on the table and to print the testimony was agreed to May 10, and an attempt on July 4 to take up the report was unsuccessful. Graves was not expelled and Wise and Jones were not censured.

speech. But a year later, on May 2, 1876, the House agreed to rescind that portion of the censure resolution condemning Brown for lying to the Speaker. The charge of insulting another member remained, however.[53]

Recent Cases

As of early 1977, neither chamber had censured any of its members since the Dodd case in 1967. However, censure was discussed in two cases, one in the Senate, one in the House, both relating to the release of confidential information.

In 1971, Sen. Mike Gravel (D Alaska), frustrated in his attempts to read from the Pentagon Papers on the Senate floor, called a one-man, late-evening subcommittee hearing on June 29, 1971, and began reading from a censored version of the papers which detailed the nation's early involvement in the Vietnam War. He then passed these portions to reporters.

Minority Leader Hugh Scott (R Pa.) said at the time that Gravel might have violated a Senate rule that prohibited the divulging of confidential communications from the President or an executive department, or other secret or confidential information. Scott added that Senate Republicans were considering asking the Senate to censure Gravel. However, Majority Leader Mike Mansfield (D Mont.) said Gravel had not broken any Senate rule, and the Senate did not reprimand him. *(Details of Gravel case, p. 120)*

The second case occurred in 1975 when the House Committee on Standards of Official Conduct formally investigated a complaint that Michael J. Harrington (D Mass.) had violated House rules in 1974 by circulating among members classified information which later was made public. Harrington was charged with disclosing secret Armed Services Investigations Subcommittee testimony by CIA Director William E. Colby on alleged U.S. efforts to prevent the 1970 election of Salvador Allende as president of Chile.

Rep. Robin L. Beard Jr. (R Tenn.), who filed the complaint, had told the Associated Press June 18, 1975, that he hoped the complaint would result in a censure resolution. But the committee, also known as the ethics committee, dismissed the charges Nov. 6, 1975, on a 7 to 3 vote, after learning that the hearing at which Colby testified was not legally an executive session and thus not a hearing covered by the House rules. *(Details, p. 114)*

Other Forms of Discipline

Faced in recent years with cases of impropriety that it has not wanted to punish by expulsion or censure, the House has imposed less stringent forms of discipline. One method has been directed toward members who have been convicted in court of criminal actions carrying certain penalties.

Suspension

In 1972, the House began a move to formalize an unwritten rule that a member indicted for or convicted of a crime should refrain from voting on the House floor or in committee. Prior to 1972, the last time a member voluntarily refrained from voting was in 1929 when, under indictment in the District of Columbia, Frederick N. Zihlman (R Md.) did not vote on the floor and temporarily turned over his chairmanship of the House Committee on the District of Columbia to the committee's ranking member.

The move to formalize that unwritten rule was prompted by the case of John Dowdy (D Texas) who was convicted Dec. 31, 1971, of charges arising from acceptance of a bribe, conspiracy and perjury. While Dowdy appealed his conviction, the ethics committee reported a resolution May 3, 1972, stating that any House member convicted of a crime for which he could receive a sentence of two or more years in prison should not participate in committee business or House votes. The maximum sentence for the crimes Dowdy was convicted of was 40 years in prison and a $40,000 fine.

Because the Rules Committee failed to act, the resolution was not enacted. But Dowdy, in a June 21, 1972, letter to Speaker Carl Albert (D Okla.) promised he would refrain from voting.[54] He retired from the House at the end of 1972. *(Details, p. 114)*

Not until April 16, 1975, did the House enact a resolution similar to the one proposed in 1972. Under the 1975 rule, the voluntary prohibition against voting would apply during an appeal of the conviction but would end on reversal or when the member was re-elected subsequent to conviction, even if the verdict was upheld on appeal.

The first member affected by the 1975 rule was Andrew J. Hinshaw (R Calif.) who was convicted Jan. 26, 1976, and sentenced to one to 14 years in prison for accepting gifts of stereo equipment and a $1,000 campaign contribution from the Tandy Corporation during his term as assessor for Orange County, Calif. Hinshaw appealed. *(Details, p. 123)*

[In the wake of Hinshaw's conviction, Rep. Charles E. Wiggins (R Calif.) June 30, 1976, introduced a resolution (H Res 1392) to expel Hinshaw from the House. The House ethics committee Sept. 1, 1976, reported the resolution adversely by a 10-2 vote. Wiggins said he would call it up for a floor vote before the House adjourned. Hinshaw lost the June 8 Republican primary election.]

Loss of Chairmanships

Another method of punishment has been to strip a member of his committee chairmanship; such action was one of several disciplinary actions taken against Adam Clayton Powell Jr. (D N.Y.). *(p. 92)* In a recent case, Rep. Wayne L. Hays (D Ohio) in mid-1976 gave up the chairmanship of both the Democratic Congressional Campaign Committee and the House Administration Committee after it was alleged that he had kept a mistress on the latter committee's payroll. Hays was pressured to resign the posts by the House Democratic leadership and it was evident that the Democratic Caucus would have forced him to do so if he had not stepped aside voluntarily. Hays resigned from Congress Sept. 1, 1976. *(Details on investigation of Hays case, p. 5)*

Sikes Reprimand

The House July 29, 1976, voted 381-3, to reprimand Robert L. F. Sikes (D Fla.) for failure to disclose certain financial holdings. It was the first time that the House had formally punished a member since 1969 when it fined Adam Clayton Powell and stripped him of his seniority. *(Details of Sikes case, p. 7)*

John J. Flynt Jr. (D Ga.), chairman of the Standards of Official Conduct Committee (ethics committee), which recommended the reprimand, said he saw no real difference between a reprimand and a censure, but that committee members decided to use the word reprimand. In the case of a vote to reprimand, no further action is taken against a member. Under censure, the member has to stand in the well and be publicly admonished by the Speaker.

House Democrats voted Jan. 26, 1977, to strip Sikes of his Military Construction Appropriations Subcommittee chairmanship.

Harrington Rebuke

Although the ethics committee decided Harrington could not be punished for releasing portions of the classified Colby testimony, the House Armed Services Committee sought to rebuke him by refusing him further access to its files. On June 16, 1975, the committee voted 16-13 to deny Harrington access to the files pending an official response from the ethics committee setting forth criteria on future access to committee files by House members.

In conflict were two House rules and a rule of the Armed Services Committee. One House rule stated that any member of Congress could inspect any committee's files but a second House rule said that no evidence or testimony taken in executive session could be released without consent of the committee. The Armed Services Committee had regulations prohibiting anyone except its members from examining classified material; Harrington was not a committee member at the time of the incident.

Although the ethics committee informally told the Armed Services Committee that the matter involved a change in House rules and was therefore under the jurisdiction of the Rules Committee, rather than the Ethics Committee, the ethics committee did not formally respond to the Armed Services Committee resolution in 1976 and Harrington technically still was denied access to the latter committee's files.

Footnotes

1. Asher C. Hinds and Clarence Cannon, *Hinds' and Cannon's Precedents of the House of Representatives of the United States* (Government Printing Office, 1935-41), vol. 1, p. 525.
2. *Ibid.*
3. *Ibid.*, vol. 2, p. 1075.
4. *Ibid.*, vol. 2, p. 847.
5. *Ibid*, vol. 1, p. 84.
6. *Ibid.*
7. *The Federalist Papers*, with an Introduction by Clinton Rossiter (Mentor, 1961), No. 60, p. 371.
8. Westel W. Willoughby, *The Constitutional Law of the United States* (Baker, Voorhis, 1929), vol. 1, p. 608.
9. U.S. Congress, Senate, Committee on Rules and Administration, *Senate Election, Expulsion and Censure Cases*, S. Doc. 92-7, 92nd Cong., 1st sess., 1971, p. 1.
10. *Ibid.*, p. 12.
11. Hinds, *Precedents*, vol. 1, p. 588.
12. William F. Willoughby, *Principles of Legislative Organization and Administration* (Brookings Institution, 1934), p. 270.
13. Hinds, *Precedents*, vol. 6, p. 58.
14. *Ibid.*, vol. 1, p. 489.
15. *Ibid.*
16. Robert S. Getz, *Congressional Ethics; The Conflict of Interest Issue* (Van Nostrand, 1966), p. 110.
17. Kent M. Weeks, *Adam Clayton Powell and the Supreme Court* (Dunellen, 1971), p. 79.
18. *Ibid.*, p. 134.
19. Floyd M. Riddick, *The United States Congress; Organization and Procedure* (National Capitol Publishers, 1949), p. 12.
20. George H. Haynes, *The Senate of the United States* (Houghton-Mifflin Co., 1938), p. 131.
21. For more background, see Congressional Quarterly, *1975 Almanac*, p. 699.
22. For additional background, see Congressional Quarterly, *Weekly Report*, March 6, 1976, p. 508.
23. George F. Hoar, *Autobiography of Seventy Years* (Scribner's, 1903), vol. 1, p. 268.
24. Quoted in DeAlva Stanwood Alexander, *History and Procedure of the House of Representatives* (Lenox Hill, 1916), p. 323.
25. William Willoughby, *Principles*, p. 277.
26. For more background, see Congressional Quarterly, *1965 Almanac*, p. 609.
27. *Congressional Record*, 84th Cong., 1st sess., Jan. 14, 1955, p. 373.
28. Hinds, *Precedents*, vol. 2, p. 817.
29. *Ibid.*, vol. 1, p. 595.
30. *Ibid.*, p. 604.
31. *Ibid.*, p. 605.
32. *Ibid.*, p. 613.
33. *Senate Election, Expulsion and Censure Cases*, p. 29.
34. *Ibid.*, p. 31-32.
35. John T. Dempsey, *Control by Congress Over the Seating and Disciplining of Members* (Ph.D. dissertation, University of Michigan, 1956), p. 294.
36. Hinds, *Precedents*, vol. 6, p. 404-405.
37. *Senate Election, Expulsion and Censure Cases*, p. 6.
38. *Ibid.*, p. 14.
39. *Ibid.*, p. 96.
40. *Ibid.*, p. 97.
41. *Ibid.*, p. 128.
42. *Ibid.*
43. *Congressional Record*, 83rd Cong., 2nd sess., July 30, 1954, p. 12730.
44. U.S. Congress, Senate, Committee on Standards and Conduct, *Investigation of Senator Thomas J. Dodd, Hearings before the Select Committee on Standards and Conduct*, 89th Cong., 2nd sess., 1966, p. 846.
45. *Ibid.*, p. 847.
46. *Senate Election, Expulsion and Censure Cases*, p. 157.
47. Hinds, *Precedents*, vol. 5, p. 103.
48. *Ibid.*, vol. 2, p. 799.
49. *Ibid.*, p. 801.
50. *Ibid.*, p. 798.
51. *Ibid.*, p. 1134.
52. *Ibid.*, p. 802.
53. *Ibid.*, vol. 4, p. 26.
54. Dowdy actually voted three times by proxy in the House District of Columbia Committee June 22 after he had said he would not vote in committee or on the floor. Dowdy explained the votes by saying that he had given his proxy to the committee for use at a meeting scheduled on June 21 which was postponed until June 22 without his knowledge. Dowdy's pledge to refrain from voting was made the evening of June 21. For details, see Congressional Quarterly, *1972 Almanac*, p. 796.

Selected Bibliography

Books

Alexander, De Alva Stanwood, *History and Procedure of the House of Representatives.* New York: Lenox Hill, 1916.

Beck, James M. *The Vanishing Rights of the States.* New York: George H. Doran Co., 1926.

Berman, Daniel M. *In Congress Assembled; the Legislative Process in the National Government.* New York: Macmillan, 1964.

Dempsey, John T. *Control by Congress Over the Seating and Disciplining of Members,* Ph.D. dissertation. University of Michigan, 1956. (Microfilm copy in Library of Congress.)

Galloway, George B. *The Legislative Process in Congress.* New York: Thomas Y. Crowell, 1953.

Getz, Robert S. *Congressional Ethics; The Conflict of Interest Issue.* New York: Van Nostrand, 1966.

Haynes, George H. *The Senate of the United States.* 2 vols. Boston: Houghton-Mifflin Co., 1938.

Hoar, George F. *Autobiography of Seventy Years.* 2 vols. New York: Scribner's, 1903.

Jacobs, Andrew Jr. *The Powell Affair: Freedom Minus One.* Indianapolis: Bobbs Merrill, 1973.

Remick, Henry C. *The Powers of Congress in Respect to Membership and Elections.* 2 vols. Privately printed, 1929.

Riddick, Floyd M. *The United States Congress; Organization and Procedure.* Manassas, Va.: National Capitol Publishers, 1949.

Weeks, Kent M. *Adam Clayton Powell and the Supreme Court.* New York: Dunellen, 1971.

Willoughby, Westel W. *The Constitutional Law of the United States.* 2nd ed., 3 vols. New York: Baker, Voorhis, 1929.

Willoughby, William F. *Principles of Legislative Organization and Administration.* Washington: Brookings Institution, 1934.

Wilson, H. Hubert. *Congress; Corruption and Compromise.* New York: Rinehart, 1951.

Articles

Curtis, Thomas B. "Power of the House of Representatives to Judge the Qualifications of Its Members." *Texas Law Review,* July 1967, p. 1199.

Eckhardt, Robert C. "Adam Clayton Powell Case." *Texas Law Review,* July 1967, p. 1205.

Fleishman, Neill. "Power of Congress to Exclude Persons Duly Elected." *North Carolina Law Review*, April 1970, pp. 655-66.

"The Power of a House of Congress to Judge the Qualifications of Its Members." *Harvard Law Review*, January 1968, p. 673-84.

Wheildon, L.B. "Challenged Elections to the Senate." *Editorial Research Reports*, 1946, vol. 2, p. 799-817.

Government Publications

Deschler, Lewis. *Procedure in the U.S. House of Representatives*. Washington: Government Printing Office, 1975.

Hinds, Asher C. and Cannon, Clarence. *Hinds' and Cannon's Precedents of the House of Representatives of the United States*. 11 vols. Washington: Government Printing Office, 1935-41.

Hupman, Richard D. *Senate Election, Expulsion and Censure Cases from 1789 to 1972*. S. Doc. 92-7, 92nd Cong., 1st sess., 1972.

Riddick, Floyd. *Senate Procedure, Precedents and Practices*. Washington: Government Printing Office, 1975.

Rowell, Chester H. *A Historical and Legal Digest of All the Contested Election Cases in the House of Representatives from the First to the Fifty-sixth Congress, 1789-1901*. H. Doc. 510, 56th Cong., 2d sess., 1901.

Wickersham, Price. *The Right of the Senate to Determine the Qualifications of Its Members*. S. Doc. 4, 70th Cong., 1st sess., 1927.

U.S. Congress. House. Committee on House Administration. *Analysis of HR 14195, a Bill to Revise the Law Governing Contests of Elections of Members of the House of Representatives and for Other Purposes*. 91st Cong., 1st sess., 1970.

U.S. Congress. House. Select Committee Pursuant to H Res 1. *Report in re Adam Clayton Powell*. H. Rept 90-27. 90th Cong., 1st sess., 1967.

U.S. Congress. Joint Committee on Congressional Operations. *House of Representatives Exclusion, Censure and Expulsion Cases from 1789 to 1973*. Committee print, 93rd Cong., 1st sess., 1973.

U.S. Congress. Senate. Select Committee on Standards and Conduct. *Hearings on Senator Thomas J. Dodd*. 89th Cong., 2nd sess., and 90th Cong., 1st sess., 1966-67.

—. *Investigation of Senator Thomas J. Dodd*. 90th Cong., 1st sess., 1967.

—. *Report on the Investigation of Senator Thomas J. Dodd of Connecticut*. S. Rept. 90-193 to accompany S. Res. 112, 90th Cong., 1st sess., 1967.

—. *Standards of Conduct for Members of the Senate and Officers and Employees of the Senate*. S. Rept. 90-1015, 90th Cong., 2nd sess., 1968.

U.S. Congress. Senate. Select Committee to Study Censure Charges, Pursuant to S. Res. 301. *Hearings on a Resolution to Censure the Senator from Wisconsin, Mr. McCarthy*. 2 pts. 82nd Cong., 2nd sess., 1954.

Ethics and Criminal Prosecutions

Under the Constitution, each house of Congress has the power to punish members for misconduct. Article I, Section 5 states: "Each House may determine the Rules of its Proceedings, punish its Members for disorderly Behavior, and with the concurrence of two thirds, expel a Member."

It is a power Congress historically has been reluctant to use. Only seven senators, 18 representatives and one territorial delegate have been formally censured by their colleagues for misconduct. Fifteen senators and three representatives have been expelled. The instances of other disciplinary actions have been equally as rare. *(Details, p. 86)*

This reluctance has stemmed from a variety of reasons. There is a belief among some that, except in cases where a member's actions are illegal and punishable by the courts, the electorate must be the ultimate judge of his behavior rather than his colleagues. Loyalty among members, especially of the same party, and toward Congress as an institution is another factor. The difficulty of agreeing on what constitutes a conflict of interest and misuse of power has also clouded the question.

It is this grey area that Congress entered into in the 1960s when a series of scandals led to the formation of ethics committees to oversee the conduct of members of Congress. From their founding until 1976, the ethics panels have frequently been derided by critics as "do-nothing" committees.

The Senate committee launched its first investigation in 1966 when it probed charges against Thomas J. Dodd (D Conn.) which led to his censure. The panel conducted few publicly known investigations in the next decade. In mid-1976, however, it was reported to be investigating one senator and an aide to another senator.

Eight years after its establishment as a permanent committee, the House Committee on Standards of Official Conduct (House ethics committee) undertook its first investigation of a member. And within weeks after it launched an investigation of Robert L. F. Sikes (D Fla.) in May 1976—which resulted in the House reprimanding Sikes—it began a probe of Wayne L. Hays (D Ohio). *(Highlights of committee activities pp. 3-12)*

Congressional Immunity

The power of each house of Congress to judge the elections and qualifications of its own members and the power to punish members for disorderly behavior are essential to the functioning of Congress as a co-equal branch of the government, free from harassment and domination by the other branches. They are reinforced by the speech or debate clause of the Constitution (Article I, Section 6), which has been broadly interpreted by the courts as granting members of Congress immunity from prosecution for nearly all actions related to their legislative functions. *(Congressional Immunity p. 118)*

Senate Ethics Committee

The Senate Rules and Administration Committee, which conducted the investigations of the misconduct of Secretary to the Senate Majority Bobby Baker, asked the Senate in 1964 to give it jurisdiction to probe infractions of Senate rules. On the floor of the Senate, however, the request was turned down and the Senate voted instead to establish a six-member bipartisan committee to investigate allegations of improper conduct by senators and Senate employees. One reason for setting up the special committee was to avoid partisan bickering between the minority of Republicans on the Rules and Administration Committee and the Democratic majority. The Republicans had charged the Democrats with "whitewashing" Bobby Baker. *(Baker case, p. 122)*

In establishing the Select Committee on Standards and Conduct (Senate ethics committee) the Senate authorized it not only to receive complaints of unethical conduct but also to recommend disciplinary action if needed and to draw up a code of ethical conduct.

The six members of the select committee were not appointed until one year later, in July 1965. John C. Stennis (D Miss.) became the first chairman.

Following are highlights of Senate ethics committee activities:

Dodd Case

As its first business, the ethics committee undertook the investigation of Sen. Thomas J. Dodd (D Conn.). On Feb. 23, 1966, Dodd had invited the panel to probe charges, being aired in the press, that he had used campaign funds for personal expenses, billed both Congress and private organizations for the same travel expenses on speaking trips, and that he had used his position to do favors for a public relations representative of West German interests.

After conducting hearings the ethics committee recommended April 27, 1967, that the senator be censured. On June 23, the Senate on a 92-5 roll-call vote censured Dodd. *(Further details, p. 102)*

Long-Teamsters Probe

In 1967, the ethics committee made its second in vestigation into the activities of a member when it scrutinized charges made by *Life* magazine that Sen. Edward V. Long (D Mo.) had used his position to aid imprisoned Teamster Union President James R. Hoffa and had accepted fees for his efforts from one of Hoffa's lawyers. On Oct. 25, Chairman Stennis announced that the ethics committee had voted unanimously to exonerate Long of the *Life* charges.[1] When *Life* raised further, more specific charges, Stennis said the panel would consider the new charges.[2] Long was defeated in the 1968 primary.

Government's Code of Ethics

Congress in 1958 approved the following Code of Ethics (H Con Res 175, 85th Congress, second session) for all government employees, including members of Congress.*

Any person in Government service should:

1. Put loyalty to the highest moral principles and to country above loyalty to persons, party, or Government department.

2. Uphold the Constitution, laws, and legal regulations of the United States and of all governments therein and never be a party to their evasion.

3. Give a full day's labor for a full day's pay; giving to the performance of his duties his earnest effort and best thought.

4. Seek to find and employ more efficient and economical ways of getting tasks accomplished.

5. Never discriminate unfairly by the dispensing of special favors or privileges to anyone, whether for remuneration or not; and never accept, for himself or his family, favors or benefits under circumstances which might be construed by reasonable persons as influencing the performance of his governmental duties.

6. Make no private promises of any kind binding upon the duties of office, since a Government employee has no private word which can be binding on public duty.

7. Engage in no business with the Government, either directly or indirectly, which is inconsistent with the conscientious performance of his governmental duties.

8. Never use any information coming to him confidentially in the performance of governmental duties as a means for making private profit.

9. Expose corruption wherever discovered.

10. Uphold these principles, ever conscious that public office is a public trust.

*The report of the House Committee on Standards of Official Conduct *In the Matter of a Complaint Against Rep. Robert L. F. Sikes* (H Rept. 94-1364, July 23, 1976) stated the following: "Although the Code of Ethics for Government Service was adopted as a concurrent resolution, and, as such, may have expired with the adjournment of the 85th Congress, the standards of ethical conduct expressed therein represent continuing traditional standards of ethical conduct to be observed by Members of the House at all times, which were supplemented in 1968 by a specific Code of Official Conduct."

Chinese Immigration Bills

A third investigation was triggered by a series of news articles in late 1969 which implied that bribes were paid to Senate employees in the offices of 13 senators for introducing hundreds of private immigration bills to help Chinese seamen stay in the United States. After holding hearings, the committee reported May 28, 1970, that although there was no evidence of senatorial misconduct, there were indications of "apparent violations of law by some of the lawyers and lobbyists who sought the introduction of some of the bills."[3]

Luxury Car Leases

Reports in August 1970 that Ford Motor Company had leased insured Lincoln Continental sedans to at least 19 members, all but two of whom were committee chairmen or ranking minority members, at lower than average prices led to a unanimous committee recommendation that the leases be quickly terminated. Ford then cancelled them.[4]

Conflict of Interest Question

A fifth case did not involve a formal investigation but exemplified the more common committee procedure of what chief counsel Benjamin R. Fern described as "nipping in the bud." On Feb. 2, 1970, Sen. George L. Murphy (R Calif.) requested an opinion from Stennis on the propriety of receiving $20,000 a year as a private corporate retainer from Technicolor Inc. Stennis March 11 stated that he and Fern decided the arrangement was "not a conflict of interest.... This was so clear that it did not seem necessary to refer the question to the full committee." The committee, he continued, "by no means requires senators to bring matters to it for resolution, but at the express request of several senators, we have rendered opinions on matters relating to standards of conduct."[5]

Campaign Contributions Probe

The Gulf Oil political contributions scandal which broke in December 1975 implicated dozens of members. But the bulk of public attention focused on charges that Senate Minority Leader Hugh Scott had received up to $100,000 in illegal campaign contributions from Gulf Oil lobbyist Claude Wild between 1960 and 1973.[6]

The Senate committee spent 10 months trying to figure out what to do about the Scott case before calling the Pennsylvania Republican in for questioning.

Then, on Sept. 15, the Committee voted 5-1 in closed session not to investigate the matter. (Scott retired from Congress at the end of 1976.) Meanwhile, several other senators involved in the Gulf matter were questioned by the special prosecutor's office or by a federal grand jury.

1968 Senate Code of Conduct

On March 22, 1968, the Senate adopted four new rules intended to guide the ethical conduct of senators and Senate employees. In an opening statement in support of the four-point committee resolution, Chairman Stennis said that the resolution would "add rules [but]...not replace that great body of unwritten but generally accepted standards that will, of course, continue in effect."[7] Stennis pointed out that the resolution contained no provisions for punishing a violator. Censure of senators and dismissal of employees, he said would continue to be the remedies. *(1977 code, p. 22)*

Regulations Governing Conduct of Members of Congress

Concern for the ethical conduct of members of Congress is reflected in the Constitution, federal statutes and Senate and House rules. Some key provisions affecting members' conduct follow:

Constitutional Provisions

"Each House may determine the Rules of its Proceedings, punish its Members for disorderly Behaviour, and, with the Concurrence of two thirds, expel a Member." (Article I, Section 5, Clause 2)

"...They shall in all Cases, except Treason, Felony and Breach of the Peace, be privileged from Arrest during their Attendance at the Session of their respective Houses, and in going to and returning from the same; and for any Speech or Debate in either House, they shall not be questioned in any other Place." (Article I, Section 6, Clause 1)

"No Senator or Representative shall, during the Time for which he was elected, be appointed to any civil Office under the Authority of the United States, which shall have been created, or the Emoluments whereof shall have been encreased during such time; and no Person holding any Office under the United States, shall be a Member of either House during his Continuance in Office." (Article I, Section 6, Clause 2)

"No Title of Nobility shall be granted by the United States; And no Person holding any Office of Profit or Trust under them, shall, without the Consent of the Congress, accept of any present, Emolument, Office, or Title, of any kind whatever, from any King, Prince, or foreign State." (Article I, Section 9, Clause 8)

"The Senators and Representatives before mentioned...shall be bound by Oath or Affirmation, to support this Constitution...." (Article VI, Clause 3)

Criminal Statutes

A series of laws in Title 18 of the U.S. Code make it a federal crime for members of Congress to engage in certain actions. Prohibited acts, excluding those relating to campaign spending, include:

Soliciting or receiving a bribe for the performance of any official act, for the violation of an official duty or for participating in or permitting any fraud against the United States. The penalty is a $20,000 fine or three times the monetary equivalent of the thing of value, whichever is greater, or imprisonment for not more than 15 years, or both, plus possible disqualification from holding office. (18 USC 201c)

Soliciting or receiving anything of value for himself or because of any official act performed or to be performed by him. The penalty is a $10,000 fine or imprisonment for not more than two years, or both. (18 USC 201g)

Soliciting or receiving any compensation for services in relation to any proceeding, contract, claim, controversy, etc., in which the United States is a party or has a direct and substantial interest, before any department, agency, court martial, officer or civil or military commission. The penalty is a $10,000 fine and imprisonment for not more than two years, or both, plus disqualification from holding office. (18 USC 203a)

Practicing in the Court of Claims. The penalty is a $10,000 fine and imprisonment for not more than two years, or both, plus disqualification from holding office. (18 USC 204)

Receiving, as a political contribution or otherwise, anything of value for promising use of or using influence to obtain for any person an appointive office or place under the United States. The penalty is a $1,000 fine, or imprisonment for not more than one year, or both. (18 USC 211)

Entering into or benefiting from contracts with the United States or any agency thereof. The penalty is a $3,000 fine and voidance of the contract. (18 USC 431) Numerous exemptions are listed in 18 USC 433 and elsewhere.

Chamber Rules

Prior to the adoption of ethics codes in 1968, the chief ethical curbs on members' activities related to voting. *(Provisions of codes, this page and p. 116)*

In 1801, when he was Vice President and presiding over the Senate, Thomas Jefferson wrote in *Jefferson's Manual:*

"Where the private interests of a Member are concerned in a bill or question he is to withdraw. And where such an interest has appeared, his voice has been disallowed.... In a case so contrary, not only to the laws of decency, but to the fundamental principle of the social compact, which denies to any man to be a judge in his own cause, it is for the honor of the House that this rule of immemorial observance should be strictly adhered to."

Jefferson's rule gave rise to Rule 8 of the House, which requires each member present to vote "unless he has a direct personal or pecuniary interest in the event of such question." In most cases this decision has been left to the member. Under an 1874 ruling, a representative may vote for his private interests if the measure is not for his exclusive benefit, but for that of a group.

Under Rule 12 senators may be excused from voting, provided they give their reasons for abstaining, and senators have been excused in the past because of such a direct interest in the outcome.

The code provided for only limited public disclosure of the personal finances of senators, Senate candidates and those Senate employees making more than $15,000 a year. On a 40-44 vote, the Senate had rejected an amendment which would have required detailed public disclosure of members' and employees' assets, liabilities and business relationships. *(Financial disclosure, next page)*

1968 Senate Code Provisions

The resolution containing the new rules declared that a senator should use the power entrusted to him by the people "only for their benefit and never for the benefit of himself or of a few."

Outside Employment (Rule 41). Stipulated that no officer or employee of the Senate might engage in any other employment or paid activity unless it was not inconsistent with his duties in the Senate. Directed employees to report their outside employment to specified supervisors, including senators, who were to take such action as they considered necessary to avoid a conflict of interest by the employee.

Contributions (Rule 42). Directed that a senator and a declared candidate for the Senate might accept a contribution from a fund-raising event for his benefit only if he had given express approval before funds were raised and if he received a full accounting of the sources and amounts of each contribution. Official events of his party were exempted from these restrictions.

Permitted a senator or candidate to accept contributions from an individual or an organization provided that a complete accounting of the sources and amounts were made by the recipient.

Specified that a senator or candidate might use such contributions for the expenses of his nomination and election and for the following purposes: travel expenses to and from the senator's home state; printing and other expenses of sending speeches, newsletters and reports to his constituents; expenses of radio, television and other media reports to constituents; telephone, postage and stationery expenses not covered by Senate allowances; and subscriptions to home-state newspapers.

Required disclosure of gifts, from a single non-family source, of $50 or more under the provisions of Rule 44. *(See below.)*

Political Fund Raising (Rule 43). Prohibited employees of the Senate from receiving, soliciting or distributing funds collected in connection with a campaign for the Senate or any other federal office. Exempted from the rule senators' assistants who were designated to engage in such activity and who earned more than $10,000 a year. Required that the senator file the names of such designated aides with the secretary of the Senate, as public information.

Financial Disclosure (Rule 44). Required each senator, declared candidate and Senate employee earning more than $15,000 a year to file with the U.S. comptroller general, by May 15 each year, a sealed envelope containing the following reports:

● A copy of his U.S. income tax returns and declarations, including joint statements.

● The amount and source of each fee of $1,000 or more received from a client.

● The name and address of each corporation, business or professional enterprise in which he was an officer, director, manager, partner or employee, and the amount of compensation received.

● The identity of real or personal property worth $10,000 or more that he owned.

● The identity of each trust or fiduciary relation in which he held a beneficial interest worth $10,000 or more and the identity, if known, of any interest the trust held in real or personal property over $10,000.

● The identity of each liability of $5,000 or more owed by him or his spouse jointly.

● The source and value of all gifts worth $50 or more received from a single source.

Specified that the information filed with the comptroller general would be kept confidential for seven years and then returned to the filer or his legal representative. If the filer died or left the Senate, his reports would be returned within a year.

Provided that the Select Committee on Standards and Conduct might, by a majority vote, examine the contents of a confidential filing and make the file available for investigation to the committee staff. Required that due notice be given to an individual under investigation and an opportunity provided for him to be heard by the committee in closed session.

Required each senator, candidate and employee earning more than $15,000 a year to file with the secretary of the Senate by May 15 each year the following information, which was to be kept for three years and made available for public inspection:

● The accounting required under Rule 42 of all contributions received in the previous year (amounts under $50 might be totaled and not itemized).

● The amount, value and source of any honorarium of $300 or more.

House Ethics Committee

Largely in reaction to the Adam Clayton Powell Jr. (D N.Y.) case, the House in 1966 took its first step toward achieving an enforceable code of ethics. The effort was minimal, for the select committee empowered to draft a code was in existence only two months before the 89th Congress expired. It could only recommend that the next Congress create a permanent committee that would not only draft a code of ethical practices but would also, like the Senate ethics committee, investigate allegations of improper conduct and recommend disciplinary action. *(Details of Powell case, p. 92)*

Still moving slowly, the House the next year, early in the 90th Congress, created a 12-member, bipartisan standing Committee on Standards of Official Conduct. Rep. Melvin Price (D Ill.) became its first chairman. The committee was given no investigative authority. Its sole function was to recommend a code of conduct and the powers it might need to enforce the code. *(1977 code, p. 18)*

Committee Powers Increased

When the House adopted the code in 1968, it also made the Committee on Standards of Official Conduct a permanent committee with investigative and enforcement powers.

The committee was given several specific powers, including the following:

● It may consider measures related to the House Code of Official Conduct or financial disclosure requirements which have been referred to it.

● It may recommend to the House such legislative or administrative actions as it deems appropriate for establishing or enforcing standards of conduct.

● It may investigate, subject to limitations, any alleged violation of the code of official conduct or of any law, rule, regulation, or other standard of conduct applicable to members, officers or employees in the performance of their duties.

● It may report, with the approval of the House, to appropriate federal or state authorities, any substantial evidence of a violation of any law by a member, officer or employee of the House applicable to the discharge of his duties and responsibilities.

● It may consider a request of a member, officer or employee for an advisory opinion respecting the general propriety of any current or proposed conduct by him.

Certain limitations had been imposed on the committee by the resolution creating it. These included:

Disclosure Requirements for House and Senate

(Prior to 1977 changes)

The House and Senate in 1968 adopted the first financial disclosure rules in the history of Congress. The regulations were different for each house, but in both cases members were required to make only limited public disclosures. *(1977 changes, p. 13)*

Senate

The Senate passed a resolution (S Res 266) March 22, 1968, setting down four new rules on conduct of members. Under the new rules, senators and senatorial candidates were required to make public the amount and source of each honorarium of $300 or more received during the preceding year. They also were asked to list the sources, amounts and disposition of the political contributions they received, as well as the source and amount of any gift in excess of $50 from persons other than relatives.

The first Senate reports were filed in 1969, and members were allowed to account for only the second half of 1968. The reports are due each year by May 15.

In practice, the political contribution and gift disclosure requirements have yielded little information, because members must list only income received by themselves directly. Most senators have indicated that all such funds are received by their campaign committees. And although candidates and defeated incumbents have been officially required to file disclosure forms, few have done so.

Besides the public disclosures, senators were required to file with the comptroller general specific information on their income, assets and debts—including U.S. income tax returns.

House

The more detailed accounting required by House members was spelled out in H Res 1099, passed April 3, 1968. The resolution established a Code of Official Conduct for members and employees, as well as the disclosure rule.

The new rules required representatives to disclose the following information by April 30 of each year:

● Interests worth more than $5,000 or income of $1,000 or more from any companies doing substantial business with the federal government or subject to federal regulatory agencies.

● Sources of any income for services (other than congressional salaries) exceeding $5,000 annually.

● Any capital gain from a single source exceeding $5,000.

In 1970, the House adopted a resolution (H Res 796) broadening the public disclosure requirements to include two new items—the source of each honorarium of $300 or more earned in one year, and the names of creditors to whom $10,000 or more was owed for 90 days or longer without the pledge of specific security. These new requirements were first added to reports for 1971.

Honoraria

Congress first limited how much its members could earn from honoraria in the 1974 campaign finance law (PL 93-443). For 1975, senators and representatives could receive no more than $15,000 annually for giving speeches and writing articles and were limited to $1,000 per item.

Under pressure from the Senate, that ceiling was raised in the 1976 amendments to the campaign law (PL 94-283) to allow members of Congress to receive $2,000 per individual event and an aggregate amount of $25,000 a year. The $25,000 limit was a net figure since members were allowed to deduct certain expenses such as booking agents' fees and travel expenditures. *(p. 57)*

Office Accounts

The 1974 campaign law also required senators and representatives to disclose contributions to and expenditures from office accounts, popularly known as "slush funds," that traditionally were used for official activities not covered by office allowances. However, the Federal Election Commission, which is responsible for enforcing the campaign law, had not implemented regulations spelling out what items were to be disclosed. The Senate rejected the initial office account regulation in late 1975. However, in March 1977, both chambers passed resolutions that abolished unofficial office accounts maintained by an unknown number of members.

● No resolution, report, recommendation or advisory opinion may be made, and no investigation of conduct undertaken, unless approved by the vote of not less than 7 of the 12 members. (This assures that no action can be taken unless at least one member of the majority or minority is willing to join with those of the opposite political party.)

● Except when the committee undertakes an investigation on its own initiative it may act only upon receipt of a complaint, in writing and under oath, made by a member. If the complaint is submitted by an individual, not a member of the House, and as many as three members of the House have refused, in writing, to transmit the complaint, the committee may act on it.

● No member of the committee may participate in any committee proceeding relating to his own official conduct.

Following are highlights of House ethics committee activities:

Probe of Voting Irregularities

The House Committee on Standards of Official Conduct in 1968 investigated a controversy over "ghost" voting in the House which arose following newspaper reports of alleged irregularities in some House roll-call voting procedures. On June 19, 1969, the committee reported that "honest errors" accounted for the discrepancies in 1968 when members who were out of Washington were recorded as having voted. The committee blamed the errors on overwork and exhaustion on the part of the tally clerk, who later was dropped from the House payroll.[8]

(Continued on p. 114)

Members of Congress and the Practice of Law

Until World War II, to be a member of Congress was to hold a part-time job. Consequently, certain occupations which demand almost full-time attention—running a business or teaching school, for example—sent few representatives to Congress while others, notably the law, sent many. For years more than half of all members of Congress have been lawyers, while few have been active businessmen (though many have been retired businessmen).

Legal Practice and Past Scandals

Lawyers have never been forbidden to practice law while holding congressional office, but the combination of the two professions has led to numerous scandals.

Sen. Daniel Webster's retainer from the Bank of the United States is familiar to many. What is not so well known is that Webster's professional relationship with the bank was no secret; he represented the bank in 41 cases before the Supreme Court. It was not an unusual arrangement for the time; neither was it universally condoned. John Quincy Adams, for example, as a member of Congress declined to practice before federal courts.

It was not until the 1850s that members were forbidden to represent claimants against the U.S. government. This restriction grew out of a scandal surrounding Senator, and later Secretary of the Treasury, Thomas Corwin of Ohio. Corwin successfully recovered half a million dollars (an enormous sum for those days) in a mining case; scandal erupted when it was revealed that both the claimant and silver mine were frauds.

Legal practice played a supporting role in the great railroad robbery known as the Crédit Mobilier scandal of the Grant administration. In that case, as brought out in a congressional hearing, promoters of the Union Pacific Railroad used stock in Crédit Mobilier, a joint stock company they controlled, to bribe members of Congress to keep up federal subsidies to the railroad.

The bribe-giver was a member of Congress, Rep. Oakes Ames of Massachusetts, and among those investigated were the Vice President Schuyler Colfax, and the Speaker of the House James G. Blaine. In the end, Ames, a Republican, and James Brooks, a Democrat from York, were censured but not expelled by the House, and censure was recommended but not carried out against Sen. James W. Patterson of New Hampshire. No unfavorable evidence was produced against Speaker Blaine, but Vice President Colfax's political career was ruined. *(Censure p. 104)*

The early 1900s again brought congressional ethics to a low spot in public opinion. Heavily promoted by publisher William Randolph Hearst, a series of articles by David Graham Phillips called *Treason of the Senate* alleged corrupt behavior by 21 senators. The series played a major role in promoting direct election of senators.

Only one of the 21 senators replied publicly to Phillips' charges. He was Sen. Joseph W. Bailey of Texas, who had received more than $225,000 in legal fees for several months' services to a Texas oilman. Bailey vehemently defended his practice of law while serving in the Senate: "...I despise those public men who think they must remain poor in order to be considered honest. I am not one of them. If my constituents want a man who is willing to go to the poorhouse in his old age in order to stay in the Senate during his middle age, they will have to find another Senator. I intend to make every dollar that I can honestly make without neglecting or interfering with my public duty...."[1]

Bar Association Actions

The legal profession moved to discourage congressional law practice in the late 1960s. The move came after a series of scandals which involved, sometimes indirectly, congressional law practices. Among those were the cases of Rep. Thomas F. Johnson (D Md.), Senate Majority Secretary Bobby Baker, Sen. Edward Long (D Mo.), Sen. Thomas J. Dodd (D Conn.) and Rep. Cornelius Gallagher (D N.J.).[2]

The American Bar Association revised its canons in 1969. Its new Code of Professional Responsibility provided that the name of a public official should not be used in the name of a law firm or in the firm's professional notices "during any significant period in which he is not actively and regularly practicing law as a member of the firm."[3]

Most state bar associations adopted the code, as well as a number of state supreme courts, thus clearing the way for formal grievance proceedings if violated.

In an extensive study of congressional ethics, conducted in 1967-69, a special committee of the Association of the Bar of the City of New York made several recommendations on congressmen and the legal profession.[4]

Income from Law Practices

In financial disclosure reports for the year 1975, 53 representatives reported at least $1,000 in income from a law practice. Nineteen of those were freshmen in the 94th Congress. Eight members of the House noted on their disclosure forms that they had withdrawn from practice.[5] (As of mid-1976, only information on the outside business activities of House members was made public.)

New Limits on Outside Earned Income

In March of 1977, both chambers included in a revised code of conduct provisions that limited to 15 per cent of official salary the amount of money a member could earn by working outside Congress. The limit did not apply to unearned income such as dividends from stocks or bonds or to income derived from family farms or businesses. *(Details, p. 13)*

1. James C. Kirby, *Congress and the Public Trust: Report of the Association of the Bar of the City of New York Special Committee on Congressional Ethics* (Atheneum, 1970), pp. 81-82.
2. For details on the involvement of law practices in these cases, see *Congress and the Public Trust*, pp. 83-85.
3. *Ibid.*, p. 103.
4. *Ibid.*, pp. 234-35.
5. Congressional Quarterly, *Weekly Report*, July 31, 1976, p. 2053.

The committee urged the installation of a modernized system of voting in the House. In 1972 the House changed its rules to allow the use of an electronic voting system for quorum calls and roll-call votes. The first recorded vote using the new system was taken Jan. 31, 1973.

Gallagher Charges

Life magazine on Aug. 9, 1968, raised charges of wrongdoing against Rep. Cornelius E. Gallagher (D N.J.), calling him a "tool and collaborator" of a reputed Mafia figure in New Jersey. The Committee on Standards of Official Conduct, after looking into the *Life* allegations, chose not to release any information on its inquiry and no action against Gallagher was taken by the committee. Chairman Price said in 1968 that "there was no proof of any violation of the code [of ethics] which the committee had adopted."[9]

On April 7, 1972, Gallagher was indicted for income tax evasion, perjury and conspiracy to hide kickbacks. He pleaded guilty to tax evasion. *(p. 123)*

Voting Ban

For the first time since its formation in 1967, the House ethics committee April 26, 1972, initiated action which would have had the effect of punishing a member. By a vote of 10-2, the committee approved a resolution stating that any representative convicted of a crime for which he might receive a sentence of two years or more in prison should refrain from participating in committee business or House votes.

The committee's report said that "the preservation of public confidence in the legislative process" demanded that guidelines be established for House members who were convicted of "serious" crimes.[10] The only member to whom the resolution was applicable at that time was John Dowdy (D Texas). *(Dowdy case, p. 122)*

The voting ban resolution never was voted on by the House in 1972 because the Rules Committee refused to recommend further action. But, on April 16, 1975, the House amended its rules to include a voluntary voting ban. *(Details, p. 105)*

Advisory Opinions on Travel

The House ethics committee on two occasions has counseled representatives on the acceptance of free trips, which long have raised ethical questions. On June 27, 1974, the committee advised members and employees of the House not to accept trips to foreign countries at the expense of foreign governments unless specifically approved by Congress.

The committee May 14, 1975, issued an advisory opinion to members recommending that they not accept free rides on noncommercial carriers—primarily company planes—when traveling to or from political campaign engagements "and the host carrier is one who would be prohibited by law from making a campaign contribution." In such cases, the committee said, the non-paid transportation would amount to a political contribution, "and should not be accepted."

Even if the trip were not for purposes of campaigning, said the opinion, representatives should not request special rides for their own convenience on a noncommercial carrier, as this could be interpreted "as an abuse of one's public position."

The committee said acceptance of free transportation would not be improper in the following situations:

Ban on Nepotism

In a move that surprised most members of Congress and reporters, the House voted in 1967 to prohibit nepotism by federal officials, including senators and representatives. The proposal was offered by Rep. Neal Smith (D Iowa) as a floor amendment to the postal rate and federal pay bill of 1967 and was adopted by a 49-33 standing vote. The Senate accepted the Smith proviso, with language extending it to less immediate relatives (sons-in-law, for example), and the ban was written into permanent law.

In explaining his amendment, Smith said it was aimed in particular at postmasters in small post offices who were inclined to hire their wives as post office clerks.

But nepotism by members of Congress—the hiring of wives, children, brothers and other close relatives for work on a member's own staff—was a frequent source of critical press comment. Columnists over the years had charged certain members with padding their official staffs or district offices with relatives who did no work for their government paycheck. *(See p. 34)*

The nepotism ban prohibited officers or employees of the federal or District of Columbia governments from appointing, or recommending for appointment or promotion, a relative to serve in the same agency or department as the official.

● If the purpose of the trip were personal or to carry out his job as a representative, and "if the host carrier's purpose in scheduling the transportation is solely for the general benefit of the host and the transportation is furnished on a space-available basis with no additional costs incurred in providing accommodations."

● If the purpose of the trip were to enable the member, as part of his official duties, to be present at an event for the general benefit of the audience—not the member.

● If the trip were in connection with the representatives' receipt of an honorarium. "Under such circumstances, the transportation may be accepted in lieu of monetary reimbursement for travel to which the passenger would otherwise be entitled."

● As a guest on scheduled airlines' inaugural flights, as long as the other conditions in the advisory opinion were met.

Complaint Against Harrington

The House ethics committee Nov. 6, 1975, dismissed a complaint brought by Robin L. Beard Jr. (R Tenn.) against Michael J. Harrington (D Mass.).

By a 7-3 vote, the committee set aside Beard's charges that Harrington had violated House rules by revealing secret information about the Central Intelligence Agency's political activities in Chile. The classified testimony had been presented to the Armed Services Investigations Subcommittee by CIA Director William E. Colby on April 22, 1974. The committee's vote came after John J. Flynt Jr. (D Ga.), who became chairman in 1975, told other members of the panel that the occasion on which Colby testified was not a legal executive session.

Flynt said no public notice of the meeting was issued, a quorum was not present, no vote was taken to meet in executive session as required by House rules and only one member of the panel was present when Colby testified.

On June 16 the House Armed Services Committee, reacting to Harrington's disclosure, had voted 16-13 to deny him future access to its files pending a ruling by the ethics panel on criteria for future access to committee files by House members. *(Details p. 105)*

Lobby Legislation

The House ethics committee shares jurisdiction with the Judiciary Committee over lobby registration legislation in the House. The ethics panel began a study of lobbying activities in 1970, and reported a bill to the House in December 1971. The bill died at the end of that Congress.

Intelligence Leak Probe

The House Feb. 19, 1976, ordered the Committee on Standards of Official Conduct to investigate the unauthorized release of the House Select Intelligence Committee's final report on U.S. intelligence operations. The House on Jan. 29 had voted to bar the report's release on grounds that it contained classified information. On Feb. 11, a New York weekly newspaper, *The Village Voice*, published extensive excerpts from the document, and CBS News correspondent Daniel Schorr later admitted that he had transmitted the report to the newspaper.

On March 3, the House approved a resolution giving the ethics committee far-reaching subpoena power. After a six-month investigation, costing $150,000, the panel concluded that the leak had originated with "someone on or very close to" the staff of the Select Intelligence Committee. Beyond that, the ethics committee was unable to pinpoint the source of the leak to Schorr. In its report, released Oct. 1, the committee recommended that the House establish a system for classifying and declassifying information related to national security.

Sikes Investigation

The House July 29, 1976, voted to reprimand Rep. Robert L. F. Sikes (D Fla.) when it accepted, by a vote of 381-3, the House ethics committee finding that Sikes was guilty of financial misconduct. It was the first time the House had punished one of its members since the Powell case in 1969 and was the result of the first known investigation of a House member by the ethics committee. *(p. 92)*

Sikes, chairman of the House Military Construction Appropriations Subcommittee, had been charged with conflicts of interest and failure to disclose certain financial holdings. *(See below.)* The complaint against Sikes had been filed by Common Cause, the self-styled citizens' lobby, and transmitted to the ethics committee by 44 House members. The formal backing for a complaint against a House member by other members was unprecedented in the history of the committee.

The ethics committee April 28 initiated an inquiry into the conflict-of-interest allegations. On May 12, by a 9-0 vote, the panel authorized a "factual investigation" into the charges. Chairman Flynt told reporters that "so far as I know" it was the first investigation of a House member by the panel. By elevating the probe from the status of an inquiry to an investigation, the panel gave itself the authority to subpoena financial records and question witnesses under oath.

Committee Findings. The committee July 21 voted 10-2 to approve a report (H Rept 94-1364) on Sikes' dealings

Senate Honoraria

Senate financial disclosure reports for 1975 showed information on both honoraria received by members and groups providing honoraria to members. Similar information was not available from House reports.

Top Earners

The following chart compares the 1974 and 1975 earnings of the 1974 top 10 recipients of honoraria. In 1974 there was no limit on the amount of honoraria a senator could receive. In 1975, the limit was $15,000.

	1974	1975
Howard H. Baker Jr. (R Tenn.)	$49,650	$ 8,500
William Proxmire (D Wis.)	46,279	13,000
Mark O. Hatfield (R Ore.)	45,677	14,964
Hubert H. Humphrey (D Minn.)	40,750	14,900
Henry M. Jackson (D Wash.)	34,350	7,700
Herman E. Talmadge (D Ga.)	32,165	14,980*
Daniel K. Inouye (D Hawaii)	29,550	14,389
Edmund S. Muskie (D Maine)	28,800	13,800
Edward W. Brooke (R Mass.)	28,700	9,000
Harrison A. Williams Jr. (D N.J.)	28,617	12,550

Highest earnings reported in 1975.

Top Spenders

The following chart shows the amounts of honoraria provided by the 10 groups which were reported as spending the most for such payments to senators in 1975.

American Mining Congress	$9,000
United Jewish Appeal	8,500
Grocery Manufacturers of America	7,000
American Podiatry Association	6,000
American Bakers Association	6,000
Heritage Foundation	5,500
Chicago Council on Foreign Relations	5,300
American Bankers Association	5,250
Brotherhood of Railway, Airline and Steamship Clerks, Freight Handlers, Express and Station Employees (AFL-CIO)	5,000
National Town Meeting	4,000

which recommended the House adopt H Res 1421 reprimanding Sikes.[11]

The report cited three instances where it said Sikes' actions "have violated standards of conduct applicable to all members of Congress." They were:

● Failure to report ownership of stock in Fairchild Industries, Inc., in annual disclosure statements from 1968 through 1973, and in the First Navy Bank at the Pensacola Naval Air Station, Pensacola, Fla., in his 1973 disclosure statement, as required by House Rule 44. (Sikes first disclosed stock ownership in both companies in his 1974 financial disclosure statement.) Although Sikes' failure to report these holdings did not appear to be "an effort to conceal" them from Congress or the public, the report declared: "The committee believes that the failure to report...is deserving of a reprimand."

● Sikes' investment in stock of the First Navy Bank which he was active in establishing violated Section 5 of the Code of Ethics for Government Service and was cause for a reprimand. *(Government code, p. 109)* "If an opinion had been requested of this committee in advance about the propriety of the investment, it would have been disapproved," according to the report.

● The sponsorship of legislation in 1961 that removed restrictions on Florida land parcels without disclosing that Sikes had an interest in the same land. The committee did not recommend any punishment for this action because, it said, it took place so long ago and "at least to some extent" the circumstances "appear to have been known to Representative Sikes' constituency which has continually re-elected him to Congress." The committee also noted that Sikes had sold some of the land after the bill he had sponsored passed the House, but before it passed the Senate. Although recommending no punishment, the committee said Sikes' involvement with the legislation "created an obvious and significant conflict of interest."

In the first two instances, the committee specified that adoption of the report would constitute a reprimand.

On another charge, the committee concluded that Sikes did not violate House rules when he voted for a fiscal year 1975 defense appropriations bill (HR 16243—PL 93-437) that contained a $73-million appropriation for an aircraft contract with Fairchild Industries. The committee determined that Sikes' ownership of 1,000 shares out of the more than 4.5 million shares outstanding in Fairchild was not "sufficient to disqualify him from voting on the bill."

But the Sikes case did not end there. On Jan. 26, 1977, the House Democratic Caucus voted 189-93 to oust him from his chairmanship of the House Military Construction Appropriations Subcommittee. Sikes' opponents argued that the integrity of the House was at stake and that a failure to remove him from his post would undermine moves to tighten up the House code of ethics.

Hays Scandal

Less than a month after undertaking the Sikes investigation, the ethics committee began a probe of a sex-and-public payroll scandal involving Wayne L. Hays (D Ohio), the powerful chairman of the House Administration Committee and the Democratic National Congressional Committee. In a story which broke in *The Washington Post* May 23, 1976, Elizabeth Ray accused Hays of giving her a $14,000-a-year job on the House Administration Committee in exchange for sexual favors.

Hays at first denied the Ray charge but then admitted to the House May 25 that he had had a "personal relationship" with Ray. However, he denied that he had hired her to be his mistress.[12]

On May 25, Hays asked the ethics committee to investigate the matter. The same day 28 House members, in a letter to ethics Chairman Flynt, asked the committee to take up the Hays case. On June 2, the committee voted 11-0 to begin an immediate investigation into the charges.

The Justice Department and FBI had entered the case soon after Ray made her charges, and by May 26, a federal grand jury in Washington, D.C., began hearing testimony relating to her allegations.

Pressure built up quickly in the House to oust Hays from his leadership positions. He relinquished June 3 his chairmanship of the Democratic Congressional Campaign Committee. Hays won renomination to his House seat in a close Democratic primary in Ohio's 18th District June 8.

Then, bowing to pressure from the House Democratic leadership, Hays resigned the chairmanship of the House Administration Committee June 18 and Aug. 13 announced he would not run for re-election to Congress in 1976. On Sept. 1 Hays resigned from Congress. The ethics panel then voted, 12-0, to end its investigation of Hays.

John Young Accused

Meanwhile, a second House member was accused of keeping a woman on his staff in return for sexual favors. Colleen Gardner, a secretary, told *The New York Times* June 11, 1976, that Rep. John Young (D Texas) increased her salary to $26,000 a year after she submitted to his sexual advances. Young denied the allegation and asked the ethics committee to look into it. The Aug. 19 *Times* reported that the Justice Department ended its inquiry into the matter because it had been unable to substantiate the charge.

House Code of Conduct

The House adopted its Official Code of Conduct April 3, 1968. The new ethics rules covered representatives, the resident commissioner from Puerto Rico and top employees of the chamber. In 1972, the definition of "members" was broadened to include the delegates from the District of Columbia, Guam and the Virgin Islands.

The House required its members to make more information public in their financial disclosure statements than did the Senate, but even the House provisions left many loopholes. The intent of the disclosure requirements, according to the House committee's report, was "to acquaint the voters with the areas in which it is possible for a conflict of interest to occur." This good intention, however, was just about nullified by strict rules the committee later laid down for members of the press or public who wanted to copy information from the non-confidential reports. *(1977 code, p. 18)*

1968 House Code Provisions

Code of Official Conduct (Rule 43). Stipulates that a member, officer or employee of the House shall:

1. "...Conduct himself at all times in a manner which shall reflect creditably on the House of Representatives."

2. "...Adhere to the spirit and the letter of the rules of the House and to the rules of duly constituted committees thereof."

3. "...Receive no compensation nor shall he permit any compensation to accrue to his beneficial interest from any source, the receipt of which would occur by virtue of influence improperly exerted from his position in the Congress."

4. "...Accept no gift of substantial value, directly or indirectly, from any person, organization or corporation having a direct interest in legislation before the Congress."

5. "...Accept no honorarium for a speech, writing for publication, or other similar activity, from any person, organization or corporation in excess of the usual and customary value for such services."

6. "...Keep his campaign funds separate from his personal funds. Unless specifically provided by law, he shall convert no campaign funds to personal use in excess of reimbursement for legitimate and verifiable prior campaign expenditures and he shall expend no funds from his campaign account not attributable to bona fide campaign purposes." [The words "Unless specifically provided by law" added in 1975.]

7. "...Treat as campaign contributions all proceeds from testimonial dinners or other fund-raising events if the sponsors of such affairs do not give clear notice in advance to the donors or participants that the proceeds are intended for other purposes."

8. "...Retain no one from his clerk-hire allowance who does not perform duties commensurate with the compensation he receives."

9. "...Not discharge or refuse to hire any individual, or otherwise discriminate against any individual with respect to compensation, terms, conditions, or privileges of employment, because of such individual's race, color, religion, sex, or national origin." [Clause added in 1975.]

10. "A member of the House who has been convicted by a court of record for the commission of a crime for which a sentence of two or more years' imprisonment may be imposed should refrain from participation in the business of each committee of which he is a member and should refrain from voting on any question at a meeting of the House, or of the Committee of the Whole House, unless or until judicial or executive proceedings result in reinstatement of the presumption of his innocence or until he is reelected to the House after the date of such conviction." [Clause added in 1975.]

Financial Disclosure (Rule 44). Requires members and officers of the House, their principal assistants and professional staff members of committees to file with the Committee on Standards by April 30 each year a report naming the sources of certain financial interests—which are to be available to the public—and a sealed report on the amounts of income from each source. The sealed report may be opened by the committee only if it determines that it is essential to an investigation.

The public listing of financial interest is to include:

● The name of any business in which the filer has a financial interest of over $5,000 or from which he derives income of $1,000 or more, but only if it does substantial business with the federal government or is under federal regulation.

● The name and type of practice of any professional organization from which the filer receives income of $1,000 or more, but only if the filer or his spouse is an officer, director, partner or adviser.

● The source of income exceeding $5,000 from a service rendered (except to the government) or a capital gain (except sale of the filer's home) and of reimbursement for expenditures exceeding $1,000.

These reports are to be available for public inspection under regulations to be set by the committee, which may require full identification of the person making the examination and the reason for it and is to notify the member involved.

The confidential reports are to give the fair market value of the business holdings reported and the amount of income from each source reported publicly.

Persons without financial interests that must be reported are required to file statements to this effect.

Additional Disclosure Requirements. In 1969 *The Wall Street Journal* ran articles about the heavy indebtedness of Rep. Seymour Halpern (R N.Y.), third-ranking Republican on the House Banking Committee. The information showed, according to the *Journal*, that: "First National City Bank of New York extended Mr. Halpern a $40,000 usecured personal loan 'at our best lending rate' when he was already in debt to 13 other banks for more than $75,000; while that loan was outstanding, First National City's lobbyists were pressing Congress to enact a mild ver-

sion of the bill bringing one-bank holding companies under federal regulation."[13]

In 1970, the House added a new financial disclosure rule: It called for public reporting of any loan of $10,000 or more outstanding for 90 days or longer without a pledge of specific collateral. The amount of the indebtedness need not be made public, only the source. The House added also a requirement, matching the existing Senate requirement, for the disclosure of the sources of honoraria of $300 or more. Again, only the sources need be made public; the amounts received would be reported in the sealed file.

Financial Disclosure Reports

In mid-1976 Congress made another move toward tightening its financial disclosure rules that for the previous eight years had provided little information to the public on the financial holdings and outside income of its members. *(Summary of Financial Disclosure Requirements box p. 112)*

The Senate July 21, 1976, passed the Watergate reform bill that set out stringent financial disclosure requirements for members of Congress, candidates for federal office, judges and top level federal government officials. That represented the fourth time in four years that tough disclosure rules had been approved by the Senate. Those provisions, included in the Senate-passed versions of the 1971, 1974 and 1976 campaign finance laws, had been dropped at the insistence of the House conferees. *(Campaign finance legislation p. 70)*

However, in mid-1976, the House reprimand of Rep. Robert L. F. Sikes (D Fla.), in part for violating House disclosure rules, appeared to weaken House resistance. And in March 1977, both the House and Senate passed resolutions requiring full financial disclosure by members and a more detailed accounting of the sources of outside earned income. *(See pp. 18, 22)*

CQ Study of Reports

Since 1969 Congressional Quarterly has examined and analyzed the House and Senate reports filed under the disclosure regulations.

Financial disclosure reports for 1975 filed by senators and representatives provided very limited information on their outside income, stock and property holdings.

A CQ study of the reports showed the following:

● The $15,000 ceiling on honoraria each member of Congress could receive in 1975—imposed in the 1974 campaign finance law (PL 93-443)—eliminated a source of substantial outside income for many senators. The campaign law also limited gratuities for speeches or articles to $1,000 per item. The total amount of honoraria senators received in 1975 fell by one-third to some $638,000 from almost $940,000 in 1974.

Senators' honoraria payments were expected to rise in 1976 following a relaxation of the limits included in the 1976 campaign finance law amendments (PL 94-283). Under the new law, members of Congress could receive $2,000 per individual event and $25,000 a year. However, the $25,000 limit was a net amount since booking agents' fees, travel expenditures, subsistence and expenses for an aide or spouse to accompany the speaker could be deducted. *(Box, Senate Honoraria p. 115)*

● Special interest groups and other organizations spent considerably less on honoraria payments to senators in 1975 than in 1974. The biggest drop was recorded in honoraria paid by academic institutions, down to $136,172 in 1975 from $242,267 in 1974.

● In the House, 231 representatives listed honoraria payments in 1975, a 20 per cent jump over 1974. Fewer representatives, however, reported receiving income from outside law practices than in previous years. *(See p. 113)*

Reports filed by representatives and senators could not be compared because the two chambers required their members to disclose different items. Senators had to reveal only honoraria payments of $300 or more as well as political contributions and gifts of over $50.

Representatives, on the other hand, were required to disclose the sources but not the amounts of their honoraria. Representatives had to list companies in which they had substantial holdings and which did business with the government or were regulated by government agencies; they also had to list capital gains of more than $5,000 and sources of outside income exceeding $5,000 a year.

Congressional Immunity from Prosecution

The concept of congressional immunity from certain legal actions was a well-established principle in England when it was added to the American Constitution. Article I, Section 6 provides that senators and representatives "shall in all cases, except Treason, Felony and Breach of the Peace, be privileged from Arrest during their Attendance at the Session of their respective Houses, and in going to and returning from the same; and for any Speech or Debate in either House, they shall not be questioned in any other Place."

The privilege from arrest clause has become practically obsolete, as various court decisions have excluded more and more acts and proceedings from the protection of the clause. As presently interpreted, the clause applies only to arrests in civil suits, such as nonpayment of debts or breach of contract; and most state constitutions or statutes prohibit arrest generally in such actions. Civil arrests were more common at the time the Constitution was adopted.

Long v. Ansell (293 U.S. 76) in 1934 and *U.S. v. Cooper* (4 Dall. 341) in 1800 declared that the clause did not apply to service of process in civil or criminal cases; nor does it apply to arrest in any criminal case. Furthermore, *Williamson v. United States* (207 U.S. 425, 446) in 1908 interpreted the phrase "treason, felony, or breach of the peace" as excluding all criminal offenses from the privilege's coverage.

The speech or debate clause has been cited more frequently by members seeking immunity from actions against them. Various court decisions have broadly interpreted the phrase "speech or debate" to include virtually everything a member does in carrying out his legislative responsibilities.

'Speech or Debate' Broadly Construed

The first Supreme Court interpretation of the speech or debate clause occurred in 1880 in *Kilbourn v. Thompson* (103 U.S. 168). The case is also widely cited for its ruling on the limits of congressional investigations. It involved a contempt of Congress citation against Hallet Kilbourn, manager of a real estate pool, for refusing to answer questions before the House Select Committee on the Real Estate Pool and Jay Cooke Indebtedness. The House ordered Kilbourn jailed for contempt. He won release on a writ of habeus corpus and sued the Speaker, members of the investigating committee and Sergeant at Arms John G. Thompson for false arrest. The Supreme Court sustained Kilbourn's claim, on the grounds that it was not a legitimate investigation.

The court decided the case on the basis of Congress' investigating powers. But the defendants, in the course of their arguments, raised the speech or debate clause as a defense, and the court also commented on this issue in its opinion. The court said the protection of the clause was not limited to words spoken in debate, but also was applicable to written reports, to resolutions offered, to the act of voting, and to all things generally done in a session of the House by one of its members in relation to the business before it.

Legislative Acts Protected

The Supreme Court on Feb. 24, 1966, held in a 7-0 decision that in prosecuting a former member of Congress the executive branch may not constitutionally inquire into the member's motives for making a speech on the floor, even though the speech was made for a bribe and was part of an unlawful conspiracy.

The holdings in *United States v. Johnson* (383 U.S. 169) left members immune from prosecution for their words and legislative deeds on the floor of Congress, with one exception reserved by the court—prosecution under a "narrowly drawn" law enacted by Congress itself "to regulate the conduct of its Members." Members of Congress already were immune from libel suits for speeches made on the floor.

Johnson was the first case of its kind. The court was unable to find among the English or American cases any direct precedent. The court did discuss cases holding that legislators were protected from private suits for their legislative words and deeds; and it cited approvingly a Supreme Court decision, the force of which appeared to extend the *Johnson* doctrine to state legislators.

Background. The *Johnson* case arose out of the conviction of former Rep. Thomas F. Johnson (D Md.) on June 13, 1963, by a federal jury in Baltimore. The government charged that Johnson, former Rep. Frank W. Boykin (D Ala.) and two officers of a Maryland savings and loan company then under indictment, J. Kenneth Edlin and William L. Robinson, entered into a conspiracy whereby Johnson and Boykin would approach the Justice Department to urge a "review" of the indictment and Johnson would make a speech on the floor of the House defending savings and loan institutions. Johnson made the speech June 30, 1960, and it was reprinted by the indicted company and distributed to the public. Johnson and Boykin allegedly received money in the form of "campaign contributions." Johnson's share was more than $20,000.

Court Rulings. Johnson was convicted on seven counts of violating the federal conflict of interest law (18 U.S.C. 281) and on one count of conspiring to defraud the United States (18 U.S.C. 371); the others were convicted of the same charges. President Johnson Dec. 17, 1965, granted Boykin a full pardon.

The 4th Circuit Court of Appeals Sept. 16, 1964, set aside Johnson's conspiracy conviction on grounds that it was unconstitutional under provisions of Article I, Section 6: "...for any Speech or Debate in either House, they [senators and representatives] shall not be questioned in any other Place." The court ordered a new trial on the other counts on grounds that evidence taken about Johnson's speech on the conspiracy count "infected" the entire case.

The Supreme Court affirmed the lower court's ruling, thus foreclosing further prosecution on the conspiracy count but permitting retrial on the other counts. In the majority opinion, Justice John Marshall Harlan said the purpose of the speech or debate clause was "prophylactic," that it was adopted by the Constitutional Convention (without discussion or opposition) because of the English experience with efforts of the Crown to intimidate and punish Parliament. The clause was intended to protect the independence and integrity of Congress, the justice said, and to reinforce the separation of powers by preventing an "unfriendly" executive and a "hostile" judiciary appointed by the executive from reaching into congressional activity for evidence of criminality.

The government's theory, rejected by Justice Harlan, was that Johnson's criminal act—acceptance of a bribe and entering into a conspiracy—predated his floor speech. Justice Harlan said the indictment particularized the speech as part of the conspiracy charged, and evidence about the speech was taken at trial.

On Jan. 26, 1968, Johnson was convicted for a second time on the conflict-of-interest charges by the U.S. District Court in Baltimore. He was sentenced to six months in prison.

Immunity Protection Narrowed

On June 29, 1972, the Supreme Court in effect narrowed the category of protected actions under the immunity clause. The court's ruling was issued in a case involving former Sen. Daniel B. Brewster (D Md.) who had been indicted, along with others, on charges of violating federal bribery laws.

Background. A federal grand jury Dec. 1, 1969, indicted Brewster, Spiegel Inc., a Chicago mail-order firm, and Cyrus T. Anderson, a lobbyist for the firm, on charges of violating federal bribery laws. The indictment announced by Attorney General John N. Mitchell, charged that Brewster received $24,500 from Spiegel Inc. and Anderson to influence his "action, vote and decision" on postal rate legislation.

The grand jury said the payments were made in five installments between Jan. 10, 1966 and Jan. 31, 1968. Brewster was a member of the Senate Post Office and Civil Service Committee during a 1967 debate on postal rate increases for regular third-class mail. Spiegel was a major user of such rates. Brewster had been defeated for re-election in 1968.

Court Rulings. Ten months after Brewster's indictment, a U.S. district court judge dismissed it on the grounds that the senator was immune from prosecution because of Article I, Section 6, Clause 1 of the Constitution—that the immunity granted members of Congress by the Constitution shielded him from prosecution for bribery related to performance of a legislative act.

The government took an appeal directly to the Supreme Court, which issued a decision June 29, 1972, narrowing the category of protected actions under the immunity clause. A six-man court majority ruled: "Taking a bribe is, obviously, no part of the legislative process or function." *(United States v. Brewster, 408 U.S. 501)*

Immunity in Washington

Members of Congress apparently were no longer to be immune from arrest in Washington, D.C., for crimes such as drunk driving and soliciting prostitutes, according to a 1976 Justice Department ruling.

Reports occasionally would appear in the press of such incidents in Washington involving a member. Invariably, once police confirmed that the suspect was a member of Congress, action against the member would be dropped.

The Justice Department ruling, which had been requested by Washington Police Chief Maurice J. Cullinane, stemmed from a case involving Rep. Joe D. Waggonner Jr. (D La.). Waggonner had been arrested after he allegedly solicited a District of Columbia policewoman posing as a prostitute. He was released when police identified him as a member of Congress.

Cullinane announced the Justice Department ruling on July 23, 1976. Based on the ruling, he said, members "and all other elected and appointed federal, state, and local officials are subject to arrest for the commission of criminal offenses to the same extent and in the same manner as all other citizens." An exception would be continued, he said, for most parking violations on private automobiles bearing congressional license plates.

Cullinane said the non-arrest policy, which had been in effect for more than 100 years, had been based on "a misinterpretation of the meaning" of the Privilege from Arrest Clause in Article I, Section 6 of the Constitution.

At least since *Williamson v. United States* (207 U.S. 425, 446) in 1908, this language was held to have been inserted in the Constitution to prevent political harassment through civil arrest. The more sweeping policy against arrest was thought to have been aimed at not offending the legislators, who controlled the D.C. police department budget.

Chief Justice Warren E. Burger, writing the opinion, continued: "The illegal conduct is taking or agreeing to take money for a promise to act in a certain way. There is no need for the government to show that [Brewster] fulfilled the alleged illegal bargain...for it is taking the bribe, not performance of the illicit compact, that is a criminal act." Importantly, the court upheld the validity of the indictment since it would not be necessary for the government to inquire into legislative acts or their motivations in order to prove a violation of the bribery statute. Brewster was ordered to stand trial, which began Oct. 30, 1972, and resulted in his conviction by a federal jury in Washington, D.C., on Nov. 17, 1972.

In its verdict, the jury found Brewster guilty of a lesser bribery charge, that of accepting an unlawful gratuity. Following the verdict, Spiegel Inc. pleaded guilty. Brewster was sentenced to two-to-six years in prison and fined $30,000. In August 1974 a federal appeals court reversed the conviction on grounds the jury had not been given proper instructions. A new trial was scheduled for August 1975. But on June 25, 1975, Brewster pleaded no contest to a felony charge of accepting an illegal gratuity while he was a senator.

Protected Acts Specified

On June 29, 1972, the Supreme Court took the unusual step of specifying in some detail certain acts of a legislator which were protected by the immunity clause. The case involved Sen. Mike Gravel (D Alaska) and his actions in releasing portions of the then-classified Pentagon Papers history of U.S. involvement in the Vietnam War.

Background. During the controversy over publication of the Pentagon Papers in 1971 by *The New York Times, The Washington Post* and several other newspapers, Sen. Gravel on June 29, 1971, convened a special meeting of the Public Works Subcommittee on Public Buildings, of which he was chairman. With the press and the public in attendance, Gravel read classified documents from the Pentagon Papers into the subcommittee record. Subsequently, the senator arranged for the verbatim publication of the subcommittee record by Beacon Press, the non-profit publishing arm of the Unitarian-Universalist Association.

In August 1971 a federal grand jury in Boston, investigating the release of the Pentagon Papers, ordered an aide to Gravel, Dr. Leonard S. Rodberg, to appear before it. Rodberg had been hired the night Gravel called the session of his subcommittee to read excerpts from the secret documents. Rodberg subsequently helped Gravel edit and make arrangements for publication of the papers. The grand jury also subpoenaed several persons associated with Beacon Press who were involved in publication of the papers.

Rodberg moved to quash the subpoena on the grounds he was protected from questioning by congressional immunity, contending such immunity extended to staff members. Gravel filed a motion to intervene on Rodberg's behalf, claiming Rodberg was acting under the senator's orders, which were immune from judicial inquiry.

The Justice Department, in a brief filed in the case Sept. 8, 1971, said no immunity existed for either Rodberg or Gravel. While not saying so directly, the department's action left open the possibility it might subpoena Gravel himself to testify.

A lower court ruled in October 1971 that the grand jury could not question any witness about Gravel's conduct at the special meeting or about his preparation for the meeting. The grand jury was also prohibited from questioning Rodberg about his own actions taken at Gravel's direction relating to the meeting.

Court Rulings. In January 1972 the Court of Appeals held that Gravel could be questioned about the subsequent publication of the subcommittee record by Beacon Press but not about the subcommittee meeting itself. The same immunities extended to Gravel were also to be applied to Rodberg, the court ruled. But third parties, the court ruled, could be questioned about any of their own actions regarding the publication and the ad hoc committee session.

In a 5-4 decision on June 29, 1972, the Supreme Court specifically enumerated the activities of Gravel and Rodberg which were protected by the immunity clause *(Gravel v. United States,* 408 U.S. 606).

The court said no witness could be questioned concerning: 1) the conduct of Gravel or his aides at the meeting of the Subcommittee on Public Buildings and Grounds of the Senate Public Works Committee on June 29, 1971; 2) the motives and purposes behind the conduct of Gravel or his aides at the June 29 meeting; 3) communications between Gravel and his aides during the terms of their employment and related to the June 29 meeting or any other legislative act of the senator; 4) any act, in itself not criminal, performed by the senator or by his aides in the course of their employment in preparation for the subcommittee meeting, except as it proved relevant to investigating possible third-party crime.

The ruling held that Sen. Gravel's constitutional immunity did not shield him or his aides from grand jury questioning regarding their activities not directly related to their legislative responsibilities. "While the Speech or Debate Clause recognizes speech, voting and other legislative acts as exempt from liability that might attach," the court stated, "it does not privilege either senator or aide to violate an otherwise valid criminal law in preparing for or implementing legislative acts."

The court concluded that the immunity of Gravel's aide was identical to that of his employer and defined the latter's as immunity from "prosecutions that directly impinge upon or threaten the legislative process."

The court majority concurred with the lower court ruling that the negotiations leading to the unofficial publication of the committee record were outside the protection of the speech or debate clause; further, however, it also held that Gravel as well as Rodberg were vulnerable to grand jury questioning and possible liability regarding their roles in the Pentagon Papers publication.

Legislative Protection Restated

The Supreme Court on Oct. 9, 1973, upheld an appellate court ruling which had reversed five of eight conspiracy, bribery and perjury convictions against former Rep. John Dowdy (D Texas) on grounds they had violated the immunity clause. The Fourth Circuit Court of Appeals in Richmond had said evidence used in the trial was an unconstitutional examination of the defendant's acts as a member of Congress.

Background. A federal grand jury in Baltimore, Md., March 31, 1970, indicted Dowdy on charges of conspiracy, perjury and the use of interstate facilities to promote bribery. The indictment alleged Dowdy had accepted a $25,000 bribe at the Atlanta, Ga., airport on Sept. 22, 1965, to intervene in a federal and District of Columbia investigation of the Monarch Construction Company of Silver Spring, Md.

Dowdy's trial was set for Sept. 14, 1970, but the opening of the case was delayed after Dowdy entered a Texas hospital Sept. 8 for treatment of a recurring back condition. Lawyers for Dowdy attempted Sept. 1 to persuade the Fourth Circuit Court of Appeals to set aside the trial on grounds of congressional immunity. The lawyers argued that federal prosecutors were attempting to question privileged legislative acts. The court turned down the petition.

Court Rulings. Dowdy was convicted on Dec. 30, 1971, in U.S. District Court in Baltimore of crossing a state line to receive a bribe, conspiracy to obstruct justice, conspiracy to violate conflict of interest statutes, and five counts of perjury. He was sentenced to 18 months in prison and fined $25,000.

On March 13, 1973, the Fourth Circuit Court of Appeals reversed five of the eight convictions and reduced Dowdy's sentence to six months in prison and a $3,000 fine. Convictions on three counts of perjury were sustained. *(Dowdy v. United States,* 479 F.2d 213)

The court of appeals found that the first trial had violated the Speech or Debate clause of the Constitution, which provides that members of Congress cannot be questioned in any other forum for any speech or debate in which they participated in Congress.

The court held that the evidence used in the first trial "was an examination of the defendant's actions as a congressman, who was chairman of a subcommittee investigating a complaint, in gathering information in preparation for a possible subcommittee investigatory hearing."

These actions were privileged under the speech or debate clause of the Constitution. Thus a conviction based on such evidence violated the privilege and was unconstitutional.

Although the alleged criminal act—bribery—was the same in both the Dowdy and Brewster cases, the major difference, which resulted in one case being upheld and one case being reversed, was the source of the evidence. In Brewster's case there was sufficient evidence available outside of Brewster's legislative activities to permit the case to go forward. In Dowdy's case so much of the evidence was based on Dowdy's legislative activities that the court reversed five of the eight convictions.

On Oct. 9, 1973, the Supreme Court upheld the ruling of the lower court *(Dowdy v. United States,* 414 U.S. 866). After losing a bid to stay out of prison for health reasons, Dowdy began his term Jan. 28, 1974.

Criminal Actions Against Members Since 1941

Following is a list of members of Congress since 1941 who have been indicted or otherwise charged in criminal courts, and the disposition of their cases. The information was compiled from Congressional Quarterly publications, *The New York Times* and *Facts on File;* Congressional Quarterly does not claim that the list is definitive.

Senate

Daniel B. Brewster (D Md. House 1959-63; Senate 1963-69)—Dec. 1, 1969, indicted for accepting bribe from a mail-order house to influence his vote on postal rate legislation; Oct. 9, 1970, charges dismissed by U.S. District Court; June 29, 1972, U.S. Supreme Court ruling ordered Brewster to stand trial; Nov. 17, 1972, convicted of accepting an unlawful gratuity, a lesser charge than bribery; Feb. 2, 1973, sentenced to two-to-six years in prison and fined $30,000; Aug. 2, 1974, U.S. Court of Appeals, D.C. Circuit, ordered a new trial on the unlawful gratuity charge; June 25, 1975, pleaded no contest and was fined $10,000.

Edward J. Gurney (R Fla. House 1963-69; Senate 1969-75)—April 26, 1974, indicted by a Florida grand jury on a misdemeanor charge of violating a state campaign finance law; May 17, 1974, indictment dismissed; July 10, 1974, indicted by federal grand jury with six other defendants for conspiracy, perjury and soliciting bribes in form of campaign contributions from Florida builders with business pending before Department of Housing and Urban Development; Aug. 6, 1975, acquitted on soliciting bribes charge, but jury failed to reach a verdict on conspiracy to create a political slush fund and perjury charges; Sept. 1, 1976, Justice Department announced that it planned retrial on the perjury charge.

House

James M. Curley (D Mass. 1911-Feb. 4, 1914; 1943-47)—Sept. 16, 1943, indicted by federal grand jury, with five others, on charge of using mails to defraud by accepting retainers on false claims of ability to obtain war contracts; Nov. 1, 1943, indictment voided by U.S. District Court, Washington, D.C., on grounds grand jury was illegally summoned; Jan. 3, 1944, indicted on same charge; Jan. 18, 1946, convicted; Feb. 18, 1946, sentenced to six-to-18 months in prison and fined $1,000; Jan. 13, 1947, U.S. Court of Appeals, D.C. Circuit, upholds conviction; June 2, 1947, U.S. Supreme Court upholds conviction; June 26, 1947, begins serving sentence; Nov. 26, 1947, President Truman commutes remainder of sentence.

Andrew J. May (D Ky. 1931-47)—Jan. 23, 1947, indicted with three other men for conspiracy to defraud U.S. government and for accepting money to influence the War Department and other agencies to give contracts to a wartime munitions combine (May was one of its directors); July 3, 1947, convicted of conspiracy and bribery; Nov. 14, 1949, Supreme Court refused to review conviction; Dec. 5, 1949, entered prison and Sept. 18, 1950, paroled after serving nine months of an eight-to-24 month sentence; Dec. 24, 1950, pardoned by President Truman.

J. Parnell Thomas (R N.J. 1937-50)—Nov. 8, 1948, indicted for conspiracy to defraud the government through padding his congressional payroll and taking kickbacks from his staff; Nov. 30, 1949, pleaded no contest and Dec. 9, 1949, sentenced to six-to-18 months in prison and fined $10,000; Sept. 10, 1950, paroled after serving eight and a half months in prison.

Theodore Leonard Irving (D Mo. 1949-53)—June 8, 1951, indicted for violation of Corrupt Practices Act and the Taft-Hartley Act for misusing funds of the labor union he headed for his 1948 House campaign; Dec. 28, 1951, acquitted.

Walter E. Brehm (R Ohio 1943-53)—Dec. 20, 1950, indicted for accepting campaign contributions from two of his congressional office employees; April 30, 1951, convicted on charges involving one employee; June 11, 1951, sentenced to five-to-15 months in prison (sentence suspended) and fined $5,000.

John L. McMillan (D S.C. 1939-73)—Jan. 14, 1953, indicted for violating law barring members of Congress from contracting with the government (he leased oil and gas lands in Utah from Department of Interior); May 16, 1953, acquitted.

Ernest K. Bramblett (R Calif. 1947-55)—June 17, 1953, indicted for making false statements in connection with payroll padding and kickbacks from congressional employees; Feb. 9, 1954, convicted; April 14, 1954, sentence stayed pending Supreme Court review; April 4, 1955, Supreme Court upheld conviction; June 15, 1955, sentenced to four-to-12 months in prison (sentence suspended) and fined $5,000.

Thomas J. Lane (D Mass. Dec. 30, 1941-63)—March 5, 1956, indicted for federal income tax evasion in 1949-51; April 30, 1956, pleaded guilty and sentenced to four months in prison and fined $10,000.

William J. Green Jr. (D Pa. 1945-47; 1949-Dec. 21, 1963)—Dec. 14, 1956, indicted, with six others, for con-

Congressional Aides Misuse Power

Misuses of power and conflicts of interest have not been limited to members of Congress. Occasionally congressional aides have used their positions and their employers' prestige for personal gain. Following are two of the most famous cases in recent years.

Bobby Baker

Bobby Baker began his Capitol Hill career as a teenage page in the Senate. Ambitious and aggressive, Baker rose to the position of secretary to the Senate majority, making himself right-hand man to his mentor, Majority Leader Lyndon B. Johnson (D Texas), in the late 1950s. When he quit his post under fire, Baker on paper was worth $2-million, most of it gained, the subsequent court records showed, from combining law practice with influence peddling. The notoriety caused by the Baker case is credited with moving the Senate to create an ethics committee.

Baker resigned from his $19,600 Senate job in 1963 after a civil suit was brought against him, charging that he used his influence to obtain contracts for a vending machine concern in which he had a financial interest. Senate investigations conducted over the next two years concluded that Baker was guilty of "gross improprieties." The investigating committee recommended that the Senate require full financial disclosures by senators and top employees of the Senate.

Baker meanwhile was brought to trial on charges of income tax evasion, theft and conspiracy to defraud the government. He was found guilty in January 1967; after appeals had been exhausted, he began his prison term four years later. The major charge on which he was found guilty was that he had collected more than $99,000 from a group of California savings and loan executives, ostensibly as campaign contributions, but that in reality he had kept about 80,000 of the total for himself.

At the trial two of the California executives testified that in 1962 they gave Baker about $66,000 for campaign contributions to seven senators and one House member, Ways and Means Committee Chairman Wilbur D. Mills (D Ark.). Mills and one of the senators, Foreign Relations Committee Chairman J. W. Fulbright (D Ark.), testified that they had received none of the funds. Defense counsel stipulated that none of the other six senators had received any of the funds. One of the savings and loan executives testified that Baker told him the California savings and loan associations could improve their standing in Congress with a "very impressive" contribution to certain senators and House members and could "win friends" in Congress at a time when a bill was pending to increase taxes on the associations.

Baker testified he turned the money over to Sen. Robert S. Kerr (D Okla.), a power on the Senate Finance Committee, for his re-election campaign. Kerr was dead by the time Baker told his story.

Sweig and the Speaker's Office

A congressional scandal which attracted nationwide attention when it was revealed in 1969 involved influence-peddling in the office of Speaker John W. McCormack (D Mass.). In the end, one of his top aides, Dr. Martin Sweig, was convicted July 9, 1970, of perjury, and Jan. 28, 1972, of misusing the Speaker's office to influence government decisions.

Sweig, who had worked for McCormack 24 years and was drawing an annual salary of $36,000 in 1969, was implicated with Nathan M. Voloshen, New York City lawyer-lobbyist and longtime McCormack friend. On June 17, 1970, Voloshen pleaded guilty to charges of conspiring to use the Speaker's office to influence matters before federal government agencies and to three counts of lying to a federal grand jury about the charges.

spiracy to defraud the government by accepting money and bond business for his insurance firm from contractors in return for influencing decisions on the construction from 1951-54 of a $33-million Army Signal Corps depot in Tobyhanna, Pa.; Feb. 27, 1959, acquitted.

Thomas F. Johnson (D Md. 1959-63)—Oct. 16, 1962, indicted with Frank W. Boykin (D Ala.) and two other defendants, for conflict of interest and conspiracy to defraud the government by trying to influence Justice Department action on indictments in a Maryland savings and loan association scandal; Johnson was accused of receiving more than $20,000 for his part in the conspiracy, which included a House speech defending savings and loan institutions; June 13, 1963, convicted; Sept. 16, 1964, Fourth Circuit Court of Appeals set aside conviction on grounds that the House speech was protected by the speech or debate clause of the Constitution, and ordered new trial for Johnson on conflict of interest charges; Feb. 24, 1966, Supreme Court upheld ruling; Jan. 26, 1968, convicted of conflict of interest; Jan. 30, 1968, sentenced to six months in prison.

Frank W. Boykin (D Ala. 1935-63)—Oct. 16, 1962, indicted with Rep. Thomas F. Johnson (D Md.) on charges of conflict of interest and conspiracy to defraud the government *(see Johnson above);* June 13, 1963, convicted; Oct. 7, 1963, Boykin placed on probation for six months and fined $40,000; Dec. 17, 1965, pardoned by President Johnson.

Adam Clayton Powell Jr. (D N.Y. 1945-67; 1969-71)—May 8, 1958, indicted for federal income tax evasion; April 5 and 7, 1960, federal judge dismissed two of three counts and trial on third count declared mistrial April 22, 1960, because of hung jury; May 23, 1960, judge refused to dismiss indictment; April 13, 1961, case dismissed at request of U.S. attorney. *(Powell's involvement in a libel suit in New York resulting in four contempt of court citations, p. 688)*

John V. Dowdy (D Texas Sept. 23, 1952-73)—March 31, 1970, indicted for bribery, conspiracy and perjury in connection with receipt of payment from a Maryland home improvements firm accused of defrauding its customers; Dec. 30, 1971, convicted; Feb. 23, 1972, sentenced to 18 months in prison and fined $25,000; March 13, 1973, Fourth Circuit Court of Appeals reversed conspiracy and bribery convictions on constitutional grounds, but left standing perjury conviction; Oct. 9, 1973, Supreme Court upheld ruling; Jan. 28, 1974, entered prison to serve a six-month term. *(p. 715)*

Martin B. McKneally (R N.Y. 1969-71)—Dec. 16, 1970, indicted for failure to file federal income tax returns for 1964-67; Oct. 18, 1971, pleaded guilty to charge that he filed no income tax in 1965 and government dropped other charges; Dec. 20, 1971, sentenced to one year in prison (sentence suspended), placed on one-year probation, and fined $5,000.

Cornelius Gallagher (D N.J. 1959-73)—April 7, 1972, indicted for federal income tax evasion in 1966-67, perjury and conspiracy to hide kickbacks for aiding two co-conspirators to evade taxes in 1966-68; Dec. 21, 1972, pleaded guilty to tax evasion charge involving his own income; June 15, 1973, sentenced to two years in prison and fined $10,000; Nov. 22, 1974, released from jail eight months before end of two-year sentence.

Frank J. Brasco (D N.Y. 1967-75)—Oct. 23, 1973, indicted for conspiracy to receive bribes from a reputed Mafia figure who sought truck leasing contracts from the Post Office and loans to buy trucks; July 19, 1974, convicted; Oct. 22, 1974, sentenced to five years in prison (all but three months suspended) and fined $10,000; June 26, 1975, began three-month sentence; Oct. 6, 1975, Supreme Court upheld conviction.

Angelo D. Roncallo (R N.Y. 1973-75)—Feb. 21, 1974, indicted for extortion of political contribution from an incinerator contractor at the time Roncallo was comptroller of Nassau County, Long Island; May 17, 1974, acquitted.

Bertram L. Podell (D N.Y. Feb. 20, 1968-75)—July 12, 1973, indicted for conspiracy, bribery, perjury and conflict of interest for receipt of payment to appear before federal agencies to help Florida Atlantic Airlines to obtain approval of a Bahaman route; Oct. 1, 1974, Podell ended nine-day trial by pleading guilty to the conspiracy and conflict of interest charges; Jan. 9, 1975, sentenced to six months in prison and fined $5,000; Nov. 3, 1975, Supreme Court refused to review the case.

J. Irving Whalley (R Pa. Nov. 8, 1960-73)—July 5, 1973, indicted for mail fraud for using mail to deposit salary kickbacks he required from congressional staff and obstruction of justice for threatening an employee to prevent her from giving information to the Federal Bureau of Investigation; July 31, 1973, pleaded guilty; Oct. 15, 1973, sentenced to three years in prison (sentence suspended) and fined $11,000.

George V. Hansen (R Idaho 1965-69; 1975-)—Feb. 19, 1975, pleaded guilty to two misdemeanor counts of campaign spending violations in 1974 (failure to file a campaign finance report and filing an erroneous report); April 18, 1975, sentenced to one year in prison (ten months suspended and one-year probation); April 25, 1975, sentence reduced to a $2,000 fine.

Andrew J. Hinshaw (R Calif. 1973-)—May 6, 1975, indicted twice—first, for soliciting a bribe involving a 1972 campaign contribution, for two counts of bribery involving Tandy Corporation and for embezzlement and for misappropriation of public funds during time he served as assessor of Orange County, Calif., and second, for conspiracy, grand theft and embezzlement in connection with the use of employees for his 1972 House campaign; Oct. 10, 1975, judge dismissed from the first indictment embezzlement and misappropriation of public funds charges, but sustained bribery charges; Jan. 26, 1976, convicted of bribery charges and acquitted of charge of soliciting a bribe; Feb. 24, 1976, sentenced to a one-to-14-year sentence, announced he would appeal: Sept. 3, 1976, Supreme Court Justice William H. Rehnquist rejected Hinshaw's plea to block a second jury trial. Dec. 3, convicted of conspiring with organized crime and other charges. Jan. 10, 1977, Supreme Court denied appeal.

James R. Jones (D Okla. 1973-)—Jan. 29, 1976, pleaded guilty to a misdemeanor charge that he failed to report a cash campaign contribution from the Gulf Oil Corp. in 1972; March 16, 1976, fined $200.

Wendell Wyatt (R Ore. Nov. 3, 1964-75)—June 11, 1975, pleaded guilty to misdemeanor charge of violating federal campaign spending laws by failing to report expenditures from a secret cash fund he controlled while heading the Nixon re-election campaign in Oregon in 1972; July 18, 1975, fined $750.

Henry J. Helstoski (D N.J. 1965-)—June 2, 1976, indicted for bribery, conspiracy, obstructing justice and perjury for his role in scheme to solicit and accept payment for the introduction of private immigration bills. Trial date set for Feb. 15, 1977.

Allan T. Howe (D Utah 1975-)—June 12, 1976, arrested in Salt Lake City on charge of soliciting two policewomen posing as prostitutes; July 23, 1976, convicted of soliciting sex acts for pay and sentenced to 30 days in prison and fined $150 (sentence suspended on payment of the fine); sentence stayed, pending appeal to state district court; Aug. 24, 1976, convicted and sentenced to 30 days in prison (suspended sentence) and assessed court costs.

James F. Hastings (R N.Y. 1969-75)—Sept. 21, 1976, indicted for operating an alleged kickback scheme with members of his congressional staff; Oct. 1, 1976, pleaded innocent to the charges; Dec. 17, 1976, convicted on 28 felony counts; Jan. 31, 1977, sentenced to serve 20 months to five years in federal prison. Hastings did not appeal the decision.

Footnotes

1. U.S. Congress, Senate, Select Committee on Standards and Conduct, *Report on the Matter of Senator Edward V. Long of Missouri,* reprinted in *Congressional Record,* 90th Cong., 1st sess., Oct. 25, 1967, pp. 30096-98.

2. *Congressional Record,* 90th Cong., 1st sess., Nov. 7, 1967, p. 31530.

3. U.S. Congress, Senate, Select Committee on Standards and Conduct, *Investigation of the Introduction of Private Immigration Bills for Chinese Crewmen, 90th and 91st Congresses,* S. Rept. 91-911, 91st Cong., 2nd sess., May 28, 1970, p. 2.

4. *Congressional Record,* 91st Cong., 2nd sess., Aug. 24, 1970, p. 29880.

5. *The New York Times,* March 13, 1970.

6. *The Washington Post,* Aug. 10, 1976, and Aug. 31, 1976. *The Washington Post* reported Sept. 16, 1976, that the Senate ethics committee Sept. 15 voted, 5-1, not to take action against Scott.

7. *Congressional Record,* 90th Cong., 2nd sess., March 18, 1968, p. 6833.

8. *Congressional Record,* 91st Cong., 1st sess., June 19, 1969, p. 16629.

9. Congressional Quarterly, *1968 Almanac,* p. 816.

10. U.S. Congress, House, Committee on Standards of Official Conduct, *Sense of the House of Representatives with Respect to Actions by Members Convicted of Certain Crimes,* H. Rept. 92-1039, 92nd Cong., 2nd sess., May 3, 1972.

11. U.S. Congress, House, Committee on Standards of Official Conduct. *In the Matter of A Complaint Against Representative Robert L. F. Sikes,* H. Rept. 94-1364 to accompany H. Res. 1421, 94th Cong., 2nd sess., July 23, 1976.

12. *Congressional Record,* 94th Cong., 2nd sess., May 25, 1976, p. H4895.

13. *The Wall Street Journal,* July 29, 1969.

Selected Bibliography

Books

Beard, Edmund and Horn, Stephen. *Congressional Ethics: The View from the House.* Washington D.C.: The Brookings Institution, 1975.

Bolling, Richard. *House Out of Order.* New York: E. P. Dutton Co., 1965.

Boyd, James. *Above the Law.* New York: New American Library, 1968.

Clark, Joseph S. *Congress: The Sapless Branch.* New York: Harper and Row, 1964.

Deakin, James. *The Lobbyists.* Washington, D.C.: Public Affairs Press, 1966.

Douglas, Paul H. *Ethics in Government.* Cambridge: Harvard University Press, 1952.

Getz, Robert S. *Congressional Ethics: The Conflict of Interest Issue.* Princeton: Van Nostrand, 1966.

Graham, George A. *Morality in American Politics.* New York: Random House, 1952.

Green, Mark J., Fallows, James M. and Zwick, David R. *Who Runs Congress?—The President, Big Business, or You.* New York: Grossman Publishers, 1972.

Kirby, James C. *Congress and the Public Trust: Report of the Association of the Bar of the City of New York Special Committee on Congressional Ethics.* New York: Atheneum, 1970.

Rienow, Robert and Rienow, Leona Train. *Of Snuff, Sin and the Senate.* Chicago: Follett Publishing Co., 1965.

Rogow, Arnold A. and Lasswell, Harold D. *Power, Corruption and Rectitude.* Englewood Cliffs: Prentice-Hall, 1963.

Weaver, Warren Jr. *Both Your Houses: The Truth About Congress.* New York: Praeger, 1972.

White, William S. *Citadel.* New York: Harper and Brothers, 1957.

Wilson, H. H. *Congress: Corruption and Compromise.* New York: Rinehart and Company, 1951.

Articles

Bernstein, Marver H. "Ethics in Government: The Problems in Perspective." *National Civic Review,* July 1972, pp. 341-47.

Clark, Joseph S. "Some Ethical Problems of Congress." *Annals of the American Academy of Political and Social Science,* January 1966, pp. 12-22.

"Bribed Congressman's Immunity from Prosecution." *Yale Law Journal,* December 1965, p. 335.

"Conflicts of Interest: A Symposium." *Federal Bar Journal,* Summer 1964.

"Conflict of Interest Acts." *Harvard Journal on Legislation,* January 1964, p. 68.

Hamer, John. "Ethics in Government." *Editorial Research Reports,* 1973, vol. 1, pp. 375-96.

Lee, Linda K. "Conflict of Interest: One Aspect of Congress' Problems." *George Washington Law Review,* vol. 32, 1963-1964, pp. 954-82.

"The Scope of Immunity for Legislators and Their Employees." *Yale Law Journal,* December 1967, pp. 366-89.

Government Publications

U.S. Congress. House. Committee on Rules. *Creating a Permanent Select Committee on Standards and Conduct.* House Report 89-1929. 89th Cong., 2nd sess., 1966.

U.S. Congress. House. Committee on Standards of Official Conduct. *Standards of Official Conduct, Hearings February 19, 1970 on House Resolution 796, Proposed Amendments to Financial Disclosure Rule.* 91st Cong., 2nd sess., 1970.

———. *Amendment of Financial Disclosure Rules.* House Report 91-938. 91st Cong., 2nd sess., 1973.

U.S. Congress. Joint Committee on Congressional Operations. *Constitutional Immunity of Members of Congress, Hearings March 21-July 19, 1973, on the Legislative Role of Congress in Gathering and Disclosing Information.* 93rd Cong., 1st sess., 1973.

———. *House of Representatives Exclusion, Censure and Expulsion Cases from 1789 to 1973.* Committee Print. 93rd Cong., 1st sess., 1973.

U.S. Congress. Senate. Committee on Labor and Public Welfare. *Hearings on the Establishment of a Commission on Ethics in Government, to Study Senate Concurrent Resolution 21.* 82nd Cong., 1st sess., 1951.

———. *Ethical Standards in Government.* Committee Print. 82nd Cong., 1st sess., 1951.

U.S. Congress. Senate. Committee on Rules and Administration. *Senate Election, Expulsion and Censure Cases from 1793 to 1972,* by Richard D. Hupman. Senate Document 92-7. 92nd Cong., 1st sess. Washington, D.C.: Government Printing Office, 1972.

U.S. Congress. Senate. Select Committee on Standards and Conduct. *Standards of Conduct for Members of the Senate and Officers and Employees of the Senate.* Senate Report 90-1015. 90th Cong., 2nd sess., 1968.

U.S. Library of Congress, American Law Division. *Provisions in the United States Code Prohibiting Conflicts of Interests by Members of Congress and by U.S. Government Officials and Employees.* By Elizabeth Yadlosky and Richard C. Ehlke. Library of Congress, 1973.

———. *Provisions in the United States Constitution, Federal Statutes and Rules of the House and Senate Governing the Conduct and Activities of Members of Congress.* By Robert L. Tienken. Library of Congress, 1972.

U.S. Library of Congress. Congressional Research Service. *The Constitutional Privileges from Arrest and of Speech or Debate of Members of Congress, U.S. Constitution Article I, Section 6: Historical Aspects and Legal Precedents.* Library of Congress, 1971.

INDEX

Flynt, John J. Jr. (D Ga.)
  Complaint against Harrington - 114
  Defense contractors' hospitality - 3
  Korean lobby probe - 9
  Sikes reprimand - 8, 115
Foote, Henry S. (Unionist Miss.) - 100
Ford, Gerald R.
  Campaign Act amendments - 72
  Exclusion proceedings - 94
  Executive, congressional pay raise - 33
Ford, Henry - 88
Foreign travel. See Perquisites, Congressional
Franking privilege - 41
Franklin, Benjamin
  Congressional pay - 30
Fraser, Donald M. (D Minn.)
  South Korean connection - 9
Freedom of Information Act
  Foreign travel abuses - 45
Frenzel, Bill (R Minn.)
  House ethics code - 13, 15, 18
Fulbright, J. William (D Ark.)
  Bobby Baker case - 122
  House ethics code - 13
Fuller, Melville W.
  Right to compel testimony - 87
Fulton, Richard (D Tenn.) - 45

G

Gallagher, Cornelius (D N.J.)
  Congressional ethics, indictment - 113, 114, 123
Gallatin, Albert
  Members-elect exclusion - 90
Galloway, George B.
  Contested elections - 95
General Accounting Office (GAO)
  Appropriations (1955-1977) - 54
  Campaign finance - 72
  House Administration audits - 6
General Services Administration (GSA)
  Senate office allowances - 39
  Travel allowances - 5, 35, 37
Gesell, Gerhard A. - 99
Giaimo, Robert N. (D Conn.)
  Perquisite changes - 5, 7
Gilbert, Jacob (D N.Y.)
  Franked mail controversy - 42
Gillett, Frederick H. (R Mass.)
  Blanton censure - 100
Glenn, John (D Ohio) - 20
Goodling, George - 39
Gould, Arthur R. (R Maine)
  Exclusion cases - 91
Gould, Kingdon - 63
Government Printing Office - 39, 49, 54
Gravel, Mike (D Alaska)
  Committee staffs - 36
  Pentagon Papers case - 104, 120

Graves, William J. (Whig Ky.) - 104
Green, William J. Jr. (D Pa.)
  Criminal indictment - 121
Griffin, Robert P. (R Mich.)
  Gulf Oil contributions - 8
  Ethics code restrictions - 20
Grinnell, Josiah B. (R Iowa) - 104
Griswold, Roger (Fed Conn.) - 103
Gross, H. R. (R Iowa) - 39, 46
Gulf Oil Corporation - 3, 8, 11, 109
Gurney, Edward J. (R Fla.)
  Criminal indictment - 121

H

Halpern, Seymour (R N.Y.)
  Financial disclosure - 117
Hamer, Fannie L.
  Mississippi Five dispute - 96
Hamilton, William R. - 59
Hammond, Samuel (Ind Ga.)
  Incompatible office - 98
Hanna, Marcus
  McKinley campaign finance - 66
Hansen, Clifford P. (R Wyo.) - 8
Hansen, George V. (R Idaho)
  Campaign spending violations - 123
Harlan, John Marshall
  Automatic expulsion - 87
  Congressional immunity - 119
Harmon, Randall S. (D Ind.)
  Allowance abuses - 39
Harrington, Michael J. (D Mass.) - 105, 114
Harris Poll - 17
Hart, George L. Jr.
  Powell case - 89
Hastings, James F. (R N.Y.)
  Criminal indictment - 12, 123
Hatch Act - 67
Hatfield, Mark O. (R Ore.) - 41
Hays, Wayne L. (D Ohio)
  Committee chairmanship loss - 1, 5, 105
  Ethics Committee investigation - 4, 116
  Foreign travel - 6, 44, 45, 46
  Honoraria limits - 41
  Misuse of committee staff - 35
  Newsletter allowance - 38
  Resignation - 7
Health care, members of Congress - 47
Heard, Alexander
  Campaign finance laws - 68
Hearst, William Randolph - 113
Heckler, Margaret M. (R Mass.)
  Travel allowance abuse - 39
Heinz, H. John III (R Pa.) - 3
Helstoski, Henry J. (D N.J.)
  Criminal indictment - 11, 123
Hinshaw, Andrew J. (R Calif.) - 3, 11, 105, 123
Hoar, George F. (R Mass.) - 96
Hoffa, James R. - 109
Holt, Marjorie S. (R Md.)
  Allowance increases - 40

Holt, Rush D. (D W.Va.) - 91
Honoraria
  CQ study of reports - 117
  Changes in limitations - 112
  Ethics code requirements - 21
  Members' honoraria - 40, 115
  Public opinion survey - 17
Hooks, Benjamin L.
  FCC equal time reversal - 65
Horton, Frank (R N.Y.)
  Criminal indictment - 12
House of Representatives
  Censure proceedings - 103
  Code of Conduct - 18-19, 116
  Committees
    Chairmen loss (discipline) - 1, 5, 8, 105
    Ethics - 15, 111
    House Administration - 4, 33, 35-37, 46, 96
    Judiciary - 94
    Post Office - 32, 33, 42
    Rules - 6
    (See also) Investigations
  Contested elections - 94
  Elections. See Elections, Congressional
  Expulsions - 99
  Financial accountability. See Reforms, Congressional
  Legislative budget (1955-1977) - 54
  Members' honoraria - 40
  Members' loans - 48
  Members' qualifications - 90
  Patronage machinery - 49
  Recording studio - 48
  Special allowances - 37-40
  Staff allowances - 33
Howe, Allan T. (D Utah)
  Criminal conviction - 3, 12, 123
Huff, Corinne A. - 44, 94
Human Events
  Campaign law challenge - 73
Humes, John F.
  Nixon campaign contribution - 63
Hunter, John W. (Ind N.Y.)
  House censure - 104

I

Immigration bills - 109, 123
Immunity
  Congressional
    Constitutional provisions - 108, 118
    Legislative acts protected - 118
    Protection narrowed, restated - 119
    Speech or debate clause - 118
    Washington, D.C., area - 119
Ingersoll, Ebon C. (R Ill.)
  Exclusion cases - 92
Inouye, Daniel K. (D Hawaii)
  Campaign funds probe - 3
  Ethics code restrictions - 20
Insull, Samuel - 67
Insurance, members of Congress - 47

Intelligence Activities
  Ethics Committee probe - 115
Interest Groups
  Campaign finance - 62, 76, 77
  Honoraria payments - 40, 115
Internal Revenue Service (IRS)
  Tax checkoff campaign fund - 70
  Taxes of members of Congress - 47, 48
Investigations
  Congressional immunity - 118
  Defense hospitality probe - 9
  Gulf Oil contributions - 8
  Ethics Committee probes - 108, 109, 112, 114-116
  Obstacles to action - 4
  South Korean lobby - 9
  Subpoena powers - 88
Irving, Theodore Leonard (D Mo.)
  Criminal indictment - 121
Irwin, John N. II - 63

J

Jackson, Andrew
  Campaign financing - 66
Jackson, Henry M. (D Wash.)
  Committee staff use - 36
James, Esther - 93
Javits, Jacob K. (R N.Y.) - 16, 20
Jefferson, Thomas
  Ethics rule - 110
Jennings, W. Pat (D Va.) - 68
Johnson, Lyndon B. - 32, 122
Johnson, Thomas F. (D Md.) - 113, 118, 122
Johnson, Waldo P. (D Mo.)
  Senate expulsion - 100
Jones, George W. - 104
Jones, James R. (D Okla.)
  Campaign law violation - 3, 11, 123
Jones, Robert E. (D Ala.) - 39
Judiciary. See also Supreme Court
  Ethics code requirements - 21
  Salaries - 1
Junketing - 44-46
Justice Department
  Campaign finance violations - 68
  Fraudulent travel claims - 11
  Hays scandal - 116
  Pentagon Papers case - 120
  South Korean lobby - 9, 14

K

Keith, Hastings R. (R Mass.) - 47
Keitt, Laurence M. (D S.C.)
  Assault on Charles Sumner - 97
Kennedy, Edward M. (D Mass.)
  Campaign finance laws - 69
  Committee staff use - 36
Kennedy, John F.
  Campaign finance - 62
  Television, use of - 64
Kerr, Robert S. (D Okla.) - 122